THE IMMIGRANT WOMAN IN NORTH AMERICA:

An Annotated Bibliography of Selected References

by

FRANCESCO CORDASCO

with a Foreword by
ROSE BASILE GREEN

The Scarecrow Press, Inc.
Metuchen, N.J., & London
1985

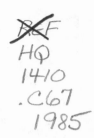

Library of Congress Cataloging in Publication Data

Cordasco, Francesco, 1920–
  The immigrant woman in North America.

  Includes index.
  1. Women immigrants--United States--Bibliography.
2. Women immigrants--Canada--Bibliography. I. Title.
Z7964.U49C67 1985   [HQ1410]   016.3054'88   85-11746
ISBN 0-8108-1824-8

Copyright © 1985 by Francesco Cordasco

Manufactured in the United States of America

In Memory of Immigrant Sisters in America

CARMELA MADROMA CORDASCO (1883-1962)

FILOMENA MADORMA TIESI (1887-1974)

Studying the mortality of Italian women (and Italian adults in general) we are confronted with a peculiar contrast; the official statistics show a small death rate, especially in regard to pulmonary tuberculosis, yet we know as all medical men, settlement workers, and others conversant with the situation know--that tuberculosis is very prevalent among them. The explanation of this descrepancy lies in the well-known fact that all adult Italians once affected by a serious disease, and so informed, board the first steamer and go back to Italy to die among the vines and orange groves. We cannot, therefore, gauge the mortality of Italian women from the tables of the Health Department, where they contribute only a small percentage (deaths from the very acute diseases, surgical operations, puerperal infection, etc.), but should count the wan-faced women that crowd the steerage of departing ships, or we should search the Bureaus of Vital Statistics of the little towns in Calabria or Sicily, where they swell the local death rate, and import from America tuberculosis where first it was unknown. The vast number of returning consumptives-- both men and women--has taken such proportions of late that the Italian Government is considering special measures of quarantine both on board the ships and the point of debarkation.

--Antonio Stella. The Effects of Urban Congestion on Italian Women and Children. New York: William Wood & Co. , 1908.

CONTENTS

FOREWORD

The ethnic consciousness which engulfed America in the 1960's has proved to be an enduring force: it has revitalized our institutions, reshaped our history, and in a very real sense, furnished both the insight and interpretation which have, for the first time, allowed us to understand our history as a people wholly, in which none of us is ignored, and in which the historical portrait is truly dimensional. Nowhere has this been more apparent than in the new attentions paid to the role of women in our history (hitherto sadly neglected) and in the invigorating new strengths that have infused the historical study of our past and present.

Out of these new appraisals have emerged a wide range of studies and broadened frames of reference; ineluctably, works of the range and power of Meredith Tax's The Rising of the Women (1980) and Hasia R. Diner's Erin's Daughters in America (1983), with a multitude of others, have illuminated dark recesses in the history of the nation. These achievements have encouraged excursions into areas formerly not only neglected, but curiously denied importance. A striking example is that of the immigrant woman, whose presence in America is everywhere manifest (if hitherto generally ignored) and who has been both a protean and a dynamic force in the creation of the nation. It is these immigrant women whose fictional representations I have studied in my The Italian-American Novel (1974) and whose fugitive essences I have elegiacally pursued in sheaves of poems. The American immigrant woman has come alive in a cornucopia of studies born of the new awareness and attention.

It is against these developments that the importance of Francesco Cordasco's The Immigrant Woman in North America is best understood. It attests the existence of an expanding scholarship which has demonstrated the elemental truth of Hasia Diner's observations: "Ethnicity can be a central determinant of human behavior. Immigrant women raised in a par-

vii

ticular culture and social milieu--that of the small village of Ireland, the shtetl of Jewish Eastern Europe, or the town in Italy's mezzogiorno--adapted and acculturated to a new set of values and to new realities in certain discernable ways" (Erin's Daughters, xv). In The Immigrant Woman in North America, Professor Cordasco has gathered the available resources for the study of the immigrant woman: he has drawn the entries from most disciplines "across a wide socio-historical spectrum," and he has wisely structured his book, portraying, in a vast kaleidoscope, immigrant women in the dynamic roles which explain the larger contexts of an expanding American society. In his more than 1100 entries (and their annotations) is revealed the richness of the resources currently available.

There can be no question of the significance, at this juncture, of The Immigrant Woman in North America, and the academic community is deeply indebted to Francesco Cordasco for providing us with this invaluable register. He has intended it as a "preliminary effort," but it stands as the best extant bibliographical guide to the world of the American immigrant woman. It is what we would expect from a scholar of the stature of Professor Cordasco, who has made many contributions to the study of American ethnic groups and immigrant historiography.

Rose Basile Green

INTRODUCTION

For some years, I contemplated doing a book on immigrant women in the United States, but for a number of reasons I was deterred from the task. The first question which posed itself was this: On what phase of immigrant experience was the book to be based and what were to be its major objectives and themes? A vast bibliography exists for the study of the immigrant experience in the United States, but, to the best of my knowledge, nobody has undertaken to survey this literature, to extract from its gargantuan corpus those titles dealing with immigrant women (directly or indirectly), and to arrange in some meaningful form an introductory bibliography which would serve as the basis from which serious study could ensue. This book is intended as that introductory bibliography. It is preliminary to my answering the question I had initially posed (what phase of the immigrant experience?); and, candidly, the question cannot be easily answered given the richness of the resources available and the complexity of the socio-historical content in which they are found.

In gathering the available resources for the study of immigrant women (and constructing an intelligible framework into which they might be placed), I was surprised to discover that the new feminism had had little discernible influence on the study of the female immigrant experience of yesterday or today. Of course, feminism, as a modern ideology, is a complex phenomenon, and its ideas, John Charvet cautions us, must

> be studied, not as purely historical entities on which the historian forbears to make critical evaluations, and certainly not as ideologies whose worth is to be understood only in relation to the practical aims of the thinkers and their adherents, but as serious contributions to an understanding of the ethical basis of relations between men and women.[1]

Professor Charvet (London School of Economics and Political Science) is, of course, correct, and in a not uncharacteristic antithesis (essentially typical of English academicians), he deals with the elusive subtleties of an intractable phenomenon. In another frame of reference, I have explained, somewhat acerbically, the feminist response (or its absence) to immigrant women:

> The leaders of the contemporary American feminist movement have, it would appear, ignored their immigrant sisters for a very simple reason. Preoccupied as American feminist leaders have been with creating a hagiology of female illuminati they have quite naturally turned their attention to earlier American women reformers (their own middle-class predecessors) who waged a battle on a wide front of social abuses. In these ideological vineyards, American feminists have found a rich and varied biographical cornucopia: heroines as diverse as Jane Addams, Lillian Wald, Florence Kelley, Lillian Betts, Emily Greene Balch, Lillian Brandt, Frances Keller, and Edith Grace Abbott, to name but a few of the intrepid workers in the social settlements which flourished in American cities between 1880 and 1920. Immigrant women, solicitously the concerns of these earlier feminist reformers, impinge on the peripatetic interests of contemporary American feminism, but, as yet, have not commanded any attention. It is, of course, a short distance (for the contemporary feminist ideologues) from the historical contexts of immigrant women (circa 1880-1930) to the contemporary contexts of Black and Puerto Rican migrant women in American cities, but the American feminist movement has yet to begin the journey. [2]

There is still another side (demonstrating its protean evolving form) to the new feminism and immigrant women. Where immigrant women have been part of political strife, labor unrest, and class conflict, they have appealed ineluctably to the new feminists, and the appeal, understandably, has been irresistible to historians (feminist and otherwise). In its best form, the genre is exemplified in Meredith Tax's stirring The Rising of the Women (1980), whose compassionate portraiture of immigrant women in the maelstrom of an insensitive, industrially expanding America (e.g., the harrowing experience of the 1912 Lawrence, Massachusetts textile strike and its starving immigrant children) attests to the richness of the subject.

Professor Tax's brilliant social history (in which immigrant women are major protagonists) does not explain away the disinclination of other historians to study immigrant women; it does, however, dismiss the untenable thesis that there is nothing to study. Hasia R. Diner has, in Erin's Daughters in America, spoken directly to the issue:

> That immigrant women have not been studied is not because the material was not there. That poor, working-class women have not been studied is not because they were "inarticulate." It may be more accurate to say that historians, with their own biases of gender, class, and culture, have been basically deaf to the voices of such women and have assumed that they could not be studied. A creative use of the best of the old descriptive histories and the best of the new quantitative studies, cemented together with internal community sources that help one view these women as they viewed themselves, can go a long way toward filling this gap.[3]

That Professor Diner is correct, is confirmed by the verisimilitude of her narrative as she follows the women of Erin's Daughters from an Ireland devastated by the famine of the 1840's to their new homes in the United States, studying post-immigration family life, their work and education, their battles against poverty, alcoholism, and mental illness; and their newly found social and economic independence which further exacerbated frail relationships with Irish men. Professor Diner is adamant in asserting that her Erin's Daughters "could be repeated for Italian women, German women, and French Canadian women as well as for internal female migrants who abandoned the rural South to make their way to the urban North."

I have structured The Immigrant Woman in North America as comprehensively as practicable, drawing its entries from most disciplines, and reaching across a wide socio-historical spectrum. I have included sections on (I.) "Bibliography and General Reference," interpreted broadly to allow the inclusion of major ethnic group studies; and in (II.) "Autobiographies, Biographies, and Reminiscences," I have collected materials that allow immigrant women to tell their own stories. It is in the multifarious entries of (III.) "The Workplace and Political Encounters," and (IV.) "The Immigrant and the Progressive Reformers," that immigrant women assume the veiled but dynamic roles which explain an

industrially expanding America, and help illuminate the well-
springs of the humanitarian reform movement in the United
States, with its concomitant organized philanthropy, charity
agents, and settlement house reformers. A focal point of
reference is (V.) "The Family, Immigrant Child and Educational Influences," where entries explore themes of asimi-
lation and enforced acculturation better measured (in the long
view) in the immigrant child's encounters with the larger
society and its schools. Section (VI.) "Miscellanea" collects
entries that are interrelated and cut across categorical lines.
The book is a preliminary effort in no way intended as complete. Others may well (out of the vast literature on immigration) have made different selections and different frame-
works may have been articulated for the register of titles.

Although fiction and belles-lettres (particularly the
ethnic novel) afford a rich resource for a multifaceted portrait
of immigrant women, I have included only a handful of these
titles since this genre deserves a separate effort. In a class
by themselves (sui generis, with distinctive historical relationships with the United States) are the Mexican-American experience and the Puerto Rican migration to the mainland; both
have been the subjects of exhaustive study and are only very
limitedly noted in this work.

A debt is owed to many individuals both within and
outside academic communities who have kindly furnished
valuable information. Librarians at the Arthur and Elizabeth
Schlesinger Library on the History of Women in America
(Radcliffe College), the Balch Institute of Philadelphia, the
Tamiment Library (New York University), and the YIVO Institute for Jewish Research (New York City) were generous with
time and assistance, and this is gratefully acknowledged. I
owe a special debt to Cynthia W. Lund of the Rolvaag Memorial Library, St. Olaf College of Northfield, Minnesota.
Professor Rose Basile Green, whose The Italian-American
Novel (1974) is an important milestone in the chronicles of
the ethnic novel, has written the Foreword for this bibliography, a generous expression of support, for which I am
thankful. Prodire tenus si non datur ultra--indulgence is
asked for those errors which may, notwithstanding a good
deal of care, have crept into the book and for which I alone
must be held responsible.

A last word. For those of us born of immigrant wom-
en in America, there is a compelling poignancy, both haunt-

ing and elusive, in any attempt to bring our mothers out of the shadows. The task is painful, yet joyous.

Francesco Cordasco
West New York, N. J.
November 1984

NOTES

1. John Charvet, <u>Feminism</u> (London: J. M. Dent, 1982), 1.

2. Francesco Cordasco, "Review Essay: Louise C. Oden-crantz: Italian Women in Industry, A Study of Conditions in New York City (1919/1979)."   <u>Italian Americana</u>, 6 (1980):   235-236.

3. Hasia R. Diner, <u>Erin's Daughters in America</u> (Baltimore: Johns Hopkins, 1983), 12.

I. BIBLIOGRAPHY AND GENERAL REFERENCE

1. Abbott, Edith. Historical Aspects of the Immigration Problem.
    Select Documents. Chicago: University of Chicago Press, 1926.
    Covers the period of the "old immigration" before 1882, when
    the control of immigration was assumed by the Federal Gov-
    ernment.

2. Abbott, Edith. Immigration: Select Documents and Case Records.
    Chicago: University of Chicago Press, 1924. Reprint. New
    York: Arno Press, 1969.
    Documents related to passage, admission, exclusion, and ex-
    pulsion of aliens, and domestic migration problems, many of
    them involving women from a wide range of European coun-
    tries. All aspects of immigration are examined by an eminent
    sociologist, who served as dean of Chicago's School of Social
    Service Administration.

3. Abbott, Edith. Women in Industry: A Study of American Eco-
    nomic History. New York: D. Appleton, 1910. Reprint. New
    York: Arno Press, 1969.
    Pioneering work on women's place in American economy from
    colonial times to the twentieth century. Appendixes include
    material on child labor prior to 1870, women's wages in cotton
    mills, statistics on women in industry, and listing of occupa-
    tions employing women in 1900. Tracing the movement of
    women from the home to the factory, presents a historical
    survey of women's role in industry. It shows how women
    were drawn into the factories and plants by the economic
    forces seeking low cost labor, and describes at length their
    movement into such new enterprises as making boots, shoes,
    cigars, books.

4. Abbott, Grace, ed. The Child and the State. Chicago: Univer-
    sity of Chicago Press, 1938. 2 vols.
    Abbott served as head of the federal Children's Bureau. Docu-
    ments on problems of dependency, delinquency, child labor,
    and legal and institutional efforts addressed to these needs.
    Notices of the immigrant child and immigrant woman. See
    also the author's Ten Years' Work for Children (Washington:
    Children's Bureau, 1923). See Edith Abbott, "Grace Abbott
    and Hull House, 1908-1921," Social Service Review, 24 (Sep-
    tember/December 1950): 374-394, 493-518; and "Grace Ab-
    bott: A Sister's Memories," Social Service Review, 13 (Sep-
    tember 1939): 351-407.

5. Aldous, Joan, and Reuben Hill. International Bibliography of
    Research in Marriage and the Family, 1900-1964. Vol. 1.
    Minneapolis: University of Minnesota Press, 1967.
        Includes listing of periodicals. Volume 2, covering the years
        1965-72, was issued in 1974. Volume 3, entitled Inventory
        of Marriage and Family Literature, covering the years 1973-
        74, was issued in 1975, and since 1975 has been issued an-
        nually.

6. Altbach, Edith H. , ed. Women in America. Lexington, Mass. :
    D. C. Heath, 1974.
        Focus on working and middle-class women employed inside
        and outside of the home from colonial period. Includes
        chronology 1617-1973.

7. [American Italian Historical Association]. "The Italian Immi-
    grant Woman in North America. " Proceedings. Tenth Annual
    Conference, October 28-29, 1977, held in Toronto, Ontario
    (Canada) in Conjunction with the Canadian Italian Historical As-
    sociation. Toronto: The Multicultural History Society of On-
    tario, 1978.
        Papers on (1) Women in the Old Country; (2) Early Years in
        North America; (3) The Italian-American Women: Genera-
        tions, Roles, and Attitudes; (4) Women, Kinship, and Net-
        works of Ethnicity; (5) Images of Italian Women in the Arts.

8. [American Italian Historical Association]. "Pane e Lavoro:
    The Italian American Working Class. " Proceedings. Eleventh
    Annual Conference, October 27-28, 1978, held in Cleveland,
    Ohio, John Carroll University. Toronto: The Multicultural
    History Society of Ontario, 1980.
        Includes papers on "Anthony Capraro and the Lawrence Strike
        of 1919"; "Italians and the Tampa General Strike of 1910";
        "Italian Involvement in the 1903-04 Coal Miners' Strike in
        Southern Colorado and Utah"; Italians in the Cherry, Illinois,
        Mine Disaster"; "The Cultural Background of the Italian Im-
        migrant Woman and Its Impact on Her Unionization in the
        New York City Garment Industry, 1880-1919"; "Angela Bam-
        bace and the International Ladies Garment Workers Union:
        The Search for an Elusive Activist"; "The Padrone System
        and Sojourners in the Canadian North, 1885-1920"; "Italian
        American Workers and the Response to Fascism"; "The Ital-
        ian American Working Class and the Vietnam War. "

9. Archdeacon, Thomas J. Becoming American: An Ethnic His-
    tory. New York: The Free Press, 1983.

10. Balch, Emily G. Our Slavic Fellow Citizens. New York:
    Charity Publications Commission, 1910.
        Based on firsthand inquiry in Europe and America, its object
        being to examine the conditions in which the Slavic immigrant
        lives in the United States, and "how far he remains the same
        man that he was at home. " A basic source for Czech, Slovak,
        Polish, Rusin (Ruthenian), Croatian, and Bulgarian immigrants.

11.   The Balch Institute.   (18 South Seventh St. , Philadelphia, Pa.
      19106).
      An educational institution devoted to North American immi-
      gration, ethnic, racial, and minority group history.   The
      Institute comprises a museum and library whose seven-point
      program includes: (1) library programs; (2) exhibitions; (3)
      educational programs; (4) outreach programs; (5) internal re-
      search; (6) information coordination; (7) Bicentennial plan-
      ning.   The Institute plans to assemble the nation's most
      comprehensive collection of books, manuscripts, and printed
      materials concerning all national groups who came to North
      America.   Plans call for a library of 400,000 volumes; 20
      million manuscripts; 20,000 reels of microfilm; and large
      numbers of ethnic and minority group newspapers.   The In-
      stitute is supported by trusts established by the late Mrs.
      Emily Swift Balch and her sons, Edwin Swift Balch and
      Thomas Willing Balch.

12.   [The Balch Institute].   Historical Reading Lists.   Philadelphia:
      Balch Institute, 1973- .
      Valuable annotated lists on American immigration and ethnic
      group history.   Handlists issued thus far include "Immigra-
      tion and Ethnicity in North America"; and individual lists on
      the Irish, Swiss, French, Ukrainians, Portuguese, English,
      Welsh, South Slavs, Finns, Greeks, Italians, Mexicans,
      Puerto Ricans, Poles, and Spanish Americans.   Others are
      projected.

13.   Barton, Josef J.   Peasants and Strangers: Italians, Rumanians
      and Slovaks in an American City, 1890-1950.   Cambridge,
      Mass. : Harvard University Press, 1975.
      The American experience of Cleveland's Italian, Rumanian,
      and Slovak communities between 1890 and 1950, with notices
      of assimilation, ethnic neighborhoods, the immigrant family,
      social mobility and the schools.

14.   Baum, Charlotte; Paula Hyman; and Sonya Michel.   The Jewish
      Woman in America.   New York: The Dial Press, 1976.
      Contends that beginning in the 1930's the image of the Jewish
      woman in literature written by Jews shifted from an ener-
      getic, warm, loving, and sentimental type to a materialistic,
      shrewish, hysterical, even castrating type.   Even if the au-
      thors do not successfully explain it, they provide a most en-
      lightening discussion and a penetrating analysis.   Recognizing
      characteristics similar to the general American family type,
      the authors point to culture and economic changes (highlighted
      by the Great Depression) in accounting for shifting family
      dynamics whereby the intergenerational conflict moves from
      father-son to son-mother.   Notable efforts are made to ex-
      plain the emergence of the "Jewish mother" and "Jewish
      American princess" types of objects of Jewish male opprobri-
      um.   Includes historical accounts of exploitation of Jewish
      women in the sweatshops of the garment industry as well as

in the heretofore taboo subject area of "Jewish prostitution."
Other "pathological" aspects of ordinarily revered Jewish
life, such as male desertion and illegitimacy, are also recognized and put into historical perspective.

15.   Baxandall, Rosalyn, et al., eds. America's Working Women:
       A Documentary History, 1600-Present. New York: Vintage
       Books, 1976.
              Includes sections on Native American, immigrant, and black
              women.

16.   Berg, Barbara. The Remembered Gate: Origins of American
       Feminism: The Woman and the City, 1800-1860. New York:
       Oxford University Press, 1978.
              Argues that the burgeoning urban growth of this era had im-
              portant impacts on women and the rise of feminism--as dis-
              tinct from the more narrowly focused issues of women's
              rights--"at once heightening women's oppression and setting
              the stage for her future efforts at emancipation."

17.   Bernheimer, Charles S., ed. The Russian Jew in the United
       States: Studies of Social Conditions in New York, Philadelphia,
       and Chicago, with a Description of Rural Settlements. Phila-
       delphia: John C. Winston, 1905. Reprint. Clifton, N.J.:
       Augustus M. Kelley, 1971.
              Includes "VI: Educational Influences," pp. 183-219, notices
              of immigrant Jewish women and children. See also the
              author's autobiography, Half a Century of Community Service
              (1917).

18.   Berthoff, Rowland T. British Immigrants in Industrial America,
       1790-1950. Cambridge, Mass.: Harvard University Press,
       1953.
              A history of how English, Scottish, and Welsh immigrants
              (with attention to immigrant women) have fared economically
              and socially in the United States based entirely on primary
              source materials. The British immigrants, as skilled work-
              ers, soon filled the higher paid jobs in textiles, iron, and
              steel, and moved on to management and ownership when
              other immigrants took their place. Since they possessed
              the same language as the native-born, the assimilation was
              easier, and quickly leveled social barriers.

19.   Bickner, Mie Liang. "The Forgotten Minority: Asian American
       Women." Amerasia Journal, 11 (Spring 1974): 1-17.

20.   Blau, Joseph L., and Salo W. Baron, eds. The Jews of the
       United States, 1790-1840: A Documentary History. 3 vols.
       New York: Columbia University Press, 1963.
              Over 300 documents arranged chronologically with introduc-
              tions to each document and general introductions to each
              major section: "The Place of the Jews in American Life";
              "Economic Life"; "The Family and Social Life"; "The First

Jews in American Politics"; "Stirrings of Cultural Activity";
"The Strains of Religious Adjustment"; "Christian and Jew";
"Widening Geographic Horizons"; and "American Jews and
World Jewry."

21. Blegen, Theodore. Norwegian Migration to America. 2 vols.
     Northfield, Minn.: Norwegian-American Historical Association,
     1931-1940. Reprint. New York: Arno Press, 1969.
        A massive history encompassing all facets of Norwegian im-
     migration to the United States, with considerable material
     on the Norwegian immigrant family.

22. Blicksilver, Edith. "The Ethnic American Woman Anthologized."
     California English, 18 (November-December 1982): 12-24.

23. Blicksilver, Edith. The Ethnic Woman: Problems, Protests,
     and Lifestyles. Dubuque, Iowa: Kendall/Hunt, 1978.
        A collection of literary materials on Asian, European and
     Hispanic immigrant women. Includes materials on Native
     American and black women.

24. Bowers, David F., ed. Foreign Influences in American Life.
     Princeton, N.J.: Princeton University Press, 1944.
        Foreign contributions to the formation of American values
     and institutions. See, particularly, Stow Persons, "The
     Americanization of the Immigrant." Essays are largely on
     the impact of immigrants on American society.

25. Brace, Charles Loring. The Dangerous Classes of New York
     and Twenty Years Among Them. 3rd ed. New York: Wynkoop
     and Hallenbeck, 1880.
        Charles Loring Brace (1826-1890), one of the founders of
     the Children's Aid Society, describes his work among the
     poor (largely the immigrant Irish) of the city, "classes with
     inherited pauperism and crime." See also Emma Brace,
     The Life of Charles Loring Brace, Chiefly Told in His Own
     Letters (1894), and Charles R. Henderson, Introduction to
     the Study of Dependent, Defective and Delinquent Classes
     (2nd ed., 1901).

26. Bremner, Robert H. American Philanthropy. Chicago: Chicago
     University Press, 1960.

27. Bremner, Robert H., et al., eds. Childhood and Youth in
     America: A Documentary History. 3 vols. in 5 vols. Cam-
     bridge, Mass.: Harvard University Press, 1971-1974.
        A vast repository of materials which provides the most com-
     plete documentary history of public provision for American
     children. For immigrant women and children, see Vol. II
     (1866-1932), parts 1-6.

28. Bremner, Robert H. From the Depths: The Discovery of
     Poverty in United States. New York: New York University
     Press, 1956.

A study of "America's awakening to poverty as a social
problem." Invaluable for the immigrant family and its
milieu; particularly, "Part Two: The Search for Truth,
1897-1917"; and "Part Three: Social Striving, 1897-1925."

29.   Brickman, William W. The Jewish Community in America:
      An Annotated and Classified Bibliographical Guide. New York:
      Burt Franklin, 1976.

30.   Brownlee, W. Elliott, and Mary M. Brownlee, eds. Women
      in the American Economy: A Documentary History, 1675-1925.
      New Haven, Conn.: Yale University Press, 1976.
      Contains primary documents related to women's evolving
      economic roles and status on farms, in factories and pro-
      fessions, and as consumers.

31.   Buenker, John D., and Nicholas C. Burckel. Immigration and
      Ethnicity: A Guide to Information Sources. Detroit: Gale Re-
      search, 1977.

32.   Buhle, Mari Jo. Women and the American Left: A Guide to
      Sources. Boston: G. K. Hall, 1983.
      Reviews sources on women and the American left beginning
      in 1871, and continuing through 1981. Within each time-
      frame (1871-1900; 1901-1919; 1920-1964; 1965-1981) sources
      are grouped under specific headings: general works and
      histories; autobiographies and biographies arranged by subject;
      books and pamphlets that specifically address the "Woman
      Question"; periodicals with a discernible socialist feminist
      content; and works of fiction, plays, novels, poetry.

33.   Bullough, Vern, et al., eds. A Bibliography of Prostitution.
      New York: Garland Publishing, 1977.
      The editors arrange their entries by topics, chronology, and
      geographic area. The scope is international, but much ma-
      terial on the United States is included, with some notices of
      immigrant women.

34.   Burgess, Thomas. Greeks in America. Boston: Sherman
      French, 1913. Reprint. San Francisco: R & E Research
      Associates, 1970.
      Information on many Greek communities in America, with
      account of organization and development of Orthodox church,
      and the acculturation of the Greek immigrant family.

35.   Cabello-Argaudona, Roberto, et al., eds. The Chicana: A
      Comprehensive Bibliographic Study. Los Angeles: Chicano
      Studies Center, University of California, 1975.
      The editors include films, articles and government publica-
      tions as well as books and monographs. The unannotated
      entries deal with Spanish-speaking women and the feminist
      movement, sex roles, discrimination in employment, health,
      family, and marriage.

36. Calhoun, Arthur W. A Social History of the American Family
     from Colonial Times to the Present. 3 vols. Cleveland:
     Arthur H. Clark, 1917-19. Reprint. New York: Arno Press,
     1973.
       Calhoun was Professor of Sociology at Clark University.
     Vol. III ("From 1865 to 1919") includes considerable materi-
     al on the immigrant woman, child, and family. See I,
     Chapters 1, 5; II, Chapter 4; III, Chapter 6.

37. Cantor, Aviva, ed. Bibliography on the Jewish Woman: A
     Comprehensive and Annotated Listing of Works Published 1900-
     1978. Fresh Meadows, N. Y.: Doris B. Gold, 1979.
       Includes general titles in history, nonsexist children's books,
     and poetry, with more specialized ones relating to Jewish
     women in American History. Lists Jewish publications
     and organizations, and feminist presses. Available from
     Biblio Press, P. O. Box 22, Fresh Meadows, New York
     11365.

38. Cantor, Milton, and Bruce Laurie, eds. Class, Sex, and the
     Women. Westport, Conn.: Greenwood Press, 1977.
       Ten contemporary views of nineteenth-century working im-
     migrant (Italian and Jewish) women, women in the West, and
     the Women's Trade Union League.

39. Caroli, Betty Boyd. "Italian Women in America: Sources for
     Study." Italian Americana, 2 (Spring 1976): 242-54.
       A general overview with important bibliographical sources
     and a number of preliminary conclusions on the Italian im-
     migrant woman.

40. Carpenter, Niles. Immigrants and Their Children. U. S. Bu-
     reau of the Census, Census Monograph, No. 7. Washington,
     D. C.: Government Printing Office, 1927.
       Statistical analysis of the distribution of immigrants, spatial
     demography, residence, national origins, race, sex, language,
     age, marriage patterns, citizenship, occupations. See also
     E. P. Hutchinson, Immigrants and Their Children (1956),
     an updating of the Carpenter data. Reference should also
     be made to Catalogs of the Bureau of the Census Library
     (Washington, D. C.), which include some 323,000 cards
     whose publication is under way (Boston: G. K. Hall, 1976-
     1981. 20 vols.).

41. Center for Migration Studies. (Brooklyn College, City Uni-
     versity of New York).
       Organized to "assist scholars in the social sciences, edu-
     cation, humanities, and related fields in the collection, pre-
     servation, and analysis of primary and secondary materials
     for the study of the migration processes." An Archives of
     Migration "will solicit manuscripts, photographs and taped
     autobiographies and interviews with significant persons in-
     volved in various aspects of migration."

8 The Immigrant Woman

42. Center for Migration Studies. (209 Flagg Place, Staten Island,
     New York, N.Y. 10304).
     A specialized library on migration and a card catalogue of
     books, articles, and dissertations on migration. Particularly
     strong (at the present time, the most comprehensive) in its
     collection of Italian-American materials. Publishes The
     International Migration Review, a scientific journal studying
     sociological, demographic, historical, and legislative aspects
     of migration. Maintains connections with Centro Studi Emi-
     grazione (Via Dondolo, 58, Roma, Italia), a Center staffed
     by the Society of St. Charles, a religious order ministering
     to migrants since 1887, which publishes Studi Emigrazione.

43. Chaff, Sandra L., et al., eds. Women in Medicine: A Bibli-
     ography of the Literature on Women Physicians. Metuchen,
     N.J.: Scarecrow Press, 1977.
     Includes history, biography, recruitment, medical education,
     specialties, missionary activity, psychosocial factors, and
     medical societies. A section on fiction is included. Entries
     are annotated. International in scope. Covers statistical
     data as well as history of physicians in general and as in-
     dividuals. Notices of women immigrant physicians.

44. Commons, John R., et al., eds. A Documentary History of
     American Industrial Society. With a Preface by Richard T.
     Ely and an Introduction by John B. Clark. 2nd edition with
     new Prefaces. Cleveland: Charles H. Clark, 1909-1911. 10
     vols. Reprint. New York: Russell & Russell, 1958.
     Invaluable resource for schools, immigrant children, and
     women, in an industrially expanding America.

45. Commons, John R., et al., eds. History of Labor in the
     United States. 4 vols. New York: Macmillan, 1918-35. Re-
     print. New York: Augustus M. Kelley, 1966.
     A collection of monographs by Commons, his colleagues,
     and students on a wide variety of labor-related topics rang-
     ing from the early nineteenth century to the New Deal era.
     Volumes 3 and 4 deal specifically with the period from 1896
     to 1932. Volume 3 focuses on the composition of the labor
     force, working conditions, employers' policies, and labor
     legislation and women in the labor force. Volume 4 deals
     with the Progressive era, the rise and fall of labor radi-
     calism, the effects of the war, and the labor doldrums of
     the 1920's.

46. Commons, John R. Races and Immigrants in America. New
     York: Macmillan, 1907.
     Surveys the historical evolution of the American demography
     and analyzes the role of immigrants in industry, labor,
     crime, poverty, and politics. Illustrates the assimilationist
     outlook of many prominent intellectuals and reformers of the
     era.

47. Conroy, Hilery, and T. Scott Miyakawa, eds. East Across
     the Pacific: Historical and Sociological Studies of Japanese
     Immigration and Assimilation. Santa Barbara, Calif.: ABC-
     Clio, 1972.
         A collection of essays with important historical backgrounds
         on Japanese communities before 1940, and the internment
         of the Japanese during World War II.

48. Conway, Jill K. The Female Experience in Eighteenth- and
     Nineteenth-Century America: A Guide to the History of Ameri-
     can Women. New York: Garland Publishing, 1984.
         Documents primary sources and secondary writings which
         have a bearing on the study of women from a variety of
         fields. It is organized to throw light on women's place in
         society in early industrial America. It analyzes women's
         work, both paid and unpaid, and lists sources for the study
         of the impact of technology both on women's place in the
         paid workforce and in domestic work. Sources are also
         provided to permit the examination of transformations of
         women's cultural roles in the wake of technological changes.
         Women's political participation is treated in both its informal
         and formal aspects and the political transfer from reform
         movements such as the temperance movement can be studied
         through the sources listed.

49. Cordasco, Francesco, and David N. Alloway. American Ethnic
     Groups: The European Heritage. Metuchen, N.J.: Scarecrow
     Press, 1981.
         Includes over 1,400 dissertations which deal with ethnic
         groups identified in the conceptual design which sets up two
         major geographical areas of origin: Western and Northern
         Europe; Central, Southern and Eastern Europe. Also in-
         cludes these sections: Multi-Group, Interethnic and Related
         Studies; Emigration/Immigration; Miscellanea; and a Check-
         list of Selected Published Bibliographies. It makes available
         the vast and largely unused doctoral dissertation resources
         that have studied the past and still evolving history of Ameri-
         can European ethnic groups.

50. Cordasco, Francesco, ed. A Bibliography of American Im-
     migration History: The George Washington University Project
     Studies. Fairfield, N.J.: Augustus M. Kelley, 1977.
         Includes "An Introductory Bibliography for the History of
         American Immigration, 1607-1955"; and "An Annotated Bibli-
         ography on the Demographic, Economic and Sociological As-
         pects of Immigration."

51. Cordasco, Francesco. Immigrant Children in American Schools:
     A Classified and Annotated Bibliography. With Selected Source
     Documents. Fairfield, N.J.: Augustus M. Kelley, 1976.
         Incorporates some 1,500 entries in a classified plan: (I)
         Basic References, General History, and Immigration; (II)
         The Immigrant Child and His World; (III) Selected Source

Documents: Edward L. Thorndike, The Elimination of Pupils
from School (1908); The Education of the Immigrant (1913);
State Americanization (1919); The Problem of Adult Education
(1920). See Review, S. M. Tomasi, International Migration
Review, 12 (Summer 1978): 277-278.

52.   Cordasco, Francesco, and Eugene Bucchioni. The Italians:
Social Backgrounds of an American Group. Clifton, N.J.:
Augustus M. Kelley, 1974.
Sources drawn from the period circa 1890-1940. Part I:
Emigration: The Exodus of a Latin People; Part II: Italian
Communities in America: Campanilismo in the Ghetto; Part
III: Responses to American Life; Part IV: Employment,
Health, and Social Needs; Part V: Education: The Italian
Child in the American School. Includes 16 halftone con-
temporary photographs and annotated bibliography.

53.   Cordasco, Francesco. Italian Americans: A Guide to Informa-
tion Sources. Detroit: Gale Research, 1978.
Includes some 2,000 entries on all aspects of the Italian
American experience. See particularly II (Social Sciences):
E. Economics and Labor; G. Education; H. Anthropology,
Folklore, and Popular Customs. IV (Applied Sciences): A.
Health and Related Concerns.

54.   Cordasco, Francesco, ed. Studies in Italian-American Social
History: Essays in Honor of Leonard Covello. Totowa, N.J.:
Rowman and Littlefield, 1975.
Includes F. Cordasco, "Leonard Covello and the Casa Italiana
Educational Bureau: A Note on the Beginnings of Systematic
Italian-American Studies," pp. 1-9; William V. D'Antonio,
"Ethnicity and Assimilation: A Reconsideration," pp. 10-27;
Jerre Mangione, "On Being Sicilian-American," pp. 40-49;
Andrew Rolle, "The American-Italians: Psychological and
Social Adjustments," pp. 105-117; Valentine R. Winsey,
"The Italian Immigrant Women Who Arrived in the United
States Before World War I," pp. 199-210; and other essays
on Italian life in the United States. Includes, also, Leonard
Covello, "The Social Background and Educational Problems
of the Italian Family in America," pp. 211-221 (Appendix I).

55.   Cotera, Martha P. The Chicana Feminist. Austin, Tex.: Information Systems Development, 1977.
Presents material on heritage, role, identity, issues, and
other areas. Bibliography partially annotated.

56.   Cotera, Martha P. The History and Heritage of the Chicana
in the U.S. Austin, Tex.: Information Systems Development,
1976.
Draws a socioeconomic profile of the Chicana and views her
as a member of the family and of society at large.

57.   Covello Papers. (East Harlem, New York City, ethnic community).

A rich collection of reports, papers, correspondence and
memorabilia collected by Leonard Covello (1887-1982) on
the life of the largest Italian community in the United States
(circa 1915-1945). Includes (1) Italian community materials;
(2) community school movement, i.e., Benjamin Franklin
High School and immigrant community; (3) Puerto Rican community materials. Deposited in Balch Institute of Philadelphia.

58. Davis, Allen F., and Mark H. Haller, eds. The Peoples of
     Philadelphia: A History of Ethnic Groups and Lower-Class
     Life, 1790-1940. Philadelphia: Temple University Press, 1973.
       Notices of Immigrant women, children and the schools in
     Chapters 10, 11, and 12: "The Immigrant and the City:
     Poles, Italians, and Jews in Philadelphia, 1870-1920";
     "Philadelphia's Jewish Neighborhoods"; and "Philadelphia's
     South Italians in the 1920's."

59. Davis, Jerome. The Russian Immigrant. New York: Mac-
     millan, 1922.
       An important early study on all phases of Russian immigrant
     life in America, with valuable notices of the immigrant fami-
     ly and women.

60. DePauw, Linda Grant. Four Traditions: Women of New York
     During the American Revolution. Albany: New York State
     American Revolution Bicentennial Commission, Office of State
     History, State Education Department, 1974.
       Examines the role of New York women of revolutionary times,
     within the context of four cultural traditions from the seven-
     teenth and eighteenth centuries: Iroquois, African, Dutch,
     and English. Shows that the cultural traditions of these
     four groups of women influenced their reactions to the Revo-
     lutionary War and also affected the way in which the war
     changed their lives. Intended as an addition to the small
     body of material available in the area of women's studies,
     the author emphasizes the effect of the war on women's
     status and includes documented stories concerning the ac-
     tivities of women during the war.

61. Diner, Hasia R. Erin's Daughters in America: Irish Immi-
     grant Women in the Nineteenth Century. Baltimore: The
     Johns Hopkins University Press, 1983.
       Described here are thousands of Irish women who saw in
     America the chance to utilize the energy, ambition, and
     ability that would otherwise have remained stifled by the
     poverty and social inflexibility of their native land. Erin's
     Daughters in America follows these women from an Ireland
     devastated by the Great Famine of the 1840's to their new
     homes in the United States. Hasia Diner explores their
     postimmigration family life, their work and education, their
     battles against poverty, alcoholism, and mental illness, and
     the network of formal and informal ethnic organizations that

developed to help them adjust to a different way of life.
Diner also discusses the stress that the immigrant women's
newly found social and economic independence put on already
frail relationships with Irish men. In terms of marriage,
work, educational achievement, and upward mobility, Irish
women were very different from--and much more successful
than--other female immigrants. Diner describes that success in detail, but her primary emphasis is on the qualities
that enabled Irish women to prosper in a new and challenging world. The origins of those qualities, she argues, can
be found only in Ireland, in a cultural tradition that the immigrant women could neither live within nor leave behind
them. A major contribution.

62. Diner, Hasia R. Women and Urban Society: A Guide to Information Sources. Detroit: Gale Research, 1979.
Provides information concerning the impact of urbanization
on women throughout the world. Deals with migration of
women and their adaptation to the urban environment, women
and the urban family, fertility patterns, employment and the
sociological and psychological impact on immigrant women.

63. Dinnerstein, Leonard, and David M. Reimers. Ethnic Americans: A History of Immigration and Assimilation. New York:
Harper & Row, 1975.
Concentrates on non-English immigrants, with particular
emphasis on the period after 1840. Important materials on
ethnic conflict and immigration restriction; ethnic background
of the American population; and provisions of major U.S.
immigration laws and programs.

64. Dinnerstein, Leonard; Roger L. Nichols; and David M. Reimers.
Natives and Strangers: Ethnic Groups and the Building of
America. New York: Oxford University Press, 1979.
Integrates the experiences of racial, religious, and ethnic
minorities into the mainstream of American history. See
review, F. Cordasco, The Annals, 444 (July 1979): 178-
179.

65. Douglass, William, and John Bilbao. Amerikanuac: The
Basques of the New World. Reno: University of Nevada Press,
1975.
Virtually an unstudied group. A basic source with materials
not easily available, with materials on the Basque immigrant
family and its acculturation.

66. Durran, Pat H., and R. Cabella-Argaudona, comps. The
Chicana: A Bibliographic Study. Los Angeles: University of
California, Chicano Studies Center, 1973.

67. [East European Jews]. YIVO Institute for Jewish Research.
(1048 Fifth Ave., New York City, N.Y.).

Institution dedicated to the study of East European culture
and Jewish ethnography. YIVO's Polish-Jewry collection includes over 10,000 photographs. Also, Jewish Museum
(1109 Fifth Ave., New York City, N.Y.). See New York
Times, March 28, 1976, for notice of photographic exhibit
covering period 1864-1939.

68. Educational Alliance. Reports. 1893- .
The Alliance was a consolidation of efforts (e.g., Hebrew
Free School Association; Young Men's Hebrew Association;
and Aquilar Free Library Society) by German Jews (earlier
immigrants) to aid East European Jews in New York City.
A major source of help to the new immigrants, the Alliance
Reports are a rich source for immigrant life. See S. P.
Rudens, "A Half-Century of Community Service: The Story
of the New York Educational Alliance," American Jewish
Year Book, (1944), pp. 73-86.

69. Ehrlich, Richard L., ed. Immigrants in Industrial America,
1850-1920. Charlottesville: University Press of Virginia for
the Eleutherian Mills-Hagley Foundation and Balch Institute,
1977.
The major theme running through the volume is the persistence of pre-migration patterns, habits, and values in an
American setting. Moreover, the family emerges as the
primary mechanism for perpetuating the pre-migration culture. Immigrant groups differed in their family structure,
in their attitude towards daughters and wives working outside the home, and in the appropriate economic contribution
of children. In coping with the urban, industrial setting,
the immigrants employed strategies which minimized the
upheavals in their family networks and values. At the same
time, family and kinship ties displayed a remarkable ability
to adapt to changing needs. The essays by Golab on Philadelphia Poles; Yans-McLaughlin on Buffalo Italians; Hareven
on Manchester, New Hampshire French-Canadians; and Carole
Groneman on Irish and German women in New York emphasize the importance of the family in the migration process.

70. Ethnic and Immigration Groups: The United States, Canada and
England. New York: The Institute for Research in History
and The Haworth Press, 1983.
The primacy of the North American experience is the point
of departure for this issue of the Trends in History series.
The essays deal with the political aspects of ethnicity, the
current debate over acculturation and pluralism in American
society, immigrant women, immigrants from Asia and Latin
America, the Canadian experience, and immigrant groups
from India who have settled in England since World War II.

71. "Ethnicity and Femininity: Special Issue." Canadian Ethnic
Studies--Etudes Ethniques Canadiennes, 13 (1981): 1-148.

The entire issue is devoted to the history of immigrant wom-
en in Canada, with articles exploring themes on acculturation, work and family roles.

72.   Ewen, Elizabeth W.   "Immigrant Women in the Land of Dollars,
       1890-1920." Unpublished Ph.D. dissertation. State University
       of New York (Stony Brook), 1979.
       Concerns itself with the migration of Jewish and Italian wom-
       en to New York City's Lower East Side during the period
       1890-1920. It locates the specific historical experience of
       immigrant women within the framework of the industrial
       transformation of the United States in the early decades of
       the twentieth century. By using a compilation of oral his-
       tory, autobiographical and literary sources, and the litera-
       ture of social work, the dissertation focuses on the relation-
       ship between the articulation of experience on the part of
       immigrant women, with the larger historical trends of the
       period, specifically industrialization and Americanization.

73.   Fairbanks, Carol, and Sara Brooks Sundberg.   Farm Women
       on the Prairie Frontier: A Sourcebook for Canada and the
       United States. Illustrations by Ted F. Myers. Metuchen,
       N.J.: Scarecrow Press, 1983.
       Four essays ("Early Agricultural Settlement on the Interior
       Grasslands of North America"; "A Usable Past: Women on
       the American Prairies"; "Farm Women on the Canadian
       Prairie Frontier: The Helpmate Image"; and "Women and
       Their Visions: Perspectives from Fiction") provide intro-
       ductions to the land and the people, the history, and the
       fiction. In Part II, the annotations direct readers and re-
       searchers to relevant materials in history and literature.
       Included here are approximately 70 works related to history
       and background; 90 works by Canadian women and 40 works
       by American women--their reminiscences, letters, diaries;
       40 Canadian novels; 60 American novels; and 80 books and
       articles providing literary backgrounds and criticism.

74.   [Finns].   The Finnish Experience in the Western Great Lakes
       Region: New Perspectives. St. Paul, Minn.: Immigration
       History Research Center, 1976.
       Proceedings of a conference held at the University of Min-
       nesota, April 25-26, and 27, 1974. Includes materials on
       the settlement and institutional growth of Finnish community
       in America, with notices of Finnish immigrant women, and
       immigrant families.

75.   Foerster, Robert F.   The Italian Emigration of Our Times.
       Cambridge: Harvard University Press, 1919. Reprint: with
       an introductory note by F. Cordasco. New York: Russell &
       Russell, 1968.
       A vast storehouse of information on the mass Italian migra-
       tions between 1876 and 1919 to all parts of the world. Chap-
       ters 17-20 (pp. 320-411) are devoted to the experience in

the United States with notices of family life, the role of
women, health, assimilation, and education.

76. Friis, Erik J., ed.   The Scandinavian Presence in North
America.   New York: Harper's Magazine Press, 1976.
The largest convocation of specialists on the Scandinavian
experience in the United States was convened in Minneapolis
on May 2-3, 1973, sponsored by the Center for Northwest
European Studies at the University of Minnesota and by SAS/
Scandinavian Airlines.   The seminar addressed, discussed,
and elaborated a single theme and its manifold refinements:
the present state of, and the future prospects for, the
Scandinavian presence in America, or Scanpresence.   Erik
J. Friis has skillfully edited the proceedings of the conference, and this volume is an invaluable contribution to
ethnic socio-historiography and appropriately appeared in
the Bicentennial of the United States focusing "attention on
the great variety of national and ethnic strains in the American amalgam and what they have contributed to the whole."
See review, R. E. Lindgren, International Migration Review,
11 (Summer 1977):   249-250.

77. Fujitomi, Irene, and Diane Wong.   "The New Asian-American
Women," in Stanley Sue and Nathaniel N. Wagner, eds., Asian
Americans: Psychological Perspectives (Ben Lomond, Calif.:
Science and Behavior Books, 1973), pp. 252-262.

78. Georges, R. A., and S. Stern.   American and Canadian Immigrant and Ethnic Folklore: An Annotated Bibliography.   New
York: Garland Publishing, 1982.
Focuses on examples and analysis of traditional expressive
forms and behaviors observed among, recorded from and
concerned with members of the immigrant generations and
their New World progeny.   The 1,900 entries cover a time
period from 1888 through 1980.   Invaluable for family customs and evolving patterns of acculturation.

79. Glanz, Rudolf.   Jew and Italian: Historic Group Relations and
the New Immigration, 1881-1924.   New York: Ktav Publishing
House, 1971.
Chapters on family building and education: citizenship, immigrant help and social work; occupational structure, etc.
See review, R. J. Vecoli, International Migration Review,
vol. 7 (Summer 1973), pp. 208-209.

80. Glanz, Rudolf.   The Jewish Woman in America: Two Female
Generations 1820-1929.   Volume 1:   The Eastern European
Woman.   Volume 2:   The German Jewish Woman.   New York:
Ktav Publishing House, 1976.   2 vols.
The great proportion of women and children among Jewish
immigrants to the U.S. resulted in the evolution of a virtu-
ally new class among the immigrants--the unmarried work-
ing girl.   Particular attention is given to the efforts of

such service organizations at the National Council of Jewish
Women to aid the immigrant working girls, as well as married women and mothers, to adjust to American life.

81.   Glazer, Nathan, and Daniel Patrick Moynihan. Beyond the
      Melting Pot: The Negroes, Puerto Ricans, Jews, Italians,
      and Irish of New York City. 2nd ed.   Cambridge, Mass.:
      M. I. T. Press, 1970.
         An influential study of American ethnic groups with special
      reference to the twin themes of the persistence of ethnicity
      in the United States, and the emergence of the "new ethni-
      city." Appeared originally in 1963; the 1970 edition incor-
      porated a 90-page introduction, "New York City in 1970."

82.   Goldfield, David R., and James B. Lane, eds.   The Enduring
      Ghetto. Philadelphia: J. B. Lippincott, 1973.
         Collection of materials on American ethnic groups, the inter-
      stitial immigrant community, and family roles, with notices
      of black inner cities and interethnic tensions.

83.   Gordon, Milton M.   Assimilation in American Life: The Role
      of Race, Religion and National Origins.   New York: Oxford
      University Press, 1964.
         Perceives seven important stages or "subprocesses" in as-
      similation and three theories that have attempted its expla-
      nation.   Rejects Anglo-Conformity theory and the Melting-
      Pot theory; integrates his own position (structural pluralism)
      with that of cultural pluralism.   See review, F. Cordasco,
      Journal of Human Relations, 13 (First Quarter, 1965): 142-
      143.   See also Gordon's Social Class in American Society
      (1958).

84.   Govorchin, Gerald G.   Americans from Yugoslavia.   Gaines-
      ville: University of Florida Press, 1961.
         Yugoslav immigration to America, with notices of schooling
      and acculturation of the Yugoslav family.   See also Branko
      M. Colakovic, "Yugoslav Migrations to America," unpub-
      lished Ph. D. dissertation, University of Minnesota, 1970.

85.   Greene, Victor R.   For God and Country: The Rise of Polish
      and Lithuanian Ethnic Consciousness in America, 1860-1910.
      Madison: State Historical Society of Wisconsin, 1975.
         Summaries of the background of Polish and Lithuanian mi-
      gration to the U. S., the building of Chicago as the "immi-
      grant capital," factionalism among Poles and Lithuanians,
      and the relationship of such tensions to ethnic and national
      consciousness.   See also Greene's The Slavic Community
      on Strike (1968).

86.   Haber, Barbara.   Women in America: A Guide to Books, 1963-
      1975.   Boston: G. K. Hall, 1978,   Reprint.   Urbana:
      University of Illinois Press, 1981.

Haber, curator of printed books at the Schlesinger Library
on the History of Women in America, Radcliffe College,
abstracted some 3,300 articles in 500 periodicals. Arranged
by subject, and with an appendix of books published 1976-
1979, the list includes many autobiographies and biographies,
works of fiction, and sources related to women's liberation.
Three chronological sections--1783 to 1865, Civil War to
World War II, and 1945 to the present--are further sub-
divided into subject divisions.

87. Hagopian, Elaine C., and Ann Paden, eds. The Arab-Ameri-
cans: Studies in Assimilation. Wilmette, Ill.: Medina University Press International, 1969.
Emphasis is on Syrians, with general studies on Arab immigrant families in the United States.

88. Hale, Frederick, ed. Danes in North America. Seattle: University of Washington Press, 1984.
Documents the stories of Danes who left their European
homeland, mostly in the latter half of the nineteenth century,
for the promise of America. In little-explored archives and
repositories throughout Denmark, Hale has searched for and
translated letters written by Danes (both men and women)
in America to friends, family, and hometown newspapers
in Denmark. Although collections of both Swedish and Norwegian immigrant correspondence have long been valuable
standard works in the field, no similar compilation of Danish
immigrant experience, as told in scores of personal letters,
has been available. Each chapter addresses a major theme
or aspect of life in nineteenth-century America. Through
letters, Danes share their observations and opinions of the
New World. They tell of crossing the Atlantic in crowded
ships, the summer heat of Iowa, having picnics in Chicago's
magnificent parks, reaching the Mormon "Zion" in Utah,
championing Bryan against McKinley in 1896, and traveling
with small children to join a husband on the vast Canadian
plains.

89. Halich, Wasyl. Ukrainians in the United States. Chicago:
University of Chicago Press, 1937.
Acculturation of Ukrainian community in the United States
with notices of the Ukrainian immigrant family.

90. Hammerton, A. James. Emigrant Gentlewomen: Genteel Poverty and Female Emigration, 1830-1914. London: Croom Helm,
1979.
Examines the distressed gentlewoman stereotype, primarily
through a study of the experience of emigration among single
middle-class women between 1830 and 1914. Based largely
on a study of government and philanthropic emigration pro-
jects, it argues that the image of the downtrodden resident
governess does inadequate justice to Victorian middle-class
women's responses to the experience of economic and social

decline and to insufficient female employment opportunities.
Although powerful factors operated to discourage distressed
gentlewomen from risking the hardships of emigration, research among emigrants' letters and other records of female
emigration societies shows that middle-class women without
economic resources persistently took advantage of the in-
variably meager facilities enabling them to emigrate.   See
review, B. B. Caroli, International Migration Review, 14
(Fall 1980):   429-430.

91.   Handlin, Oscar; Carl Wittke; and John Appel, advisory eds.
       The American Immigration Collection. 41 vols. New York:
       Arno Press/New York Times, 1969.
           A massive reprint program/ of basic materials on the history
           of American immigration.   Also (Series II), Victor Greene,
           Oscar Handlin, and John Appel, advisory eds., The Ameri-
           can Immigration Collection, 33 vols. (1970).

92.   Handlin, Oscar. Boston's Immigrants. Cambridge, Mass.:
       Harvard University Press, 1941; rev. ed., 1959. New York:
       Atheneum, 1968.
           Actually a study of acculturation, with emphasis on the Irish
           immigrant community.

93.   Handlin, Oscar. The Uprooted: The Epic Story of the Great
       Migrations That Made the American People. Boston: Little,
       Brown, 1951; 2nd ed., 1973.
           The immigrant urban experience and its background, with
           perceptive assessments of immigrant family adjustment.
           An epic narrative of the life of immigrants: the ocean cross-
           ing, work, religion, generational differences, conflict/
           acculturation, and restriction.

94.   Hansen, Marcus Lee.   The Immigrant in American History.
       Cambridge, Mass.: Harvard University Press, 1941.
           Also, Hansen's influential The Problem of the Third Genera-
           tion Immigrant (Rock Island, Ill.: Augustana Historical So-
           ciety, 1938); and Eugene I. Bender and George Kagiwada,
           "Hansen's Law of 'Third Generation Return' and the Study
           of American Religio-Ethnic Groups," Phylon, 29 (Winter
           1968):   360-370.

95.   Harrison, Cynthia E., ed. Women in American History. Santa
       Barbara, Calif.: American Bibliographical Center, Clio Press,
       1979.
           Includes 3,500 entries from 650 key journals in the period
           from 1963 to 1976.   All deal with the literature on women
           in the United States and Canada.   The entries are arranged
           by chronological periods, which are subdivided topically.

96.   Higham, John. Strangers in the Land: Patterns of American
       Nativism, 1860-1925. Corrected with a new Preface. New
       York: Atheneum, 1973.

American attitudes toward immigrants and immigration. See also the author's Send These to Me: Jews and Other Immigrants in Urban America (1975), much broader than its title suggests, and particularly, "Chapter 10: Ethnic Pluralism in Modern American Thought" (pp. 196-230), which includes an incisive commentary on family adaptation.

97.   Hinding, Andrea, and Clarke A. Chambers, eds. Women's History Sources: A Guide to Archives and Manuscript Collections in the United States. 2 vols. New York: R. R. Bowker, 1979.
         Lists twenty thousand sources located in two thousand repositories. Introduction discusses origins and status of women's history, as well as historical methodology.

98.   Hinding, Andrea, and Rosemary Richardson. Archival and Manuscript Resources for the Study of Women's History: A Beginning. St. Paul: University of Minnesota Libraries, 1972.
         Arranged geographically, the list has a brief description of manuscript holdings of various depositories.

99.   Hoglund, A. William. Finnish Immigrants in America. Madison: University of Wisconsin Press, 1960.
         Basic source on the Finnish community in America. A full portrait of the Finnish immigrant community (with valuable vignettes of women's roles) and its evolving acculturation.

100.   Howe, Irving. World of Our Fathers: The Journey of the East European Jews to America and the Life They Have Found and Made. New York: Harcourt Brace Jovanovich, 1975.
         The East European Jews in the United States, 1880 to the present. See the review of Theodore Solotaroff, New York Times Book Review, February 1, 1976. A vast panoramic portrait of the immigrant community. A social and cultural history of the East European Jewish community in New York City. See a critique-essay review by Leon Wieseltier, New York Review of Books, July 15, 1976.

101.   Immigration History Research Center. University of Minnesota (826 Berry Street, St. Paul, Minnesota 55114).
         An international center for the collection and preservation of the historical records of immigrants who came to the United States and Canada. See Rudolph J. Vecoli, "The Immigrant Studies Collection of the University of Minnesota," American Archivist, 32 (April 1969): 139-145.

102.   "The Immigrant Woman." Mirror, 3, No. 1 [Spring 1977]: 1-136. Extension Division, University of Rhode Island.
         A collection of oral histories of Armenian, French, Italian, Canadian, Polish, and Jewish women, mostly long resident in Rhode Island.

103.   James, Edward T., ed. Notable American Women, A Bio-
        graphical Dictionary. Cambridge, Mass.: Harvard University
        Press, Belknap Press, 1971. 3 vols.

104.   Japanese-American Project. (University of California, Los
        Angeles, 405 Hilgard Ave., Los Angeles, Calif. 90024).
        The largest collection of manuscripts, memorabilia, and
        other materials of the Japanese community. See Jyji
        Ichioka, A Buried Past: An Annotated Bibliography of the
        Japanese-American Research Project Collection (Berkeley:
        University of California Press, 1974).

105.   Jones, Maldwyn Allen. American Immigration. Chicago:
        University of Chicago Press, 1960; rev. ed., 1970.
        A richly textured history, and one of the best introductions
        to the history of the migrations to America.

106.   Joseph, Samuel. Jewish Immigration to the United States,
        1881-1910. New York: Columbia University Press, 1914.
        The fullest study of its kind: invaluable data and sources
        on the Jewish immigrant community, roles of women, pat-
        terns of acculturation and adjustment.

107.   Kastrup, Allan. The Swedish Heritage in America: The Swedish
        Element in America and American-Swedish Relations in Their
        Historical Perspective. Minneapolis: Swedish Council of
        America, 1975.
        The contributions and major events in the American-Swedish
        experience. A massive (863 pp.) catalogue of broad themes
        and detailed narrative, with detailed notices of the immi-
        grant family.

108.   Katzman, D. M. Seven Days a Week: Women and Domestic
        Service in Industrializing America. New York: Oxford Uni-
        versity Press, 1978.
        Presents material by and about women (largely immigrant)
        domestic servants in the United States from 1870-1920.
        Concludes that the influences of status, race and ethnicity,
        and sex are more salient features in household labor than
        are economic factors. Presents a statistical overview of
        domestic service, showing a predominance of native-born
        servants in small towns, immigrant servants in large cities
        and black servants in the South.

109.   Kessner, Thomas. The Golden Door: Italian and Jewish
        Immigrant Mobility in New York City, 1880-1915. New York:
        Oxford University Press, 1977.
        Compares the social and residential mobility, patterns of
        the two groups and finds that, while Jews fared better
        than Italians, both groups experienced significant progress
        over two generations. Also discusses similarities and dif-
        ferences between New York and other cities with regard to
        evolving social mobility. See review, F. Cordasco, Edu-
        cational Studies, 9 (Spring 1978): 86-89.

110.	Kessner, Thomas, and Betty Boyd Caroli. Today's Immi-
	grants: Their Stories. A New Look at the Newest Ameri-
	cans. New York: Oxford University Press, 1981.
		An overview of the American immigration experience since
	the 1965 Immigration Act. Historical analysis combined
	with oral history (recent immigrants to New York City).
	See review, D. M. Reimers, International Migration Re-
	view, 16 (Winter 1982): 900.

111.	Koltun, Elizabeth, ed. The Jewish Woman: New Perspec-
	tives. New York: Schocken Books, 1976.

112.	Konnyu, Leslie. Hungarians in the United States. St. Louis:
	American Hungarian Review, 1967.

113.	Krichmar, Albert, et al., eds. The Women's Rights Move-
	ment in the United States. ·Metuchen, N. J.: Scarecrow Press,
	1972.

114.	Lebeson, Anita L. Recall to Life--The Jewish Woman in
	America. New York: Thomas Yoseloff, 1970.
		An informative, suitably documented study of the role of
	women in the history of Jewish welfare, culture, religion,
	education, and society in the United States.

115.	Lee, Rose Hum. The Chinese in the United States of Ameri-
	ca. Hong Kong: Hong Kong University Press, 1960.

116.	Lemons, J. Stanley. The Woman Citizen: Social Feminism
	in the 1920's. Urbana: University of Illinois Press, 1973.
		Beginning with a description of feminism at the time of
	the ratification of the 19th Amendment, deals with social
	welfare activities of the feminists to increase education,
	health, and work opportunities. Describes the activities
	of the League of Women Voters, National Consumers League,
	Women's Trade Union League, and Women's Joint Congres-
	sional Committee. Contrasts the social feminists who
	fought these battles with the hard-core feminists who con-
	centrated on the Equal Rights Amendment.

117.	Lengyel, Emil. Americans from Hungary. Philadelphia:
	J. B. Lippincott, 1948.

118.	Leonard, Eugenie, and Sophia Drinker. The American Wom-
	an in Colonial and Revolutionary Times: 1565-1800: A Syl-
	labus with Bibliography. Westport, Conn.: Greenwood Press,
	1975.

119.	Lerner, Gerda. Bibliography in the History of American
	Women. 3rd rev. ed. Bronxville, N. Y.: Sarah Lawrence,
	1975.
		Unannotated. Listings in bibliography; historiography;
	theories regarding women; general history; family;

motherhood; work; education; sexuality; women, law, and
crime; women and art; black and other minority, and immigrant women; biography and autobiography.

120.   Lerner, Gerda.   The Female Experience: An American Documentary.   Indianapolis: Bobbs-Merrill, 1977.

121.   Logan, Mary S., et al.   The Part Taken by Women in American History.   Wilmington, Del.:   Perry-Nolle Publishing,
1912.   Reprint.   New York: Arno Press, 1972.
Background and biographical material.   Special attention to
immigrant women, particularly Catholic and Jewish women.

122.   Lopata, Helene Z.   Polish Americans: Status Competition in
an Ethnic Community.   Englewood Cliffs, N.J.:   Prentice-
Hall, 1976.
A fully detailed history of the Polish community in America: (1) Background to the Study of Polish Americans; (2)
Poland and Polonia; (3) Developing and Maintaining an
Ethnic Community; (4) Polonia's Relations with the Rest
of American Society; (5) Patterns of Change in Polonia;
(6) Life in Polonia; (7) The Long View.

123.   Lyman, Stanford M.   Chinese Americans.   New York: Random House, 1974.

124.   McCaffrey, Lawrence J.   The Irish Diaspora in America.
Bloomington: Indiana University Press, 1975.

125.   McFeeley, Mary Drake.   Women's Work in Britain and America from the Nineties to World War I: An Annotated Bibliography.   Boston: G. K. Hall, 1982.
Surveys primary sources and historical studies on women's
work and related issues in the Anglo-American world from
1890 to 1914.   The volume brings together widely disparate
published material on women's occupations at all levels, as
well as on trade unions, protective legislation, professional
training, and occupational choices.   Books, articles, pamphlets, and government documents are listed in separate
sections for Great Britain and the U.S., with multiple
access by subject, author, and title indexes.

126.   Marcus, Jacob R.   The American Jewish Woman, 1654-1980.
New York: Ktav Publishing House, 1980.
In this work, the distinguished historian of the American
Jewish experience, Jacob Rader Marcus, narrates the 300-
year history of the American Jewish woman.   With a style
that is both scholarly and popular, provoking and explana-
tory, Professor Marcus challenges the standard chronicles
of American Jewry which have consistently ignored the
history of American Jewish women.   As the author states
in the preface to this book: "There can be no question:
there is an American Jewish woman's history that goes

back to September, 1654." Based upon archival documentation that includes letters, memoirs, congregational minutes
and other historical materials.

127. Marcus, Jacob R. The American Jewish Woman, 1654-1980:
A Documentary History. New York: Ktav Publishing House,
1981. Published jointly with the American Jewish Archives,
Cincinnati, Ohio.
Consists of nearly two hundred printed documents which
give historical meaning to three centuries of American
Jewish women's experience. Presented in a chronological
format, the documents demonstrate that American Jewish
women understood themselves to be a distinct group with
a special history well before the beginning of the twentieth
century. The documents highlight specific aspects of that
history, in particular the religious evolution of American
Jewish women, the development of women's voluntaristic
organizations, the participation of Jewish women in the
American labor movement, in American politics and in
the American feminist movement.

128. Marcus, Jacob R. Jewish Americana: A Supplement to A.
S. W. Rosenbach's An American Jewish Bibliography. New
York: Ktav Publishing House, 1978.
In 1926, the American Jewish Historical Society published
An American Jewish Bibliography, being a list of books
and pamphlets by Jews or relating to them printed in the
United States from the establishment of the press in the
colonies until 1850. This work supplements that with de-
scriptions of books, pamphlets, and articles that have since
come to light and that are in the Hebrew Union College,
Jewish Institute of Religion Library in Cincinnati.

129. Marlow, H. Carleton, ed. Bibliography of American Women.
Part I. Woodbridge, Conn.: Research Publications, 1975.
Microfilm includes all monograph materials by and about
American women to 1904. Fifty thousand titles arranged
chronologically, alphabetically, and topically. Part 2 to
be announced. Available in 16mm and 35mm silver emul-
sion film from Research Publications, Inc., 12 Lunar
Drive, Woodbridge, Connecticut 06525.

130. Matheson, G., ed. Women in the Canadian Mosaic. Toronto:
P. Martin Associates, 1976.

131. Melville, B., ed. Twice a Minority: Mexican American
Women. St. Louis: C. V. Mosby, 1980.
Includes a variety of empirical data on Mexican American
women collected by both Mexican American and Anglo
American social scientists. Its purpose is to modify the
stereotypes of the women found in much of the social
science literature, which often views females as passive
sufferers. It is a work of political and social advocacy.

132. Miller, Sally M., and Mary Wedegaertner, eds. "Experiences of Immigrant Women." Pacific Historian, 26 (Summer 1982): 1-65.

133. Miller, Wayne C., et al. A Comprehensive Bibliography for the Study of American Minorities. New York: New York University Press, 1976. 3 vols.
      Includes 29,300 entries, the most comprehensive biblio-graphical coverage of American ethnic groups extant, and includes references to more specialized bibliographies for every ethnic group. Vol. 3 assembles the historical-biblio-graphical essays preceding each section on individual groups. See review, F. Cordasco, Contemporary Sociology, 6 (September 1977): 594-595.

134. [Minnesota Historical Society]. The Picture Collection of the Minnesota Historical Society. St. Paul: Audio-Visual Library, Minnesota Historical Society, 690 Cedar Street, St. Paul, Minnesota, 55101.
      Some 100,000 photographs and other graphics. The So-ciety was founded in 1849. Collection is indexed by subject areas (e.g., education, ethnic groups, immigration, women, urban life). Emphasis is on Minnesota and the Upper Mid-west.

135. Mirandé, Alfredo, and Evangelina Enríquez. La Chicana: The Mexican-American Woman. Chicago: The University of Chicago Press, 1981.
      Examines a number of dualities in the Mexican and Chicana experience that impinge on the Mexican American woman, some at odds with each other and others complementary.

136. Monk, Una. New Horizons: A Hundred Years of Women's Migration. London: Mansell, 1963.

137. Mora, Magdalena, and Adelaida R. Del Castillo, eds. Mex-ican Women in the United States: Struggles Past and Present. Los Angeles: University of California Chicano Studies Re-search Center Occasional Paper No. 2, 1980.
      The primary objective of this book is to document and ap-praise Mexican women's activism in struggles against "national oppression, class exploitation, and sexism." The essays, case studies, and profiles of individual wom-en indicate the extent to which women of Mexican heritage have been involved in such struggles and the dilemmas they face when they are active. See review, H. Hartman, Inter-national Migration Review, 16 (Spring 1972): 228-229.

138. Moser, Charlotte, and Deborah Johnson. Rural Women Work-ers in the Twentieth Century: An Annotated Bibliography. Central Rural Manpower and Public Affairs Special Paper, no. 15. East Lansing: Michigan State University, 1973.

Includes material on immigration, education, full- and part-
time employment, day care, organizing, women's liberation, and international trends.

139.   Museum of the City of New York.   (Fifth Ave. at 103rd St.,
        New York City, N.Y. 10029).
        A very rich collection of memorabilia, photographs, and
        other materials, particularly strong for the period 1880
        through 1920.   Includes the Jacob A. Riis Collection and
        the Byron Collection, photographic archives rich for immi-
        grant life in New York City.   Many of the photographs of
        the Riis Collection have appeared in editions of Riis's
        books (q. v.).   Many of the Byron photographs are repro-
        duced in Grace M. Mayer, Once upon a City (1958); Roger
        Whitehouse, New York: Sunshine and Shadow (1974); John
        A. Kowenhoven, The Columbia Historical Portrait of New
        York (1953); and Oscar Handlin, Statue of Liberty (1971).

140.   [National Council of Jewish Women.   Pittsburgh Section].   By
        Myself I'm a Book!   An Oral History of the Immigrant Jewish
        Experience in Pittsburgh.   Waltham, Mass.:   American Jewish
        Historical Society, 1972.

141.   Nee, Victor G., and Brett de Bary Nee.   Longtime California:
        A Documentary Study of an American Chinatown.   New York:
        Pantheon Books, 1973.
        The contemporary Chinese community in San Francisco,
        with extensive notices of the immigrant Chinese family and
        women's roles.   Based on oral histories of first and second
        generation immigrants.   See also Gunther Barth, Bitter
        Strength: A History of the Chinese in the United States,
        1850-1870 (Harvard University Press, 1964).

142.   Neidle, Cecyle S.   American Immigrant Women.   Boston:
        G. K. Hall, 1975.   Reprint.   New York: Hippocrene Books,
        1976.
        Surveys the contribution of immigrant women to American
        social and political development.   Beginning in the colonial
        period, the author details the deeds of wives and daughters
        of the British settlers.   In later chapters focuses on groups
        from continental Europe and concludes with a brief treat-
        ment of successful professional women in the midtwentieth
        century.   Chapters, which cover the peak period of Euro-
        pean immigration, record the activities of mainly Irish
        and Jewish women in the trade-union movement.

143.   Nelli, Humbert S.   Italians in Chicago: 1880-1930; A Study
        in Ethnic Mobility.   New York: Oxford University Press,
        1970.
        "The new urban surroundings profoundly affected other
        traditions and viewpoints, although immigrants themselves
        believed that in America they were re-creating homeland
        village life.   In the process they created a myth that they

have nurtured to the present." A challenging study whose conclusions are controversial.

144.   Nelson, Barbara J. American Women and Politics: A Bibliography and Guide to the Sources. New York: Garland Publishing, 1983.
A comprehensive bibliography with over 2,500 entries on American women and politics, this volume goes beyond the narrow definition of women's political activities and examines the many ways in which individuals and groups are connected to the state. Among the 13 topics explored are Women in Social Movements, Feminist Theory, Women and the Family, Women and Education, Women at Work and at Leisure, Political Participation, and Women as Political Leaders. A chapter on research resources and an index are included.

145.   New York Public Library. (Fifth Avenue and 42nd St., New York, N.Y. 10018).
The general collections contain extensive materials on American ethnic groups. Invaluable for New York City immigrant archives; also, collections of papers and letters in the Library's Manuscript Division, e.g., the papers and letters of Gino Charles Speranza (1872-1927), a major figure in the early history of the Italian immigrant community; the letterbooks and scrapbooks of Joseph Barondess, a Jewish immigrant leader who in 1904 ran unsuccessfully as a candidate for Congress; the papers of the social reformer Lillian Wald (1867-1940); and the unpublished manuscripts of the Italian political reformer Carlo Tresca.

146.   Norwegian-American Historical Association. (St. Olaf College, Northfield, Minnesota 55057).
Publishes Norwegian-American Studies (1925-), a cumulative bibliography of publications on Norwegian-American history. See Odd Lovoll and Kenneth O. Bjork, The Norwegian-American Historical Association, 1925-1975 (1975).

147.   Oakes, Elizabeth H. Guide to Social Science Resources in Women's Studies. Santa Barbara, Calif.: ABC-Clio Books, 1978.

148.   Oakley, Ann. The Sociology of Housework. New York: Pantheon Books, 1975.

149.   Oakley, Ann. Woman's Work: The Housewife, Past and Present. New York: Random House, 1976.

150.   O'Connor, Richard. The German Americans: An Informal History. Boston: Little, Brown, 1968.

151.   Papachristou, Judith. Women Together: A History in Documents of the Women's Movement in the United States. New York: Alfred Knopf, 1976.

152.   Pebotsky, Bessie.   The Slavic Immigrant Woman [1925].

153.   Pitkin, Thomas M.   Keepers of the Gate: A History of Ellis
       Island.   New York: New York University Press, 1975.
           Ellis Island (one of the islets off the New Jersey shore of
       the Upper Bay of New York City) was the principal gateway
       for millions of immigrants to America.   Formally inaugu-
       rated as a federal immigration station on January 1, 1892,
       it continued to function until March 4, 1955.   Pitkin's
       history is the "administrative side of the Ellis Island
       story."   See review, F. Cordasco, Italian Americana, 2
       (Autumn 1975):   121-125.   See also Ann Novotny, Strangers
       at the Door: Ellis Island, Castle Garden, and the Great
       Migration to America (Riverside, Conn.:   Chatham Press,
       1971); Ludovico Caminata, Nell'Isola delle Lagrime: Ellis
       Island (New York: Stabilimento Tipografico Italia, 1924);
       Edward Corsi, In the Shadow of Liberty: The Chronicle
       of Ellis Island (New York: Macmillan, 1937); and B.
       Severn, Ellis Island: The Immigrant Years (New York:
       Simon and Schuster, 1971).

154.   Pratt, Norma Fain.   "Jewish Women Through the 1930's."
       American Quarterly, 30 (Winter 1978):   681-702.

155.   Renoff, Richard, and Stephen Reynolds, eds.   Proceedings of
       the Conference on Carpatho-Ruthenian Immigration.   Cam-
       bridge, Mass.:   Harvard Ukrainian Research Institute, 1975.
           Includes a bibliography of English language materials.   Im-
       portant for notices of immigrant woman and family.

156.   Rischin, Moses.   The Promised City: New York's Jews,
       1870-1914.   Cambridge, Mass.:   Harvard University Press,
       1962.
           Based on the author's doctoral dissertation, "Jewish Life
       and Labor in New York City, 1870-1914" (Harvard Uni-
       versity, 1957).   German and East European Jews; notices
       of immigrant women, the family, and patterns of adjust-
       ment.

157.   Rischin, Moses.   "Since 1954:   A Bicentennial Look at the
       Resources of American Jewish History."   Immigration History
       Newsletter, 7 (November 1975):   1-6.
           See also the author's An Inventory of American Jewish
       History (Harvard University Press, 1954), an earlier guide
       to American Jewish historical resources.

158.   Ritchie, Maureen.   Women's Studies: A Checklist of Biblio-
       graphies.   London: Mansell, 1980.

159.   Roberts, Peter.   The New Immigration: A Study of the In-
       dustrial and Social Life of Southeastern Europeans in America.
       New York: Macmillan, 1912.

The new immigration is that movement to America of the
peoples of Southern Europe, which began in a small way
in the early eighties and continued unabated until the im-
position of immigration restrictions in the 1920's. Deals
with the inducements that lead to emigration and first impressions of the immigrant; industrial life; community
conditions (with special attention to the immigrant woman
and family); social relations; assimilation and hindrances.

160.   Robet-Petitat, C. "Bibliographie sur les femmes immigrées."
        Migrants-Formation, 32-33 (March 1979): 149-154.

161.   Rossi, Alice S., ed. The Feminist Papers: From Adams to
        de Beauvoir. New York: Columbia University Press, 1973.
        A comprehensive collection of documents which Rossi calls
        "the essential works of feminism."

162.   Roucek, Joseph S. The Immigrant in Fiction and Biography.
        New York: Bureau for Intercultural Education, 1945.

163.   Ryan, Mary. Womanhood in America: From Colonial Times
        to the Present. New York: Franklin Watts, 1975.

164.   Saloutos, Theodore. The Greeks in the United States. Cam-
        bridge, Mass.: Harvard University Press, 1964.
        A comprehensive account with chapters on political and
        sociocultural conditions in Greece which motivated migration
        at the end of the century. A panoramic overview of Greek
        life in the United States with special attention to Greek
        immigrant women and the family.

165.   Sanders, Ronald. The Downtown Jews: Portraits of an Immi-
        grant Generation. New York: Harper and Row, 1969.
        The Jewish community of the Lower East Side, New York
        City. Materials on the Jewish community, family, and
        women.

166.   Saveth, Edward N. American Historians and European Immi-
        grants, 1875-1925. New York: Columbia University Press,
        1948. Reprint. New York: Russell & Russell, 1965.
        The development of racism in America with special refer-
        ences to immigrants. Ideas of racial superiority which
        were developed in the nineteenth century are traced in the
        writings of Theodore Roosevelt, Woodrow Wilson, and
        twentieth-century historians. Bibliographies include (1)
        writings by historians; (2) writings about historians; (3)
        general references. See also Saveth, "Race and Nationalism
        in American Historiography: The Late Nineteenth Century,"
        Political Science Quarterly, 64 (September 1939): 421-441.

167.   Scarpaci, Jean, ed. "Immigrant Women and the City" [Special
        Issue]. Journal of Urban History, 4 (May 1978): 251-360.

Five essays explore the role of Irish women in New York
City in the 1850's; the impact of economic and ecological
environments upon the lives of Scandinavian women in
Seattle; women immigrants (Jews, Slavs, and Italians) in
Pittsburgh; women immigrants and adult education in Ameri-
ca; and the work experience of Mexican, Black and Anglo
(including foreign-born white) women in Atlanta, New
Orleans and San Antonio during the Depression.

168.   Scarpaci, Jean. "La Contadina. The Plaything of The Middle
       Class Woman Historian." Occasional Papers on Ethnic and
       Immigration Studies. The Multicultural History Society of
       Ontario, October 1978.
            Discusses four concepts (the monad theory, the general
       sequence pattern, the creation of a woman's culture, and
       history through empathy) which dominate current literature
       concerning Italian American women's studies. Suggests
       that each fails to document women's history in a way that
       illustrates women's full participation in and interaction
       with the many worlds they inhabit.

169.   [Arthur and Elizabeth Schlesinger Library on the History of
       Women in America, Radcliffe College]. Catalogs of the Books,
       Manuscripts, and Pictures of the Arthur and Elizabeth
       Schlesinger Library. Boston: G. K. Hall, 1983. 10 vols.
            The Schlesinger Library's holdings have tripled since publi-
       cation of the original catalog in 1973, reflecting the dra-
       matic growth in women's studies during the past decade.
       Included are some 18,000 bound books, more than 400
       manuscript collections, and an extensive corpus of im-
       portant photographs. Among the major subjects covered
       are education, employment, women's rights and suffrage,
       social welfare and reform, family and domestic history,
       women's organizations. The Library's collections in these
       and affiliated areas form an invaluable documentary history
       of American women in the nineteenth and twentieth centuries.

170.   Schoener, Allon, ed. Portal to America: The Lower East
       Side, 1870-1925. New York: Holt, Rinehart and Winston,
       1967.
            New York City's Lower East Side and the Eastern European
       Jewish immigrant community.

171.   Seller, Maxine S. "Beyond the Stereotype: A New Look at
       the Immigrant Woman, 1880-1924." Journal of Ethnic Studies,
       3 (Spring 1975): 59-70.

172.   Seller, Maxine S., ed. Immigrant Women. Philadelphia:
       Temple University Press, 1981.
            The only comprehensive sourcebook on the American immi-
       grant woman. The book's strength lies in the use of pri-
       mary source materials: "Using documents written by immi-
       grant women themselves, or by others who knew them

intimately, Immigrant Women offers a different perspective,
a woman-centered perspective on American immigration
history" (Intro.).   Contents: I.   Why They Came; II.
Surviving in a New Land; III.   Work; IV.   Family; V. Community Life; VI.   Education; VII.   Social Activists; VIII.
Daughters and Granddaughters; Bibliographical Essay.

173.   Seller, Maxine S.   To Seek America: A History of Ethnic
       Life in the United States.   Englewood, N. J.:   Jerome S.
       Ozer, 1977.
           A felicitously written history of immigrant life in America.
       Particularly Chapter 6:   "The Urban Ghetto: Immigrants
       in Industrial America, 1880-1924"; and Chapter 7:   "Pro-
       gressive America: Home, School, and Neighborhood, "
       which includes a section on the immigrant woman.   Excel-
       lent bibliographical essay.

174.   Sinclair, Andrew.   The Better Half: The Emancipation of the
       American Woman.   New York: Harper and Row, 1965.
           Examines the evolution of feminism from colonial times to
       the adoption of female suffrage.   Concentrates on the inter-
       action between feminism and wider reform currents in the
       progressive and other eras.

175.   Smuts, Robert W.   Women and Work in America.   New York:
       Columbia University Press, 1959.   Reprint.   New York:
       Schocken Books, 1971.
           Investigates the different women who work, and the personal
       qualities and social attitudes underlying employment.   Con-
       siderable data on the economics of women in the work-
       place with attention to the immigrant woman.

176.   Sochen, June.   Herstory: A Woman's View of American
       History.   New York: Alfred A. Knopf, 1974.

177.   Soltow, Martha Jane, and Mary K. Wery, eds.   American
       Women and the Labor Movement, 1825-1974:   An Annotated
       Bibliography.   Metuchen, N. J.:   Scarecrow Press, 1976.
           Includes over 700 entries arranged alphabetically by topic,
       with short descriptive statements about each.   Topics cov-
       ered are employment, trade unions, working mothers,
       strikes, legislation, worker education, labor leaders, and
       supportive efforts.

178.   Soltow, Martha Jane, and Susan Gravelle.   Worker Benefits.
       Industrial Welfare in America 1900-1935.   An Annotated Bibliog-
       raphy.   Metuchen, N. J.:   Scarecrow Press, 1983.
           Consists of selected books, articles and government docu-
       ments relating to employee benefits during the first third
       of this century.   Included here are 1) surveys of existing
       industrial welfare programs; 2) descriptions of specific
       industry programs; 3) descriptions of specific company pro-
       grams; 4) descriptions of a particular benefit; 5) biographies

of leaders in the field; and 6) scholarly works of an analytical nature. A section has been added on labor's response to welfare capitalism. Sources included are secondary and are comprised of books, special surveys and reports of industry and private organizations, government and state documents, publications of the American Federation of Labor, pamphlet material, and above all, periodical literature.

179.   Soltow, Mary Jane; Carolyn Forche; and Murray Massre. Women in American Labor History, 1825-1935: An Annotated Bibliography. East Lansing: School of Labor and Industrial Relations, Michigan State University, 1972.

180.   [Sophia Smith Collection]. Catalog of the Sophia Smith Collection. Women's History Archive: Smith College, Northampton, Mass. 7 vols. Boston: G. K. Hall, 1975.
       Volumes 1 and 2 contain author catalogs and volumes 3, 4, and 5 a subject catalog. Volumes 6 and 7 relate to manuscript collections and volume 7 deals with photographs.

181.   Suomi College Library. (Quincy St., Hancock, Mich. 49930).
       Includes a collection of materials on Finns in America.

182.   Tachiki, Amy, et al., eds. Roots: An Asian-American Reader. Los Angeles: University of California, Asian-American Study Program, 1971.
       A sourcebook on the history, community, and identity of Asian American peoples (with special attention to the role of women) with most of the material drawn from memoirs and short stories.

183.   Talbot, Jane M., and Gilbert R. Cruz. A Comprehensive Chicano Bibliography, 1960-1970. Austin, Tex.: Jenkins Publishing, 1973.
       Particularly "Women, Marriage, and the Family" and "Machismo."

184.   Tamiment Library. (New York University, Bobst Library).
       A rich collection of books, periodicals, pamphlets, manuscripts, and miscellanea illustrating the history of American labor, and radical movements from the midnineteenth century to the present. Important materials on women, the Women's Trade Union League, and other women's organizations.

185.   Taravella, Louis, and Graziano Tassello. Les Femmes Migrantes: Bibliographie Internationale (1965-1982). Rome: Centro Studi Emigrazione, 1983.
       A largely annotated bibliography on migrant women (worldwide) intended to point up the state of extant research on the phenomenon. Annotations are in French, with primary attention to Europe. Includes 488 entries: "Nous avons

analysé surtout des ouvrages, des essais et des articles
edités en France, Italie, et dans les Pays de langue an-
glaise. "

186.   Taylor, Philip.   The Distant Magnet: European Immigration
       to the U.S.A.   New York: Harper & Row, 1972.
       Both a history and an analysis of the patterns and signifi-
       cance of American immigration, with attention to evolving
       patterns of acculturation.

187.   Terris, Virginia R.   Woman in America: A Guide to Infor-
       mation Sources.   Detroit: Gale Research, 1980.
       A collection of some 2,500 references intended "to suggest
       possibilities for research into the lives of American women
       rather than to define the direction the research should
       take."   See particularly Chapter 6 (Sociology), which in-
       cludes some references to immigrant women.

188.   Thernstrom, Stephan, ed.   Harvard Encyclopedia of Ameri-
       can Ethnic Groups.   Cambridge, Mass.:   Harvard University
       Press, 1980.
       A guide to the history, culture, and distinctive character-
       istics of the more than 100 ethnic groups who live in the
       United States.   Each ethnic group is described in detail.
       The origins, history, and present situation of the familiar
       as well as the virtually unknown are presented.   Not only
       the immigrants and refugees who came voluntarily, but
       also those already in the New World when the first Euro-
       peans arrived, those whose ancestors came involuntarily
       as slaves, and those who became part of the American
       population as a result of conquest or purchase and sub-
       sequent annexation.   The group entries are at the heart
       of the book, but it contains, in addition, a series of thema-
       tic essays that illuminate the key facets of ethnicity.   Some
       of these are comparative, some philosophical, some his-
       torical, and others focus on current policy issues or relate
       ethnicity to major subjects such as education, religion, and
       literature.   American identity and Americanization, immi-
       gration policy and experience, and prejudice and discrimina-
       tion in U.S. history are discussed at length.   Several es-
       says probe the complex interplay between assimilation and
       pluralism--perhaps the central theme in American history--
       and the complications of race and religion.

189.   Thomas, Roy R.   Women in American History, 1896-1920:
       Their Manuscripts in the Library of Congress.   Bowie, Md.:
       Bowie Street College, 1972.
       A brief checklist prepared for Workshop in Archival and
       Manuscript Sources for the Study of Women's History, organ-
       ization of American Historians.

190.   Thomas, William I., and Florian Znaniecki.   The Polish
       Peasant in Europe and America.   5 vols.   Boston: Richard

G. Badger, 1918-1920. Reprint. Ed. by Eli Zaretsky. Ur-
bana: University of Illinois Press, 1984.
   A classic work which alleges a disintegration of the Polish
   family in America. Essential for study of the Polish immi-
   grant woman and family in America. See Herbert Blumer,
   "Critiques of Research in the Social Sciences: An Ap-
   praisal of Thomas and Znaniecki's The Polish Peasant in
   Europe and America" (New York: Social Science Research
   Council, Bulletin 44, 1939); and Konstantin Symmons-
   Symonolewicz, "The Polish-American Community--Half a
   Century After the Polish Peasant," The Polish Review, 11
   (Summer 1966): 67-73.

191.   Tingley, Elizabeth, and Donald F. Tingley. Women and Femi-
       nism in American History: A Guide to Information Sources.
       Detroit: Gale Research, 1981.
          Includes "the primary and most important resources on
          women and history, women today, and the feminist struggle."
          See Chapter 22: "Ethnic and Minority Women."

192.   Tolzmann, Don Heinrich. German Americana. Metuchen,
       N.J.: Scarecrow Press, 1975.
          A comprehensive bibliography on most aspects of German
          American history and life (including women and family).
          Includes listing of archives containing material on German
          Americans.

193.   U.S. Bureau of the Census. Census Monograph, 7. Niles
       Carpenter. Immigrants and Their Children. Washington:
       Government Printing Office, 1927.
          Statistical analysis of the distribution of immigrants, spatial
          demography, residence, national origins, race, sex, lan-
          guage, age, marriage patterns, citizenship, occupations.
          See also E. P. Hutchinson, Immigrants and Their Children
          (1956), an updating of the Carpenter data. Reference should
          be made to Catalogs of the Bureau of the Census Library
          (Washington, D.C.), which include some 323,000 cards
          (Boston: G. K. Hall, 1976-1981, 20 vols.).

194.   U.S. Congress. Senate. Report on the Condition of Women
       and Children Wage-Earners in the United States. 61st Cong.
       2d sess. Senate doc. nos. 86-104. Washington, D.C.:
       Government Printing Office, 1912. 19 vols.
          An invaluable repository of data on "industrial, social,
          moral, educational, and physical condition" of women and
          children. Begun in 1907. The nineteen volumes are en-
          titled as follows: 1. The Cotton Textile Industry; 2.
          Men's Ready-Made Clothing Industry; 3. The Glass Industry;
          4. The Silk Industry; 5. Wage-Earning Women in Stores
          and Factories; 6. The Beginnings of Child Labor Legisla-
          tion. Prepared by Elizabeth L. Otey; 7. Conditions Under
          Which Children Leave School to Go to Work; 8. Juvenile
          Delinquency and Its Relation to Employment; 9. History

of Women in Industry in the United States. Prepared by
Helen L. Sumner; 10. History of Women in Trade Unions.
Prepared by John B. Andrews and W. D. P. Bliss; 11.
Employment of Women in Metal Trades. Prepared by
Lucian W. Chaney; 12. Employment of Women in Laun-
dries. Prepared by Charles P. Neill; 13. Infant Mor-
tality and Its Relation to the Employment of Mothers; 14.
Causes of Death Among Women and Child Cottonmill Opera-
tives. Prepared by Arthur R. Perry; 15. Relation Be-
tween Occupation and Criminality of Women. Prepared by
Mary Conyngton; 16. Family Budgets of Typical Cotton-
mill Workers. Prepared by Wood F. Worcester and Daisy
W. Worcester; 17. Hookworm Disease Among Cottonmill
Operators. Prepared by Charles W. Styles; 18. Employment of Women and Children in Selected Industries; 19.
Labor Laws and Factory Conditions.

195.   [United States Department of Commerce]. Statistical Ab-
       stract. [Annual].
       Convenient source for current'information on immigrants,
       refugees, foreign labor, and naturalization.

196.   United States Immigration Commission. Report of the Immi-
       gration Commission. 41 vols. Washington: Government
       Printing Office, 1911. The Children of Immigrants in Schools,
       vols, 29-33. Republished with an introductory essay by F.
       Cordasco, Metuchen, N. J.: Scarecrow Reprint Corp, 1970.
       The five-volume report is a vast repository of data on
       immigrant children (analyses of backgrounds, nativity,
       school progress, home environments, etc.). In all, 2, 036,-
       376 school children are included (in both public and paro-
       chial schools in 37 cities). Also, data on 32, 882 students
       in higher education and 49, 067 public school teachers.
       "The purpose of the investigation was to determine as far
       as possible to what extent immigrant children are availing
       themselves of educational facilities and what progress they
       make in school work."

197.   United States Immigration Commission. Report of the Immi-
       gration Commission. (61st Congress, 2nd and 3rd Sessions).
       Washington: Government Printing Office, 1911. 41 vols.
       Abstracts, vols. 1-2. Includes statistical review of immi-
       gration; emigration conditions in Europe; dictionary of races
       and peoples; immigrants in industries; immigrants in cities,
       occupations of immigrants; fecundity of immigrant women;
       children of immigrants in schools; immigrants as charity
       seekers; immigration and crime; steerage conditions; bodily
       form of descendants of immigrants; federal immigration
       legislation; state immigration and alien laws; other coun-
       tries; statements and recommendations. The Index of Re-
       ports of the Immigration Commission (S. Doc. No. 785,
       61st Congress, 3rd Session) was never published. The
       Report was restrictionist in its basic recommendations,

and the chairman of the Commission was Senator (Mass.)
William P. Dillingham. The Report is summarized in
Jeremiah W. Jenks and W. Jett Lauck, The Immigration
Problem: A Study of Immigration Conditions and Needs
(New York: Funk & Wagnalls, 1912; 6th ed., 1926).
Isaac A. Hourwich, Immigration and Labor: The Eco-
nomic Aspects of European Immigration to the United
States (New York: G. P. Putnam Sons, 1912; 2nd ed.,
1922), subsidized by the American Jewish Committee, was
a statistical attack on the Commission's Report.

198.   United States Immigration and Naturalization Service. Annual
Report. 1892-
      Began as the Annual Report of the United States Commis-
      sioner General of Immigration in 1892. Also, the USINS
      publishes the quarterly I and N Reporter.

199.   U. S. Treasury Department. Tables Showing Arrivals of Alien
Passengers and Immigrants in the United States from 1820 to
1888. Prepared by the Bureau of Statistics. Washington,
D. C.: Government Printing Office, 1889.
      Includes breakdowns by sex according to nationality and
      numbers, by quarter and financial years.

200.   Vlachos, Evangelos. The Assimilation of Greeks in the United
States. Athens: National Centre of Social Research, 1968.
      Assimilation and the patterns of immigrant adjustment.
      Includes a case study of the Greek community in Anderson,
      Indiana, and the experiences of three generations (women)
      of Greek-Americans.

201.   Weber, Gustavus A. The Women's Bureau: Its History, Activities and Organization. Baltimore: Johns Hopkins Press,
1923.
      A short description of the early history of the Women's
      Bureau of the Department of Labor in the years 1919 to
      1923. Includes a list of the Bureau's publications of the
      period.

202.   Whaley, Sara S., and Margrit Eichler. "A Bibliography of
Canadian and United States Resources on Women." Women's
Studies Abstracts, (part 1) 2, no. 4 (1974): 1-5; (part 2) 3,
no. 1 (1974): 1-20.
      Annotated. Listings of general reference works, biblio-
      graphies in book and pamphlet form, additional library re-
      sources, and books and bibliographies in preparation.

203.   Wheat, V., ed. Hispanic Women and Education: Annotated
Selected References and Resources. San Francisco: Far
East Laboratory for Educational Research and Development,
1978.

204.   Wihtol de Wenden, Catherine, ed. "La Donna nei Fenomeni
Migratori." Studi Emigrazione, 20 (June 1983): 130-254.

The whole issue is devoted to the phenomenon of female
migration, with primary attention to Europe (Italy, France,
Belgium) and Brazil. Invaluable in delineating the socioeconomic patterns out of which migration evolves, and the
special circumstances which influence the migrant woman.

205.   Williams, Selma R. Demeter's Daughters: The Women Who
        Founded America, 1587-1787. New York: Atheneum Publish-
        ers, 1975.
        Women's roles in settlement of and growth of America.
        Includes all social classes and Native American women.

206.   Wilson, Joan H., and Lynn B. Donnan. "Women's History:
        A Listing of West Coast Archival and Manuscript Sources--
        Part 1." California Historical Quarterly, 55 (September
        1976): 74-83.

207.   Wirth, Louis. The Ghetto. Chicago: University of Chicago
        Press, 1928.
        A classic study of Jews in Chicago. See also Albert J.
        Reiss, Jr., ed., Louis Wirth on Cities and Social Life
        (1964); and Amitai Etzioni, "The Ghetto--A Re-evaluation,"
        Social Forces, 37 (March, 1959): 255-262, which uses
        Wirth's Ghetto to explore the shift of ethnicity from a
        basis in the ecological community to a reference group
        concept.

208.   Women Studies Abstracts. Rush, N.Y.: Women Studies Ab-
        stracts, 1972- . Quarterly.
        An attempt is made to abstract articles on women in more
        than two thousand periodicals concerning education, sex
        roles, characteristics and differences, employment, society
        and government, sexuality, family, women in history and
        literature, and the women's liberation movement. Most
        issues contain a bibliographical essay on some pertinent
        topic on women.

209.   [Women's Study Staff]. A Selected Bibliography of Works by
        Chicanas and Other Women Interested in Chicana Culture.
        Monticello, Ill.: Vance Bibliographies, 1979.

210.   Wright, Carroll D. The Slums of Baltimore, Chicago, New
        York and Philadelphia. Seventh Special Report of the Com-
        missioner of Labor [Washington: Government Printing Office,
        1894]. Reprint. With an Introduction by Francesco Cordasco.
        New York: Garrett Press, 1970.
        Areas which conformed to the common dictionary definition
        of slum ". . . dirty back streets, especially such streets
        as are inhabited by squalid and criminal population; they
        are low and dangerous neighborhoods" were chosen for this
        detailed statistical survey of slum life in Baltimore, Chicago,
        New York, and Philadelphia. Some of the findings were
        predictable--high illiteracy, crime, saloons, insufficient

sanitary facilities, overcrowding--but others were totally unexpected. The idea of the slum as an area of sickness and disease was proved untrue: "The statistics show no greater sickness prevailing in the districts canvassed than in other parties of the cities involved, and while the most wretched conditions were found here and there, the small number of sick people discovered was a surprise to the canvassers." Detailed information on housing rentals, costs, and on wages and hours of workers (including women, mostly immigrant) engaged in almost every conceivable task are also included.

211.   Yoshika, Robert, et al. "Asian American Women." <u>Civil Rights Digest</u>, 6, no. 3 (Spring 1974): 43-53.
On Chinese, Japanese and other Asian-American women.

212.   Zurawski, Joseph W. <u>Polish American History and Culture: A Classified Bibliography</u>. Chicago: Polish Museum of America, 1975.
Some 1,700 entries concentrating on three basic categories: the Old World Polish heritage; transplantation and transformation in America (special attention to the Polish immigrant family); and its evocation in prose and poetry by Americans. Excludes Polish-language materials.

II. AUTOBIOGRAPHY, BIOGRAPHY, AND
REMINISCENCES

213. Adorno, Elvira. "Italian Immigrants Tell Their Story," in
S. L. La Gumina, ed., The Immigrants Speak (New York:
Center for Migration Studies, 1979), pp. 189-199.
Autobiographical account of Italian immigrant who taught
Italian in the New York City public school system and
served as executive director of the Italian Cultural Council.

214. Anderson, Mary. Woman at Work: The Autobiography of
Mary Anderson as Told to Mary N. Winslow. Minneapolis:
University of Minnesota Press, 1951.
Anderson (1872-1964) served as chief of the Women's
Bureau, U.S. Department of Labor. Born in Sweden, she
emigrated to the United States in 1888. She was one of
the founders of the National Women's Trade Union League.

215. Antin, Mary. The Promised Land. With a foreword by Oscar
Handlin. Boston: Houghton Mifflin, 1958.
This classic memoir (1912) by a Russian immigrant, Mary
Antin (1881-1949), of the immigrant experience begins in
anti-Semitic Tsarist Russia, describes the hardships of
ghetto life in Boston, and ends with a remarkable self-
identification with America.

216. Antin, Mary. At School in the Promised Land, or the Story
of a Little Immigrant. Boston: Houghton Mifflin, 1912.
A selection of chapters on school life from Antin's The
Promised Land (1912) for use as a textbook in high school.
See also Antin's They Who Knock at Our Gates (1914), "a
complete gospel of immigration."

217. Austin, Mary. A Woman of Genius. New York: Doubleday,
Page, 1912.
Austin (1868-1934) fashions a largely autobiographical novel
about a famous actress fighting against the social conventions of a small town.

218. Bacon, Albion Fellows. Beauty for Ashes. New York: Dodd,
Mead, 1914.
An autobiographical account of a woman who spent her life
working to help the harassed and overworked inhabitants of
the slums.

219. Badt-Strauss, Bertha. White Fire: The Life and Works of
Jessie Sampter. New York: G. P. Putnam's Sons, 1956.

The biography of a Jewish-American poet and writer who became an ardent Zionist and immigrated to Palestine in 1919.

220. Baker, S. Josephine. Fighting for Life. [1939] New York: Arno Press, 1974.
The autobiography of Dr. Baker (1873-1945), a pediatrician who organized and directed the New York City Bureau of Hygiene, the first tax-supported agency in the United States concerned exclusively with improving child health. For forty years she took part in the fight to reduce the staggering rate of infant and maternal mortality (largely in immigrant contexts), and lived to see that hope being realized. This vital and witty autobiography sums up the work and philosophy of a woman who, in her words, enjoyed "a glorious, and exhilarating, and an altogether satisfactory life."

221. Bannan, H. M. "Warrior Women: Immigrant Mothers in the Works of Their Daughters." Women's Studies, 6 (Winter 1979): 165-177.

222. [Barolini, Helen]. Director: Kay Bonetti. Produced and dist. by American Audio Prose Library, 915 E. Broadway, Columbia, Missouri 65201, 1983. 2 audiocassettes. 56 min. ea. Helen Barolini Interview, 83-740100; Helen Barolini Reading, 83-740099.
Helen Barolini's Italian-American ancestry and especially her immigrant grandmother were the major influences on her first novel, Umbertina (1979), a multigenerational saga. In the first of two audiotapes the author describes her own family history, the origins and motivations of her major characters, and the way she researched and structured her story. She also explores the nature of ethnic literature and discusses her work in progress, a nonfiction study of Italian-American women writers. The interview is conducted by Kay Bonetti. On the second audiotape Barolini, who believes her work is as much feminist as ethnic, reads three excerpts from her novel. Each excerpt focuses on one major character: Umbertina, the immigrant matriarch, her granddaughter Marguerite, and Tina, Marguerite's daughter.

223. Barschak, Erna. My American Adventure. New York: Ives Washburn, 1945.
A refugee psychology professor who, as a Jew, had been dismissed by the Nazis from her professorship in Berlin in 1933 recounts with humor and insight her experiences on coming to America in 1940.

224. Barton, H. Arnold, ed. Letters from the Promised Land: Swedes in America, 1840-1914. Minneapolis: University of Minnesota Press, 1975.

Edited corpus of letters sent back home by Swedish immigrants; valuable commentaries on immigrant family life.

225.   Bjorn, Thyra Ferre. Papa's Wife. New York: Rinehart, 1960.
        Swedish immigrants in America.

226.   Bjorn, Thyra Ferre. This Is My Life. New York: Rinehart and Winston, 1966.
        Autobiography of the novelist, an immigrant from Sweden.

227.   Blanc, Madam [Marie Therese de Solms]. (Th. Bentzon pseud.). The Condition of Woman in the United States: A Traveller's Notes. Translated by Abby Langdon Alger [1895]. New York: Arno Press, 1976.
        A noted French authoress travelled throughout the United States, met and talked with organized women's groups, visited women's colleges, women's clubs and private homes and observed women at work in the industrial East. The result is a perceptive report enriched by comments from a visitor with the background of a different but cognate culture.

228.   Blegen, Theodore C. "Immigrant Women and the American Frontier: Three Early 'American Letters.'" Norwegian American Studies and Records [Northfield, Minn.: Norwegian American Historical Association], 5 (1930): 27-28.

229.   Blegen, Theodore C., ed. Land of Their Choice: The Immigrants Write Home. Minneapolis: University of Minnesota Press, 1955.

230.   Blicksilver, Edith. "Monica Krawczyk: Chronicler of Polish-American Life." Melus 7 (1980): 13-20.

231.   Bloor, Ella R. We Are Many: An Autobiography. New York: International Publishers, 1940.
        Bloor (1862-1951), better known as "Mother Bloor," describes her long career as a social reformer. Valuable for insights on activist social groups with biographical information on many immigrant women social reformers.

232.   Boe, A. Sophie. The Story of Father's Life. [St. Paul, 1929].
        Includes many details of immigrant life between 1846 and 1929. The author's father was one of the first Norwegian Lutheran pastors in America.

233.   Boelhower, William. Immigrant Autogiography in the United States. Four Versions of the Italian American Self. Venezia: Essedue Edizioni, 1982.
        An attempt "to restore the new system of self-description implicit in immigrant autobiography, to raise to the level

of a structural condition what has previously been considered an amorphous and mixed corpus of texts." Considers
autobiographies of Constantine Panunzio, Pascal D'Angelo,
Emanuel Carnevali, and Jerry Mangione, which exemplify
four axiological procedures: (1) confirmation of the codes
of the dominant culture; (2) a variation of these codes;
(3) a negation of the dominant codes; (4) a substitution of
the dominant culture with a counterculture alternative.

234.   Borenstein, Audrey.   Chimes of Change and Hours: Views
of Older Women in Twentieth-Century America.   Cranbury,
N.J.:   Fairleigh Dickinson University Press, 1983.
An interdisciplinary study of "older women as seen through
social science and literature, and as seen in life by themselves and others." In this "symposium," as the author
calls the "spirit" of her work, sociology, anthropology,
psychology, history, oral history, and literature are mined
for information about the older woman (largely immigrant)
in the U.S.

235.   Bowen, Ralph H., ed.   A Frontier Family in Minnesota:
Letters of Theodore and Sophie Bost, 1851-1920.   Minneapolis:
University of Minnesota Press, 1981.
Sophie Bonjour, the well-educated daughter of a school-
master, had joined Theodore on June 4, 1858, and had
married him the next day after a protracted courtship by
letter only.   Her reports show deep affection for Theodore's
parents and reveal a woman of strength, deep love for life,
and versatile competence.   Although she missed the com-
forts of her former French Swiss world, she became deeply
attached to life on a frontier farm.   Her reports touch on
her pregnancies and the birth of her children, on cooking,
sewing, and gardening, on the vagaries of the economy, and
on the anxieties derived from the Civil War and the 1862
uprising of the Sioux.   After 1874 her letters unfortunately
vanish from the collection.

236.   Brinks, Herbert J.   Schrijf Spoedig Terug: Brieven van Immi-
granten in Amerika 1847-1920 [Write back soon: letters of
immigrants in America 1847-1920].   The Hague: Uitgeverij
Boekencentrum, 1978.
Written in Dutch, this work makes the use of Dutch immigrant letters (sent to friends and relatives in the Netherlands) to describe the emigration, resettlement, and adjustment of the Dutch emigrants to America.   The narrative,
interspersed with excerpts from letters, includes eight main
chapters covering the topics of the emigration experience
(descriptions of the leaders and accounts of the journey),
the major settlements in Michigan, the Chicago area, Wisconsin, and the West (South Dakota, Nebraska, Kansas,
Colorado), the role of the church, and the immigrants'
perception of American society and politics.

237. Brody, Catherine. "A New York Childhood." American Mercury, (May 1928): 57-66.

238. Brown, Harriet Connor. Grandmother Brown's Hundred Years, 1827-1927. Boston: Little, Brown, 1929.
      The narrative of a courageous nineteenth-century woman constitutes a vivid picture of a long and hardship-filled life in an America expanding to cover a continent.

239. Burland, Rebecca, and Edward Burland. A True Picture of Emigration. Or 14 years in the interior of North America, Being a full and impartial account of the various difficulties and ultimate success of an English family who emigrated from Barwick-In-Elmet, near Leeds, in the year 1831. New York: Citadel Press, 1968. [Edited by Milo Milton Quaife].

240. Canuteson, Richard L. "Lars and Martha Larson: 'We Do What We Can for Them.'" Norwegian-American Studies, 25 (1972): 142-166.
      Mainly concerned with Lars Larson, one of the first Norwegian immigrants to America on the sloop Restoration. Included are many details on the life of his wife, Martha. Together they settled in Rochester, New York, where he prospered as a canal boat builder. She became the mother of eight children and later provided food, shelter, and located work for many subsequent Norwegian immigrants. Martha became a widow left with children whose ages were 1 to 20. She lived until the age of 84. The article sheds light on the influence of Quakerism on Norwegians in Norway and in America. Both Martha and her husband were Quakers.

241. Carhart, Alfreda Post. It Happened in Syria. New York: Fleming H. Revell, 1940.
      Immigrant reminiscences on early life in the Middle East.

242. Carlozzi-Rossi, Angela. "Italian Immigrants Tell Their Story," in S. L. La Gumina, ed., The Immigrants Speak (New York: Center for Migration Studies, 1979), pp. 153-163.
      Autobiographical account of an Italian immigrant who was a social worker in Philadelphia's settlement houses, and served as executive secretary of the Italian Welfare League.

243. Cather, Willa. My Antonia. Boston: Houghton Mifflin, 1918; 1961.
      A classic novel of pioneer Czech life in Nebraska, with many biographical vignettes woven into the text of the narrative.

244. Chavchavadze, Paul. Marie Avinov: Pilgrimage Through Hell. An Autobiography as told to Paul Chavchavadze. Englewood Cliffs, N.J.: Prentice-Hall, 1968.
      Autobiography of Russian émigree to the United States.

245. Child, Lydia Maria [Francis]. Letters from New York. New
      York: C. S. Francis, 1843.
         Child (1802-1880) describes her impressions of New York
         City in the mid-nineteenth century, its surroundings, and
         many of the social and ethnic problems it faced. Includes
         The Jews, Fear of Public Opinion, and Anecdotes of the
         Irish. See also her Good Wives (1833); and The History
         of the Condition of Women in Various Ages and Nations
         (1835).

246. Chou, Cynthia L. My Life in the United States. North Quincy,
      Mass.: Christopher Publishing House, 1970.
         The author grew up in China, coming to the United States
         after World War II.

247. Clausen, C. A., ed. The Lady with the Pen: Elise Waeren-
      skjold in Texas. Northfield, Minn.: Norwegian-American
      Historical Association, 1961.
         Letters written between 1851 and 1895 from Texas to which
         place this woman emigrated in 1847 from Norway. Inter-
         ested in languages, writing, and painting, Elise Waeren-
         skjold was a "premodern" woman with advanced ideas for
         her time about the role of women. She was also an ardent
         supporter of the abolition of slavery and of the temperance
         movement. The introduction to these letters provides inter-
         esting background on this woman's personal history as well
         as the events in Norway and America which were the back-
         drop for her dramatic life.

248. Cohen, Rose. Out of the Shadows. Garden City, N. Y.:
      Doubleday, Doran, 1918.

249. Covello, Leonard, with Guido D'Agostino. The Heart Is the
      Teacher. New York: McGraw-Hill, 1958. Reprint. With
      an Introduction by F. Cordasco, Teacher in the Urban Com-
      munity: A Half-Century in City Schools. Totowa, N. J.:
      Littlefield, Adams, 1970.
         Autobiography of Leonard Covello (1887-1982), leading
         American educator and long-time principal of Benjamin
         Franklin High School, East Harlem, New York City. In-
         cludes accounts of Italian immigrant women, and a detailed
         account of the Canadian social reformer, Anna C. Ruddy,
         who devoted her life to working with Italian immigrant
         families in East Harlem, New York City. See also Robert
         Peebles, "Leonard Covello: An Immigrant's Contribution
         to New York City." Unpublished Ph.D. dissertation, New
         York City, 1967.

250. Dahl, Borghild Margarethe. Homecoming. New York: E. P.
      Dutton, 1953.
         This autobiographical novel by a second-generation Nor-
         wegian immigrant, is written from the point of view of a
         young girl and presents the theme of the conflict between

first- and second-generation immigrants. According to the
view of the author, assimilation is inevitable, but from the
conclusion of Homecoming we understand that she also considers retention of the Old World heritage necessary. Her
definition of assimilation thus includes total Americanization.

251.   De Capite, Michael. Maria. New York: John Day, 1943.
        An autobiographical novel spanning three generations of
        Italian life in Cleveland, with vivid portraits of immigrant
        women. See also De Capite's No Bright Banner (1944).

252.   [Dertzeilt, Celia Adler]. The Celia Adler Story. New York:
        Shulsinger Bros., 1959. 2 vols.
        An autobiographical reminiscence (in Yiddish) with con-
        siderable information on the Yiddish theatre and glimpses
        of immigrant Jewish life.

253.   Di Donato, Pietro. Christ in Concrete. Indianapolis: Bobbs-
        Merrill, 1939.
        Autobiographical novel of Italian proletariat life in America.
        See also Di Donato, This Woman (1958), and Three Circles
        of Light (1960), variations on the same theme which include
        vividly strong portraits of Italian immigrant women.

254.   Di Donato, Pietro. Immigrant Saint. Life of Mother Cabrini.
        New York: McGraw-Hill, 1960.
        A biography of Frances Xavier Cabrini (1850-1917), prioress
        of her foundation, the Institute of the Missionary Sisters
        of the Sacred Heart. Sent to the United States by Pope
        Leo XIII to help Italian immigrants. She was canonized
        in 1946.

255.   Drinnon, Richard. Rebel in Paradise: A Biography of Emma
        Goldman. Chicago: University of Chicago Press, 1961. Re-
        print. New York: Harper Colophon Books, 1976.
        The first full biography of Goldman. Despite limitations,
        provides a sound and succinct narrative of Goldman's life
        based on exhaustive research into formerly untapped primary
        sources.

256.   Duffus, Robert L. Lillian Wald: Neighbor and Crusader.
        New York: Macmillan, 1938.
        Biography of Lillian Wald (1867-1940), a leader in nursing
        who was active in health and social work among immigrants
        on New York City's Lower East Side. Founded Henry
        Street (N.Y.C.) Settlement House, whose visiting nurse
        services were pioneering efforts.

257.   Edelman, Fannie. The Mirror of Life: The Old Country and
        the New. Foreword and translated from Yiddish by Samuel
        Pasner. New York: Exposition Press, 1961.
        Autobiography of a Galician Jew who arrived in New York
        at sixteen and educated herself while raising three children.

258.   Epstein, Beryl W. Lillian Wald, Angel of Henry Street. New
       York: Julian Messner, 1948.

259.   Ferber, Edna. Fanny Herself. [1917]. New York: Arno
       Press, 1975.
          Edna Ferber (1887-1968) of "Show Boat" fame, turns to
       her own life story in the quasi-autobiographical novel,
       Fanny Herself. This is the story of a bright, plucky Jew-
       ish girl growing up in Winnebago, Wisconsin in the early
       1900's. In her teens, Fanny Brandeis helps her widowed
       mother establish a china specialty shop. After Mrs. Brandeis
       dies, Fanny, determined to succeed, moves to Chicago
       where she hides her Jewish origin. There she joins a
       women's wear mail-order merchandising house, trans-
       forming its sluggish infant's wear section by introducing
       the idea of selling packaged layettes. Fanny rises to top
       buyer and is offered a business and a love partnership.
       As Fanny comes to self-knowledge, Ferber's art of detail
       and wit make this a memorable and endearing story.

260.   Fermi, Laura. Atoms in the Family: My Life with Enrico
       Fermi. Chicago: University of Chicago Press, 1954.
          Wife of the Italian physicist Enrico Fermi (1901-1954), who
       received the Nobel Prize in Physics in 1938, soon after
       which Fermi and his wife (who was Jewish) left Italy for
       the United States.

261.   Fetherling, Dale. Mother Jones, the Miners' Angel: A Por-
       trait. Carbondale: Southern Illinois University Press, 1974.
          Assesses the significance of the contribution to the labor
       and Socialist movements of Mary Harris Jones (1830-1930),
       an Irish immigrant, familiarly known as "Mother Jones."
       Acknowledges that no coherent or consistent philosophy
       guided her work; she was, rather, a "benevolent fanatic."
       Nevertheless, Mother Jones was "a folk heroine whose in-
       spiration reached down to those people who were unimpor-
       tant in name or wealth or title but all-important in numbers."

262.   Flynn, Elizabeth Gurley. I Speak My Own Piece: Autobio-
       graphy of "The Rebel Girl." New York: Masses & Main-
       stream, 1955. Reprint. New York: International Publishers,
       1973.
          Reminiscences of Elizabeth Gurley Flynn (1890-1964), social
       activist among unskilled, unorganized, mostly immigrant
       workers.

263.   Forbes, Kathryn. Mama's Bank Account. New York: Har-
       court, Brace, 1943.
          An autobiographical novel about an immigrant family in
       urban San Francisco at the turn of the century. The
       mother of this Norwegian family is the main character and
       the main theme of the novel is apparently love of the mother.
       First-generation Norwegian-Americans are seen to be "con-
       sciously conforming to Yankee requirements of behavior."

264.   Forsythe, Hilda J.   Grandeur in Simplicity.   New York: [The
       Author].   1963.
       The author remembers her childhood in Wisconsin and her
       Norwegian-born farmer father.

265.   Goldman, Emma.   Living My Life.   New York: Alfred A.
       Knopf, 1931.   2 vols.   Reprint.   New York: De Capo Press,
       1970.
       Born in Kovno, now Lithuania, Goldman (1869-1940) moved
       with her family to Koenigsberg, Prussia, where she gained
       a preliminary education despite her resistance to discipline.
       She rapidly became a political radical and dissident.   Immi-
       grated to the United States to gain freedom from her family.
       For a brief spell she lived and worked in Rochester, New
       York, but emotional reaction to the murder of the Hay-
       market strikers sent her on a new course.   She moved to
       New York City where she became acquainted with the lead-
       ing anarchist personalities.

266.   Goldman, Emma.   Living My Life.   Edited by Richard and
       Anna Maria Drinnon.   New York: New American Library
       1977.
       Richard and Anna Maria Drinnon have reduced Goldman's
       lengthy autobiography by preserving the significant sections
       that deal with her years of activism in the United States.
       They cut the last six chapters of the original version pub-
       lished in 1931 and have replaced them by an afterword
       summarizing the last two decades of Goldman's life, the
       years since 1919, which she spent in exile.   A new index
       and bibliographical essay are added.

267.   Goldmark, Josephine.   Impatient Crusader: Florence Kelley's
       Life Story.   Urbana: University of Illinois Press, 1953.
       Josephine Goldmark (1877-1950), an investigator of labor
       conditions and legislative reformer, was a close friend of
       Florence Kelley (1859-1932) and co-worker in the National
       Consumers' League.   Focuses primarily on Kelley's efforts
       to improve the working conditions of women and children.
       The descriptions of her early years are drawn almost en-
       tirely from Kelley's personal reminiscences published
       serially in the Survey in 1926 and 1927.

268.   Grant, Anne McVicar.   Memoirs of an American Lady, with
       Sketches of Manners and Scenery in America, as They Existed
       Previous to the Revolution.   London: Longman, Hurst, Rees,
       and Orme, 1808.   2 vols.   Reprint.   New York: Research
       Reprints, 1970.
       Grant, born in Glasgow (1755), came to America at a
       young age and settled, with her mother, at Claverack on
       the Hudson.   She learned the Dutch language and became
       interested in the social life and customs of the New York
       area.   Memoirs consists of her early recollections of
       Margarita Schuyler of Albany, descriptions of the manners

and customs of the descendants of the early Dutch settlers, historical sketches of New York, and tales about the Indians of New York.

269. Grillo, Clara Corica. "Italian Immigrants Tell Their Story," in S. L. La Gumina, ed., The Immigrants Speak (New York: Center for Migration Studies, 1979), pp. 113-123.
Autobiographical account of a Sicilian immigrant on life in Cleveland, Ohio, with notices of the Italian theatre activities in the city.

270. Guttersen, Alma A., ed. Souvenir "Norse-American Women" 1825-1925: A Symposium of Prose and Poetry, Newspaper Articles, and Biographies, Contributed by One Hundred Prominent Women. [St. Paul, Minnesota and Mrs. Regina Hilleboe Christensen, Portland, Oregon]. St. Paul, Minn., 1926.
Contains articles in English with a few in Norwegian as well as numerous photographs. An interesting collection of information on a variety of topics and a rich source for names and biographical information.

271. Hamilton, Alice. Exploring the Dangerous Trades. The Autobiography of Alice Hamilton, M.D. Boston: Little, Brown, 1943.
Alice Hamilton (1869-1970) was an American physician and educator. Her Autobiography is valuable for the description of industrial areas (and their hazards) in which immigrants formed the majority of workers.

272. Hardy, Mary (McDowell) Duffus. Through Cities and Prairie Lands: Sketches of an American Tour. New York: R. Worthington, 1881.
Lady Duffus Hardy (1825?-1891) describes her trip through urban and rural regions of nineteenth-century America.

273. Hartman, [Mrs.] Gustave. I Gave My Heart. New York: Citadel Press, 1960.
Autobiography of woman workers for Jewish charitable causes.

274. Hasanovitz, Elizabeth. One of Them: Chapters from a Passionate Autobiography. Boston: Houghton Mifflin, 1918.
Jewish social activist.

275. Helsenrad, Helen. Brown Was the Danube. New York: Thomas Yoseloff, 1966.

276. Henley, Gail. Where the Cherries End Up. Boston: Little, Brown, 1978.
Unusual background of Polish immigrants in Ontario, and a young woman's experience.

277. Hilf, Mary Asia [as told to Barbara Bourns]. No Time for Tears. New York: Thomas Yoseloff, 1964.

Autobiography of a Jewish immigrant woman from Russia
who settled on the West Coast and devoted herself to working for others.

278.   Hourwich, Andrea Taylor, and Gladys L. Palmer, eds. I
       Am a Woman Worker: A Scrapbook of Autobiographies. New
       York: Affiliated School for Workers, 1936.
       A collection of women's experiences as workers which grew
       out of the summer schools for workers run by a coalition
       of labor movement groups. The women speak out about
       life in the factory, losing their jobs, organizing unions,
       and strikes they have been involved in. Unadorned reports
       by working women in the early days of the New Deal, of
       strikes, exploitation, organizing efforts, work with men,
       and confrontations with their bosses.

279.   Houston, Jeanne Wakatsuki, and James D. Houston. Fare-
       well to Manzanar: A True Story of Japanese American Ex-
       perience During and After the World War II Internment. Bos-
       ton: Houghton Mifflin, 1973.
       An autobiographical account delineating the experiences of
       Jeanne W. Houston's family. She was seven years old
       when the internment began.

280.   [Ishvani]. The Brocaded Sari. Philadelphia: John Day, 1946.
       Autobiography of Indian girl who married an American.

281.   Jacob, Henrick E. The World of Emma Lazarus. New York:
       Schocken Books, 1949.
       Best known for writing the inscription on the base of the
       Statue of Liberty, Lazarus (1849-1887) was a champion of
       Jewish immigrants and wrote on Jewish themes.

282.   Jannopoulo, Helen P. And Across Big Seas. Caldwell, Ida.:
       Caxton Publishers, 1949.
       Greek woman immigrant from Romania.

283.   Janson, Drude Krog. En saloonkeepers datter; fortaelling.
       Minneapolis: C. Rasmussen, 1891.
       Originally published in Copenhagen in 1887, this "autobio-
       graphical novel of manners fused with elements of the con-
       fession or autobiography" went through at least seven edi-
       tions. It was written by a Norwegian woman immigrant
       who settled in Minneapolis during the 1880's. The main
       character of the novel is a young Oslo girl who comes to
       Minneapolis. Opinions expressed in the novel reflect the
       author's sympathies with the women's suffrage movements
       in Norway and America.

284.   Jaworski, Irene D. Becoming American: The Problems of
       Immigrants and Their Children. New York: Harper, 1950.

285.   Jean, [Sister] Patricia. Only One Heart: The Story of a
       Pioneer Nun in America. New York: Doubleday, 1963.

Mother Praxedes of the Sisters of Loretto (originally Susan Carty, Irish immigrant).

286. Jones, [Mother] Mary. The Autobiography of Mother Jones. Edited by Mary Field Parton: Foreword by Clarence Darrow; Introduced by Fred Thompson. Chicago: Charles H. Kerr, 1925. Reprint. New York: Arno Press, 1971.
Born in Cork, Ireland, Mary Harris Jones (1830-1930) was a major force in the American labor movement. First published in 1925, the Autobiography is a chronicle of her strike activity. Jones offers few insights into her personal life but rather presents a picture of the famed agitator as she liked to be recognized: e.g., she narrates her many adventures; her renditions of the 1903 march of the mill children, and the great strikes in Colorado in 1903 and 1913-1914.

287. Joyce, Rosemary O. A Woman's Place: The Life History of a Rural Ohio Grandmother. Columbus: Ohio State University Press, 1983.
Traces the counterpoint of local economic history and the family life of a rural woman. The author conducted the study mainly through lengthy interviews from 1975 through 1982 with an anonymous woman, her sister, and her daughter. The subject, a "rural Ohio Grandmother," is rooted in her community and can trace her family back five generations. A fluent speaker, she provided the many remembrances that the author taped and presents in the book. Stimulated by the work of L. L. Langness and his associates, the book is a response to the newly awakened field of life history of ordinary (and immigrant) people, an area of research largely dormant in North America from the 1940's through the 1970's. Joyce provides an excellent 38-page introduction to life history creation.

288. Kelly, Myra. Little Citizens: The Humours of School Life. New York: Macmillan, 1904.
An Irish schoolteacher's experience with East Side (New York City) Jewish immigrant children. See also Little Aliens (1910) and Wards of Liberty (1907).

289. Kikumura, Akemi. Through Harsh Winters: The Life of a Japanese Immigrant Woman. Novato, Calif.: Chandler and Sharp, 1981.
The author tells the story of her family's immigration to the United States through an extended life-history of her mother.

290. Kingston, Maxine Hong. The Woman Warrior: Memoirs of a Girlhood Among Ghosts. New York: Random House, 1976.
Acculturation and conflict for Chinese daughter of immigrants.

291.   Knauff, Ellen Raphael. The Ellen Knauff Story. New York:
        W. W. Norton, 1952. Introduction by Arthur Garfield Hays.
        A chronicle of a three-year detention on Ellis Island.

292.   Kohn, Frida. Generation in Turmoil. Great Neck, N. Y.:
        Channel Publishing, 1960. Introduction by Joseph Machlis.
        Autobiography of a woman musician who moved from Russia
        to Germany and finally to the United States.

293.   Kohut, Rebekah. As I Knew Them: Some Jews and a Few
        Gentiles. New York: Doubleday, 1929.

294.   Kohut, Rebekah. My Portion: An Autobiography. New York:
        Thomas Seltzer, 1925.
        Reminiscences of the wife of the scholarly Alexander Kohut,
        especially of her participation in American Jewish life and
        overseas activities, and in education and social work. Dur-
        ing the period of the women's suffrage movement, Kohut,
        a founder of the National Council for Jewish Women, was
        an important activist whose recollections provide the reader
        with glimpses of Jewish life in late nineteenth-century San
        Francisco.

295.   Kohut, Rebekah. More Yesterdays: An Autobiography (1925-
        49): A Sequel to "My Portion." Foreword by Fannie Hurst.
        New York: Bloch Publishing, 1950.

296.   Kramer, Sydelle, and Jenny Masur, eds. Jewish Grand-
        mothers. Boston: Beacon Press, 1976.
        Contains the reminiscences of ten immigrant women drawn
        out of their experiences of their lives.

297.   Krause, Corinne Azen. Grandmothers, Mothers, and Daugh-
        ters: An Oral History Study of Ethnicity, Mental Health, and
        Continuity of Three Generations of Jewish, Italian, and Slavic
        American Women. New York: American Jewish Committee,
        1978.

298.   Kugler, Israel. "The Trade Union Career of Susan B. Anthony."
        Labor History, 2 (1961): 90-100.

299.   Lang, Lucy Robins. Tomorrow Is Beautiful. New York:
        Macmillan, 1948.

300.   Larcom, Lucy. A New England Girlhood. Outlined from
        Memory. Boston: Houghton Mifflin, 1889.

301.   Larsen, Karen. Ingeborg Astrup Larsen: Her Family and
        Her Girlhood in Norway. Northfield, Minn., 1958.
        Biographical materials about the second wife of Laurence
        Larsen, president of Luther College. The author's mother
        came to America in 1872. Various genealogical tables are
        included.

302. Lee, Sirkka Tuomi. "The Finns." Cultural Correspondence,
      6, 7 (Spring 1978): 41-49.
      Lee recalls her childhood in a Finnish-American radical
      community. Her account of women's activities is especially
      interesting: women taught Sunday schools in Finnish, of-
      fering as their counterpart to biblical tales the story of
      Spartacus and the legacy of Finnish peasant uprisings; they
      directed the children's chorus in songs of proletarian trial
      and revolution; and they led the children's theatre, with a
      combination of skits, recitations, music, and Isadora Dun-
      can-style dancing. Recalls children's activities of the
      1920's and 1930's and emphasized their participation in
      virtually all phases of adult cultural life.

303. Levy, Harriet Lane. 920 O'Farrell Street. [1947]. New
      York: Arno Press, 1975.
      On the north of San Francisco's O'Farrell Street, in the
      1890's lived Jewish families of a mid-century German
      emigration who had become solid householders and pros-
      perous city merchants. Number 920, where Harriet Lane
      Levy grew up, offered a view of once-upon-a-time San
      Francisco. Her story of a house is carried to that moment
      in 1906 when earthquake and fire demolished this neighbor-
      hood enclave, along with much of the West's most fabled
      city.

304. Lilienthal, Meta. Dear Remembered World: Childhood Memo-
      ries of an Old New Yorker. New York: Richard R. Smith,
      1947.
      Lilienthal (1876-1947) was one of the important journalists
      among women in the Socialist party. She produced several
      pamphlets, scores of leaflets and short essays, and edited
      a women's page in the New Yorker Volkszeitung and a
      "Votes for Women" column in the New York Call. Her
      autobiography does not focus on her political accomplish-
      ments; it relates her childhood memories of New York City.
      Lilienthal provides scattered insights into the German immi-
      grant radical milieu of the late nineteenth century, for her
      parents were ardent Socialists and prominent activists in
      the Socialist Labor party. Lilienthal's parents emigrated
      from Germany in 1861.

305. Ljone, Oddmund. Mine tårer fløt rikelig: Fortellingen om
      utvandrerkvinnen Gro Nilsdatter fra Hallingdal. Oslo: Glyden-
      dal Norsk Forlag, 1975.
      Stories about the wife of a Norwegian emigrant based on
      the subject's own letters home to Norway. The author
      was a journalist who visited the American sites associated
      with Gro Svendsen. He has written other books for chil-
      dren and directs this work to young as well as older adults.
      The title in English is translated My Tears Flow Abun-
      dantly: Stories About Emigrant Wife Gro Nilsdatter from
      Hallingdal.

306.   Loggins, Vernon. Two Romantics and Their Ideal Life. New
        York: Odyssey, 1946.
        Life of Elizabeth Ney, German-born Texas sculptor during
        the nineteenth century.

307.   Long, Priscilla. Mother Jones, Woman Organizer. Cam-
        bridge, Mass.: Red Sun Press, 1976.
        Focuses on the charismatic, maternal quality of Mother
        Jones to explain her organizing success among miners
        and their wives. Examines Jones's conservative view of
        women's role and her reluctance to leave "her boys" for
        the six million women in paid employment at the turn of
        the century. Even the Women's Trade Union League could
        not change her hostility toward middle-class women or
        change her fundamental belief that women belonged at home,
        not in industry.

308.   Lowenthal, Marvin. Henrietta Szold: Life and Letters. New
        York: Viking Press, 1942.
        A biographical portrait of an outstanding Jewish leader of
        the American Zionist movement. Many letters in the text.
        Szold (1860-1945) founded Hadassah in 1912, serving as
        president until 1926.

309.   Manley, Sean. My Heart's in the Heather. New York: Funk
        & Wagnalls, 1968.
        Autobiography of woman who grew up in the Scottish-Ameri-
        can colony in New York City and who later became an
        author and critic.

310.   Maynard, Theodore. Too Small a World. The Life of Fran-
        cesca Cabrini. Milwaukee: Bruce Publishing, 1945.

311.   Meir, Golda. My Life. New York: G. P. Putnam's Sons,
        1975.
        Born in Kiev, Russia in 1898, Golda (Mabovitch) Meir's
        family migrated to the United States in 1906. Served as
        Israeli Prime Minister, 1969-1974.

312.   Merriam, Eve. Emma Lazarus: Woman with a Torch. New
        York: Citadel Press, 1956.
        A popular biography of the noted American Jewish poet.
        The text includes several poems.

313.   Michelet, Maren. Glimpses from Agnes Mathilde Wergeland's
        Life. Memorial Edition. Privately published. Minneapolis:
        Folkebladet Publishing, 1916.
        Biographical sketch of Mathilde Wergeland, an unusual
        Norwegian immigrant woman. She was an academic and
        intellectual person who came to America in 1890 after
        living in various places in Europe for her studies. Al-
        though she made trips back to Norway and Europe, she be-
        came an American citizen and was on the history faculty

at the University of Wisconsin.   She was an artist, poet,
and musician as well as scholar.   An independent thinker,
she was a reserved and quiet person by nature.   She was
closely involved with the women's suffrage movements both
in Norway and America.

314.   Miller, Karen.   A Diary.   Translated from the Danish by
Olaf Morgan Norlie.   Published by her Grandson, Daniel
Milford Peter Hansen.   Northfield, Minnesota, 1952.
A collection of notes penned from time to time recording
the life and thoughts of a Minnesota Danish immigrant.
They give a realistic picture of the life of this farm house-
hold in the year 1894, and the immediate neighborhood.

315.   Modjeska, Helena.   Memories and Impressions of Helena Modjeska: An Autobiography.   New York: Macmillan, 1910.
Born in Cracow, Poland, Modjeska (1840-1909) was both
a famous actress in her homeland and an activist in the
cause of Polish nationalism.   In 1876 she joined a group
of Polish immigrants who formed a cooperative farm in
the Santa Ana valley of California.   Modjeska devotes a
small portion of her memoirs to her encounter with communal living.   By January 1877 the farm began to fail and
Modjeska, to provide the needed funds, resumed her acting
career.   She learned English and conducted a successful
tour of eastern United States, but by the summer of 1878
the colony had disbanded.

316.   Molek, Mary.   Immigrant Woman.   Dover, Del.:   M. Molek,
1976.
Mary Molek (1909-1982), an archivist and museum curator,
was a member of the Yugoslav Socialist Federation in the
1930's and 1940's and leading contributor to its newspaper,
Prosveta (Chicago), edited by her husband, Ivan Molek.
Portrays Slovenian-American working-class life in the first
decades of the twentieth century.

317.   Moodie, Susanna.   Roughing It in the Bush, or, Life in Canada.
New York: G. P. Putnam, 1852.
Autobiographical account of experiences of immigrant's wife
in the Canadian backwoods.   See also Life in the Backwoods (1887), a sequel.

318.   Munch, Helen, and Peter A. Munch, trans. and eds.   The
Strange American Way: Letters of Caja Munch from Wiota,
Wisconsin, 1855-1859--An American Adventure.   Carbondale:
Southern Illinois University Press, 1970.
The grandson of Caja Munch and his wife gathered these
letters which are presented together with excerpts from
Caja Munch's husband's autobiography.   He was pastor of
the Lutheran church in Wiota, Wisconsin from 1855-1859.
An article by Professor P. A. Munch entitled "Social
Class and Acculturation" is also included.

319.   Nathan, Maud. Once upon a Time and Today. [1933]. New
        York: G. P. Putnam's Sons, 1933. Reprint. New York:
        Arno Press, 1975.
            After her marriage Maud Nathan (1862-1946) gave much of
            her time to such genteel and philanthropic causes as the
            New York Exchange for Women's Work and the Hebrew
            Free School Association. As president of the National
            Consumers' League she worked with Josephine Shaw Lowell
            in the drive to make women aware of their power as con-
            sumers. She was active in the National Council of Jewish
            Women.

320.   Nelson, David T., ed. and trans. The Diary of Elisabeth
        Koren 1853-1855. Northfield, Minn.: Norwegian-American
        Historical Association, 1955.
            Provides an unusually detailed account of the Atlantic cross-
            ing in 1853 and the overland trip to Iowa. Koren describes
            her first year as a young minister's wife in Iowa, six miles
            southeast of what is now Decorah in Washington Prairie
            where her husband had responded to a call for a Norwegian
            Lutheran minister. As the editor notes, the diary reveals
            "the intelligence, interest, fortitude and clear vision with
            which Mrs. Koren met the problems of the frontier and
            made the transition from her assured station in the old
            country." The diary is supplemented by her letters to
            family in Norway. Historians will appreciate the descrip-
            tions of a woman adjusting to a new place, adapting to the
            homes and habits of other church members until her own
            house has been built, and coping with the frequent absences
            of her husband.

321.   Nestor, Agnes. Woman's Labor Leader, An Autobiography.
        Rockford, Ill.: Bellevue Books Publishing, 1954.
            Nestor (1880-1948) was elected president of the International
            Glove Workers Union in 1903. Member of the executive
            board of the National Women's Trade Union League, active
            in behalf of immigrant women and children.

322.   Newby, Elizabeth Loza. A Migrant with Hope. Nashville,
        Tenn.: Broadman Press, 1977.
            Mexican-American chronicle of acculturation and social
            mobility.

323.   Nilsen, Frida R. Growing Up in the Old Parsonage. Lake
        Mills, Iowa, 1975.

324.   Nilsen, Frida R., trans. and ed. Letters of Longing: The
        Story of A Trans-Atlantic Courtship. Minneapolis, 1970.
            Letters of the Reverend Ole Nilsen of Northwood (Iowa) to
            his future wife, still in Europe, 1881-1882.

325.   Noren, Catherine Hanf. The Camera of My Family. New
        York: Alfred Knopf, 1976.

The hundred-year album of a German-Jewish family. Includes photos of five generations from their lives in Germany
before the turn of the century to the American present.

326.   Olsson, Anna. A Child of the Prairie. Trans. by Martha
        Winblad. Ed. by Elizabeth Jaderborg. Lindsborg, Ka.:
        privately printed, 1978. [En Prärieunges Funderinger, 1917].
        Olsson's story for children covers the years 1869 to 1873
        in Lindsborg, Kansas, and provides a child's perception of
        Swedish immigrant customs and American ways.

327.   Orpen, Mrs. [Doaty]. Memories of the Old Emigrant Days
        in Kansas, 1862-1865. Edinburgh & London: William Black-
        wood & Sons, 1926.
        Doaty Orpen recalls the three years when she pioneered
        in Kansas. Unconventional female roles for both girls and
        women in the new territory are compared with ways "back
        East." Doaty thrived during this period in her life when
        she could live as a boy. Describes the variety of people
        settling in Kansas, bouts with ague, attitudes toward slavery,
        and the adjustments that had to be made while her father
        was away fighting in the Civil War.

328.   Osterweis, Rollin G. Rebecca Gratz: A Study in Charm.
        New York: G. P. Putnam's Sons, 1935.
        An illustrated, popular biography of a leader of early nine-
        teenth-century Jewry in Philadelphia and a founder of the
        Hebrew Sunday School in 1838. The bibliographical note
        includes references to primary sources. Gratz (1781-1869)
        was secretary of the Philadelphia Orphan Society for forty
        years.

329.   Pesotta, Rose. Bread upon the Waters. New York: Mead,
        1944.

330.   Peyton, Karen. The World So Fair. Philadelphia: John
        Day, 1963.
        Norwegian immigrant life is presented in this autobio-
        graphical novel set in Duluth.

331.   Philipson, David, ed. Letters of Rebecca Gratz. Edited with
        an Introduction and Notes. Philadelphia: Jewish Publication
        Society of America, 1929. Reprint. Arno Press, 1975.
        These letters, extending from the years 1808 to 1866,
        capture the warmth, family devotion and piety of a nine-
        teenth-century Jew, Rebecca Gratz (1781-1869). One of
        five children of the distinguished mercantile family of Phila-
        delphia, Rebecca is known in Jewish history as a founder
        of the Philadelphia Orphan Society (1815) and the Jewish
        Sunday School movement (1838). In literary history she
        holds an equally honored place--as the prototype of Rebecca
        in Sir Walter Scott's Ivanhoe. Rebecca Gratz's character
        traits reportedly described to Scott by Washington Irving,
        are amply corroborated by this volume of correspondence.

332.   Pieracci, Bruna. "Italian Americans Tell Their Story," in
        S. L. La Gumina, ed., The Immigrants Speak (New York:
        Center for Migration Studies, 1979), pp. 33-47.
        Autobiographical account of Italian immigrant woman from
        the Northern Apennines on the harsh life in a mining camp
        in Iowa.

333.   Preus, Caroline Dorothea Margarethe [Keyser]. Linka's
        Diary On Land and Sea 1845-1864. Trans. and ed. by
        Johan Carl Keyser Preus and his wife Diderikke Margrethe,
        née Brandt. Minneapolis, Augsburg, 1952.
        The diary of the orphaned daughter of a Norwegian pastor,
        and later professor of sacred theology at the University
        of Christiana, who immigrated to America in 1851. She
        settled with her husband in Spring Prairie, Wisconsin. The
        editor writes the following about his grandmother's diary:
        "For want of an intimate friend to whom she could unburden
        herself, she had confided to the pages of her book the deep
        and sacred thoughts of her lonely heart."

334.   Prisland, Marie. From Slovenia to America: Recollections
        and Collections. Chicago: Slovenian Women's Union of
        America, 1968.

335.   Raaen, Aagot. Grass of the Earth: Immigrant Life in the
        Dakota Country. Northfield, Minn.: Norwegian-American
        Historical Association, 1950.
        Theodore Blegen's "Foreword" notes that the Raaen family
        was not "wholly typical of the Norwegian immigrants who
        turned the prairie sod and made garden of wilderness."
        The value of the book lies in its analysis of experiences
        not always found in other memoirs. It is about a family
        that values intellect and creativity more than materialistic
        comforts and security, for one thing. While the author
        says in her "Introduction" that she has omitted "the most
        tragic scenes," she still gives readers insight into the
        life of a family coping with a disillusioned male (Far) who
        turns to alcohol, and into a female's response (Mor) who
        becomes a militant (and on one occasion saloon-smashing)
        prohibitionist on the Dakota prairies in the 1870's and
        1880's.

336.   Raaen, Aagot. Measure of My Days. Fargo, N.D.: North
        Dakota Institute for Regional Studies, 1953.
        The sequel to Grass on the Earth, this book records the
        education and world travels of the author, the daughter of
        Norwegian immigrants who settled in North Dakota during
        the middle period of Norwegian immigration. "Though her
        travels ultimately encompass the world, she is always going
        home."

337.   Rachlin, Nahid. Foreigner. New York: W. W. Norton,
        1978.

Novel about Iran and Iranian women by an Iranian-American woman; one of the few works, fiction or otherwise, about this immigrant group.

338. Rasmussen, Anne-Marie. <u>There Once Was a Time</u>. New York: Dell, 1975.
      Autobiography of a Norwegian girl who came to work for Nelson Rockefeller and who married his son, Steven.

339. Razovsky, Cecilia. <u>Making Americans.</u> New York: National Council of Jewish Women, 1938.
      A manual on naturalization.

340. Richards, Marilee, ed. "Life Anew for Czech Immigrants: The Letters of Marie and Vavrin Strítecký, 1913-1934." <u>South Dakota History</u>, 11 (Fall-Winter 1981): 253-304.
      Beginning in 1913, these letters from South Dakota (near Colombe) cover two decades, demonstrating changing attitudes and perspectives of immigrants adapting to a new land and a different culture. Commentary on American customs and political issues, crops, livestock, and prices.

341. Richardson, Dorothy. <u>The Long Day: The Story of a New York Working Girl, as Told by Herself.</u> New York: Century, 1905.

342. Rogow, Sally. <u>Lillian Wald: The Nurse in Blue.</u> Philadelphia: Jewish Publication Society of America, 1966.

343. Rölvaag, Ole. <u>Giants in the Earth.</u> New York: Harper, 1927; New York: Harper, 1955.
      A classic portrayal of immigrant life whose message is the survival of Norwegian farmers in Minnesota and the Dakotas.

344. Rosten, Leo C. (Leonard Q. Ross, pseud.). <u>The Education of Hyman Kaplan.</u> New York: Harcourt, Brace, 1937.
      Humorous sketches about Americanization classes in a New York City night school. See also <u>The Return of Hyman Kaplan</u> (1959).

345. Ruskay, Sophie. <u>Horsecars and Cobblestones.</u> New York: Beechhurst Press, 1948.
      Fully dimensional portrait of life in the Jewish immigrant community written as a sheaf of reminiscences.

346. Rybacki, Stella. <u>Thrills, Chills, and Sorrows.</u> New York: Exposition Press, 1954.
      The Polish working-class community.

347. Salverson, Laura Goodman. <u>Confessions of an Immigrant's Daughter.</u> Toronto: University of Toronto Press, 1981.

348. Schappes, Morris U., ed. The Letters of Emma Lazarus,
      1868-1886. New York: New York Public Library, 1949.
         Letters by the American Jewish poet to Ralph Waldo Emer-
      son, Rabbi Gustav Gottheil, Henry George, Philip Cowen,
      and others. Introduction and notes by the editor.

349. Schappes, Morris U. "Three Women." Jewish Currents,
      29 (September 1975): 5-7.
         As a backdrop for International Women's Year proclaimed
      by the United Nations for 1975, Schappes contributes very
      brief biographical sketches of Ernestine L. Rose, Emma
      Lazarus, and Clara Lemlich.

350. Schneiderman, Rose, and Lucy Goldthwaite. All for One.
      New York: Paul S. Eriksson, 1967.
         Schneiderman (1882-1972), an immigrant from Russian
      Poland, served as president of the New York Women's
      Trade Union League from 1918 until 1949. A close as-
      sociate of Eleanor Roosevelt.

351. Schoen, Carol. "Anzia Yezierska: New Light on the 'Sweat-
      shop Cinderella.'" Melus, 7 (1980): 3-11.

352. Segale, Sister Blandina. At the End of the Sante Fe Trail.
      Milwaukee: Bruce Publishing, 1948.
         Nuns who worked with poor Indians and Chicanos in the
      American Southwest.

353. Seifer, Nancy. Nobody Speaks for Me! Self-Portraits of
      American Working Class Women. New York: Simon and
      Schuster, 1976.

354. Semmingsen, Ingrid. "A Pioneer: Agnes Mathilde Wergeland,
      1857-1914." In Odd S. Lovoll, ed., Makers of an American
      Immigrant Legacy: Essays in Honor of Kenneth O. Bjork.
      (Northfield, Minn.: The Norwegian-American Historical As-
      sociation, 1980), pp. 111-130.
         This article was translated by Sigvald Stoylen and is a
      revision of an article published in Kvinner og bøker.
      Festskrift til Ellisiv Steen/på hennes 70-årsdag 4. februar
      1978, 25-41 (Oslo, Norway, 1978). This work was edited
      by Edvard Beyer, et al. Describes the life of a scholarly
      Norwegian woman who emigrated to America in 1890.
      "Agnes Mathilde Wergeland's academic and scholarly career
      calls to our attention the inspiring influence of America on
      Norwegian feminism" according to Odd Lovoll.

355. Shank, Margarethe Erdahl. Call Back the Years. Minneapo-
      lis: Augsburg, 1966.
         An autobiographical novel about a young girl's emigration
      from Norway to Minnesota.

356. Shank, Margarethe Erdahl. The Coffee Train. New York:
      Doubleday, 1953.

This autobiographical novel is the story of a young girl
living in Grand Prairie, North Dakota with her immigrant
grandparents. Although technically third-generation, Margrit lives the life of a second-generation immigrant child.
Conscious retention of Norwegian heritage is made by the
family with little conflict with American patterns. The
novel is "a document of loving commemoration of a late
grandparent."

357.   Simkhovitch, Mary K. Neighborhood: My Story of Greenwich
       House. New York: W. W. Norton, 1938

358.   Sjoborg, Sofia Charlotte. "Journey to Florida." Swedish
       Pioneer Historical Quarterly, 26 (1975): 24-45.
           Concerns a woman emigrating from Uppsala, Sweden to
       Florida in 1871.

359.   Sone, Monica. Nisei Daughter. Boston: Little, Brown,
       1953.
           Story of one woman's experience of growing up as a
       Japanese-American in the mid-twentieth century. Of special
       interest is Sone's account of life in a relocation camp dur-
       ing World War II.

360.   Steel, Edward M. "Mother Jones in the Fairmont Field,
       1901." Journal of American History, 57 (1970): 290-307.

361.   Steen, Ragna, and Magda Hendrickson. Pioneer Days in
       Bardo, Alberta. Introduced by N. N. Ronning. Published
       by the Historical Society of Beaver Hills Lake. Tofield,
       Alberta, 1944.
           Includes sketches of early surrounding settlements with
       vivid accounts of immigrant settlers' lives.

362.   Stern, Elisabeth G. I Am a Woman--and a Jew. New York:
       J. H. Sears, 1926. Reprint. New York: Arno Press, 1969.
           Autobiography of "Leah Morton." This unusual document
       is an autobiographical account of the clash between Jewish
       and American cultures.

363.   Stoll, Joseph. The Lord Is My Shepherd: The Life of Eliza-
       beth Kemp Stutzman. Aylmer, Ont.: Pathway, 1965.
           Biography of a member of the Old Order Mennonite Church.
       Setting is the Midwest.

364.   Straus, Leonore Thomas. The Tender Stone. New York:
       W. W. Norton, 1964.
           The author describes her voyage from America to Norway.
       She was an artist and the daughter of a Norwegian immi-
       grant.

365.   Svendsen, Gro. Frontier Mother: The Letters of Gro Svend-
       sen. Northfield, Minn.: Norwegian-American Historical So-
       ciety, 1950.

The "American letters" of the wife of a Norwegian emigrant
written to her parents in Norway beginning in 1862. The
letters show the "life, character, and growth of a frontier
woman." The story of Gro Svendsen is also told in a
short novel written by her brother, Ole Nilsen, published
about 1877 in Norwegian in a small midwestern edition:
Dalrosen: fra virkelighetens verden paa begge sider av
havet. (Minneapolis: Augsburg, 19?.) In English the
title is Rose of the Valley: From the World of Reality on
Both Sides of the Sea.

366.   Talbot, Toby. A Book About My Mother. New York: Farrar,
        Straus and Giroux, 1980.
        A daughter's reminiscences of her mother, a Jewish immi-
        grant from Poland.

367.   Thompson, Ariadne. The Octagonal Heart. Indianapolis:
        Bobbs-Merrill, 1956.
        Reminiscences of a Greek-American childhood spent in St.
        Louis, where the author's father was the Greek consul.
        The octagonal heart refers to the octagonal house, owned
        by her uncle in Webster Groves, St. Louis, where the two
        families spent summers together.

368.   Truax, Rhoda. The Doctors Jacobi. Boston: Little, Brown,
        1952.
        A popular biography of Dr. Mary Corrina Putnam and her
        husband, Dr Abraham Jacobi, a Prussian-born Jewish
        immigrant--two important pediatricians of the late nine-
        teenth and early twentieth centuries.

369.   Vietor, Agnes C., ed. A Woman's Quest: The Life of
        Marie E. Zakrzewska, M.D. [1924]. New York: Arno
        Press, 1976.
        Having overcome the numerous obstacles faced by women
        venturing into medicine, Marie Zakrzewska (1829-1902) be-
        came a doctor and carried her personal crusade into the
        big city where ignorance and poverty battered immigrant
        women and children into sickness and early death. Story
        of one who strove successfully to found hospitals for women
        and children in Boston and New York. Marie Zakrzewska
        was the first Resident Physician of the New York Infirmary
        for Women and Children.

370.   [Waerenskjold, Elise]. The Lady with the Pen: Elise Waer-
        enskjold in Texas. Edited by C. A. Clausen with a Fore-
        word by Theodore C. Blegen. Northfield, Minn.: Norwegian
        American Historical Society, 1961.
        These letters by a strong leader in her community span a
        period of Texas history from 1851 to 1895. As an abo-
        litionist, journalist, temperance worker, and supporter of
        public education, Waerenskjold retained an optimistic point
        of view and encouraged Scandinavian immigration to the
        South.

371. Williams, Margaret. Second Sowing: The Life of Mary
      Aloysia Hardey. New York: Sheed & Ward, 1942.
      Biography of an early French missionary to the United
      States.

372. [Woerishoffer, Carola]. Carola Woerishoffer, Her Life and
      Work. Bryn Mawr, Pa.: Published by the Class of 1907,
      Bryn Mawr College, 1912.

373. Wong, Jade Snow. Fifth Chinese Daughter. New York:
      Harper and Row, 1965.

374. Xan, Erna Oleson. Home for Good. New York: Ives Wash-
      burn, 1952.
      Autobiographical stories about the author's move with her
      family to a farm in east-central Wisconsin in the years
      1910-1912. The stories reveal the flavor of a Norwegian-
      American home and the author's midwestern childhood.

375. Xan, Erna Oleson. Wisconsin My Home. Madison: Uni-
      versity of Wisconsin Press, 1950.
      Told by the author's mother, Thurine Oleson, this book is
      a detailed account of life in a Norwegian immigrant family
      in Wisconsin. Family genealogical tables and photographs
      are included.

376. Yezierska, Anzia. Bread Givers. New York: Doubleday,
      1925.
      Anzia Yezierska (1885-1970) was an immigrant novelist.
      See also companion novels Arrogant Beggar (1927) and All
      I Could Never Be (1932). See also her Salome of the Tene-
      ments (1923) and Red Ribbon on a White Horse (1950).

377. Yezierska, Anzia. Children of Loneliness: Stories of Immi-
      grant Life in America. New York: Funk & Wagnalls, 1923.
      In this volume of seven autobiographical short stories and
      three factual pieces, the author has written an emotional
      short story volume on American-Jewish life. The senti-
      mental, honest and stirring experiences of the Jewish im-
      migrants of the early 1900's are vividly evoked in this
      book.

378. [Yurka, Blanche]. Bohemian Girl: Blanche Yurka's Theatri-
      cal Life. Columbus: Ohio University Press, 1970.
      Czech-American actress.

379. [Zakrzewska, Marie Elizabeth]. Marie Elizabeth Zakrzewska,
      1829-1902. A Memoir. Boston: New England Hospital for
      Women and Children, 1903.

380. Zeitlin, Rose. Henrietta Szold: Record of a Life. New
      York: Dial Press, 1952.

III.   THE WORKPLACE AND POLITICAL ENCOUNTERS

381.   Abbott, Edith, and Sophonisba P. Breckinridge. "Employment of Women in Industries." Journal of Political Economy,
14 (January 1906): 14-40.

382.   Andrews, John B., and P. D. Bliss. History of Women in
Trade Unions. Washington, D. C.: Government Printing Of-
fice, 1911. [61st Congress, 2nd Session, Senate Document
No. 645].

383.   Baker, Elizabeth F. Technology and Women's Work. New
York: Columbia University Press, 1964.
Traces women's place in the labor force from colonial
times. Covers changing occupational patterns and protective
labor legislation beginning in the nineteenth century.

384.   Barnum, Gertrude. "The Story of a Fall River [Mass.] Mill
Girl." Independent, 58 (January-June 1905): 241-243.

385.   Beard, Mary Riter. Women's Work in Municipalities. [1915].
New York: Arno Press, 1976.
Best known for the popular American history text written
in collaboration with her husband, the historian Charles
Beard, Mary Beard was also the author of the pioneering
Women as Force in History. Women's Work is a balanced
attempt to evaluate, on the eve of the passage of the 19th
amendment, the female force for good in civic enterprise.
It draws on vast contemporary literature to depict, with
a sense of visceral commitment, the contributions being
made by women in social movements for community improvement, education, public health, integration, social
services and in the fight against "the social evil."

386.   Berman, Hyman. "Era of the Protocol: A Chapter in the
History of the International Ladies Garment Workers Union,
1910-1916." Unpublished Ph. D. dissertation. Columbia University, 1956.
Traces the organization of the labor force of the ladies
garment industry into effective and stable trade unions
during the early decade of the twentieth century and then
examines the workings of a pioneering trade agreement,
known as the Protocol, which was in effect in many branches
of the industry from 1910 to 1916. Provides economic
bird's-eye view of the industry and relates the faltering
attempts of the union to organize the labor force from 1900

to 1910. Chapters III through V, dealing with the Shirtwaist Makers' Strike of 1909, the Cloakmakers' Strike of
1910, and the strikes in the women's trades in 1913, relate
the successful efforts at trade union organization. Union
and manufacturer tactics are explored and the role of the
socially conscious outsiders, such as Brandeis, Filene,
Marshall, Schiff, is examined. Without the interference
of the social workers and progressives it is doubtful whether
trade union organization would have been successful as
early as 1910 in the ladies' garment industry.

387. Best, Harry. "The Extent of Organization in Women's Garment Making Industries of New York." American Economic
Review, 9 (December 1919): 789-791.

388. Blackwelder, Julia Kirk. "Women in the Work Force: Atlanta,
New Orleans, and San Antonio, 1930 to 1940." Journal of
Urban History, 4 (1978): 331-58.
Compares the work experiences of Chicano, black, native
white, and immigrant women in the three cities and examines the impact of proportion in the population, cultural
preferences, race discrimination, and female head of household upon the employment structure.

389. Boone, Gladys. Women's Trade Union Leagues in Great
Britain and United States. New York: Columbia University
Press, 1942.

390. Boseworth, Louise M. The Living Wage of Women Workers:
A Study of Income and Expenditures of 450 Women in the City
of Boston. Philadelphia: American Academy of Political
and Social Sciences, 1911. Reprint. New York: Arno Press,
1976.
Information on nominal and actual income as well as expenditures for lodging, food, clothing, health, savings, and
debt. Offers insight into urban living conditions.

391. Branca, Patricia. "A New Perspective on Women's Work:
A Comparative Typology." Journal of Social History, 7
(1974): 407-28.

392. Bryner, Edna. The Garment Trades. Cleveland: Survey
Committee of the Cleveland Foundation, 1916.

393. Buhle, Mari Jo. "From Sisterhood to Self: Woman's Road
to Advancement in the 20th Century." In Howard H. Quint
and Milton Cantor, eds., Men, Women, and Issues. Vol. 2,
rev. ed. (Homewood, Ill.: Dorsey Press, 1980), pp. 170-84.
Examines three Socialist women--Kate Richards O'Hare,
Rose Schneiderman, and Margaret Sanger--as archetypal
"new women" of the turn of the century, and their varying
degrees of reliance on networks of women. O'Hare's
social purity agitation, Schneiderman's activity within the

Women's Trade Union League, and Sanger's birth-control
campaigns are interpreted as symbols of the progressive
dissolution of the female collectivity that sustained women's
reform activities in the nineteenth century.

394. Buhle, Mari Jo. "Socialist Women and the 'Girl Strikers,'
Chicago, 1910." Signs, 1 (Summer 1976): 1039-51.
In 1910 women led a strike of over 41,000 workers in the
Chicago garment industry. Describes the role of Socialist
women in strike activities and reprints selections from the
Chicago Daily Socialist which state their expectations.

395. Buhle, Mari Jo. Women and American Socialism, 1870-
1920. Urbana: University of Illinois Press, 1981.
Traces the story through three generations and several
ethnic groups to understand the complex tradition of Socialist feminist struggles in the early decades of the
twentieth century. Uncovers little-known collective en-
deavors, reveals their influence upon the larger Socialist
movement, and finds their political forms in the lives of
activists themselves. Presents brief biographies of leading
activists such as Augusta Lilienthal and her daughter Meta,
Theresa Malkiel, Kate Richards O'Hare, Josephine Conger-
Kaneko, and May Wood Simons, among others. Also describes the networks that served the political movement.

396. Butler, Elizabeth Beardsley. Women and the Trades. Pittsburgh, 1907-1908. New York: Charities Publication Committee, 1909. Reprint. New York: Arno Press, 1971.
The first general survey of women-employing trades in a
major American city. Based on a survey of 400 Pittsburgh
establishments employing 22,000 women, investigates the
effects of industry on women: how well they submit to the
industrial pace and managerial direction; how they perform:
how they relate to other women in the plant: how their
employment affects the male wage earner in the family, the
children, and the family position in the community. Fully
documented with facts, figures and human interest, the
book explores female employment in pickle-canning factories,
cracker bakeries and casket-making firms, as well as
women employed as tobacco strippers, laundry workers,
lamp assemblers, glass decorators, makers of paper boxes,
brooms, and candies.

397. Calvert, Bruce T. The Story of a Silk Mill. New York:
Belding Brothers, 1914.
A narrative description of the development and operations
of Belding Brothers and Company silk mill. The Belding
Brothers believed it was their responsibility to care for
the welfare of the girls (largely immigrant) who worked in
the mill because "If we want fine people we must have fine
mothers." Stresses the need for cleanliness in the mill to
make conditions as pleasant as possible. Describes the
model factory town with clean, modern facilities, schools,

churches, sports and recreational facilities, a park, low-cost housing, and a company doctor.

398.   Campbell, Helen.   Women Wage Earners: Their Past, Their
        Present, and Their Future.   With an Introduction by Richard
        T. Ely.   Boston: Roberts Brothers, 1893.   Reprint.   New
        York: Arno Press, 1976.
        This pioneer study by a leading home economist was ex-
        panded from the 1891 award-winning monograph done for
        the American Economic Association.   It traces the manner
        in which barriers to women's entry into the industrial
        labor force were removed, the impact of their entry on
        the male-female wage differential and the nature of women's
        initial industrial experiences.   Richard T. Ely, in his
        introduction, points out that this distinctive study provides
        the positive information upon which wise legislative action
        must depend.

399.   Carsel, Wilfred.   A History of the Chicago Ladies' Garment
        Workers Union.   Chicago: Normandie House, 1940.

400.   [Chicago Trade and Labor Assembly].   The New Slavery:
        Investigation into the Sweating System.   Chicago: Detwiler
        Printers, 1891.
        In 1891, Elizabeth Morgan and two other members of the
        Trade and Labor Assembly formed a committee to begin
        a systematic campaign to alert the public to the injustices
        levied against the city's working women and children.   In
        her report, Morgan detailed the conditions in twenty-six
        clothing establishments and argued for the abolition of the
        sweating system by drawing a parallel between the horrors
        of chattel slavery and the suffering endured in the "new
        slavery" of the garment industry.

401.   "Company Housing in the Cotton Textile Industry in Massa-
        chusetts."   Monthly Labor Review, 19 (August 1924):   437-38.
        Results of a questionnaire on workers' housing sent to all
        Massachusetts textile companies in 1924.   Lists percentage
        of companies that owned workers' housing and the percentage
        of employees that lived in company housing.   Describes
        types of houses, rents, and various facilities provided.

402.   Cook, Blanche Wiesen.   "Female Support Networks and Po-
        litical Activism: Lillian Wald, Crystal Eastman, Emma Gold-
        man."   Chrysalis, (1977):   44-61.
        Examines the female networks that allowed politically active
        women to conduct their work.   Each section begins with a
        statement outlining the political beliefs of the individual and
        then turns to a detailed description of the nature of close
        friendships and emotional attachments.

403.   Cordasco, Francesco.   "Review Essay: Louise C. Odencrantz:
        Italian Women in Industry: A Study of Conditions in New York
        City (1919/1979)."   Italian Americana, 6 (1980):   235-242.

404.   Dancis, Bruce. "Socialism and Women in the United States,
        1900-1917." Socialist Revolution, 6 (January-March 1976):
        81-144.
            Offers an analysis of the women's sector of the Socialist
            Party of America. Discusses the Socialist position on
            several political issues: marriage, free love, the home,
            sexual relations, woman suffrage, the nature of womanhood,
            and the interrelation of socialism and feminism. An ex-
            amination of Socialists' participation in the major contempo-
            rary campaigns for women's equality.

405.   D'Andrea, Vaneeta. "The Ethnic Factor and Role Choice of
        Women: Ella Grasso and Midge Costanza, Two Firsts for
        American Politics," In Remigio U. Pane, ed., Italian Ameri-
        cans in the Professions (New York: Italian American His-
        torical Association, 1983), pp. 253-264.

406.   Davis, Allen F. "The Women's Trade Union League: Origins
        and Organization." Labor History, 5 (1964): 3-17.
            Examines the organization and activities of the Women's
            Trade Union League and concludes that it was "a prime
            example of the cooperation that existed between reformers
            and labor leaders, and also of the support given organized
            labor by at least a portion of those who crusaded for so-
            cial justice in the progressive era."

407.   Delzell, Ruth. The Early History of Women Trade Unionists
        of America. Chicago: National Women's Trade Union League
        of America, 1919.

408.   Dickinson, Joan Y. The Role of the Immigrant Women in the
        United States Labor Force 1890-1910. New York: Arno
        Press, 1980.
            In the decades between 1890 and 1910 immigrant women
            from Europe and Canada comprised one-fourth of the white
            female labor force of the United States. Primarily con-
            cerned with occupational roles, Dickinson brings forward
            and interprets neglected data. Immigrant women were
            found chiefly in three kinds of "women's work" in these
            decades: domestic service, textile work, and in the needle
            trades. Clustering by ethnic (or nativity) groups within
            these work areas was very marked. Documents distinctions
            between the work roles of English, Irish, German, and
            Scandinavian immigrant women (the "old" immigration), and
            those of Italian, Russian, Polish, and Slavic immigrant
            women (the "new" immigration); most of the former were
            engaged as domestic workers: the latter were in manu-
            facturing. A major conclusion is drawn from this study:
            "The menial role of the immigrant women workers between
            1890 and 1910 served to advance the women of other nativity
            classes both in the labor force itself, and outside, for it
            is probable that without the presence of the immigrant wom-
            en workers in the kitchens, nurseries, textile mills, and

clothing factories, the turn-of-the-century leisure class of
women volunteers in church, community, and suffrage
work might not have been possible." Originally, Ph.D.
dissertation, University of Pennsylvania, 1975.

409. Doubilet, Ann. "The Illinois Woman's Alliance, 1888-1894."
Unpublished M.A. thesis, Northern Illinois University, 1973.

410. Dublin, Thomas. "Women, Work and Protest in the Lowell
Mills: 'The Oppressing Hand of Avarice Would Enslave Us.' "
Labor History, 16 (Winter 1975): 99-116.

411. Dubofsky, Melvin. "Organized Labor and the Immigrant in
New York City, 1900-1918." Labor History, 2 (1961): 182-
201.
Traces the efforts of Samuel Gompers and the American
Federation of Labor to limit the power and effectiveness
of the Socialist-oriented immigrant unions, primarily in
New York's needle trade unions. Generally, the unions
succeeded despite Gompers' opposition.

412. Dye, Nancy Schrom. "Creating a Feminist Alliance: Sisterhood and Class Conflict in the New York Trade Union League."
Feminist Studies, 2 (1975): 72-86.

413. Dye, Nancy Schrom. As Equals and as Sisters: Feminism,
Unionism, and the Women's Trade Union League of New York.
Columbia: University of Missouri Press, 1980.
The Women's Trade Union League, formed in 1903, attracted
radical women to its ranks, especially during the first
decade of activity. A cross-class alliance of trade unionists and middle-class "allies," the League also tested the
individual's loyalty to the women's movement or labor
movement. Covers the history of New York League until
the 1920's.

414. Dye, Nancy Schrom. "Feminism or Unionism? The New
York Women's Trade Union League and the Labor Movement."
Feminist Studies, 3 (1975): 106-121.

415. Dye, Nancy Schrom. "The Women's Trade Union League of
New York, 1903-1920." Unpublished Ph.D. dissertation, University of Wisconsin, 1974.
Traces the evolution of the League from a small organization of workers dedicated to unionizing the city's women
workers during the Progressive era to an efficient welfare
organization lobbying for protective legislation in the 1920's.
Evaluates the League's efforts at creating a coalition across
class and ethnic lines.

416. Eckert, William Albert. "Ethnicity, Reformism, and Public
Policy in American Cities." Unpublished Ph.D. dissertation,
Florida State University, 1976.

Finds great variations among ethnic groups with regard to
both preference of urban political forms and attitudes toward particular public policy areas. Examines the various
factors that account for these differences, with some notices
of the role of immigrant women.

417.   Feder, Leah Hannah.   Unemployment Relief in Periods of
Depression: A Study of Measures Adopted in Certain American Cities, 1857 Through 1922. [1936]. New York: Arno
Press, 1971.
An important historical account of the ways in which American communities in the nineteenth and twentieth centuries
reacted to the problems of cyclical unemployment. Feder
describes the increasing complexity of local relief measures,
and the spread of the idea that unemployment was an economic and not a moral problem.

418.   Feeley, Dianne. "Antoinette Konikow: Marxist and Feminist."
International Socialist Review, 33 (January 1972): 42-46.
Antoinette Buchold Konikow (1869-1949), Russian-born revo-
lutionary, spent her life in the Socialist movement. After
emigrating to the United States in 1893, she helped organize
the Boston Jewish Workmen's Circle and joined the Socialist
Labor party and later, the Socialist Party of America. She
participated in the founding of both the Communist party in
1919 and the Socialist Workers party in 1938. Konikow
was firmly committed to women's rights, particularly their
right to control their bodies. She was an early pioneer
of the birth-control movement. A physician and lecturer,
she continued to advocate reforms in medical law through
the 1930's and 1940's.

419.   Fenton, Edwin.   Immigrants and Unions: A Case Study
Italians and American Labor, 1870-1920. New York: Arno
Press, 1975.
A comprehensive examination of the evolving experience of
Italian and other immigrants and their relation to the development of American trade unionism in the critical half
century from 1870 to 1920. Although Fenton's greatest
concern is with the southern Italian peasant immigrants
who became factory workers and construction laborers in
an expanding urban and industrial America, he also deals
with a great number of Italian anarchist, socialist, and
syndicalist artisans who had emigrated from northern Italy
and who became leaders of the peasants in the large American cities. The author also considers the unstable organization of many A. F. of L. unions, policies of socialist
groups, and divisions within the ranks of the Italian-American radicals. Particularly graphic are Fenton's descriptions of the spectacular strikes taking place between 1910
and 1913. These were led by the IWW in industries in
which Italian workers predominated, such as the great textile mill strike of 1912 in Lawrence, Massachusetts, in

which immigrant women workers played a decisive role.
Originally a Ph.D. dissertation, Harvard University, 1957.

420.   Foner, Philip S., ed.   The Factory Girls: A Collection of
Writings on Life and Struggles in the New England Factories
of the 1840's by the Factory Girls Themselves, and the Story,
in Their Own Words, of Women Workers in the United States.
Urbana: University of Illinois Press, 1977.
         Gathers writings by the exploited women who spearheaded
         formation of women's industrial unions.   Includes essays,
         tracts, poems, and songs.

421.   Foner, Philip S.   Women and the American Labor Movement
from Colonial Times to the Eve of World War I.   New York:
The Free Press, 1979.
         On the role of Socialist women in the labor movement.   In-
         cludes a section on the Illinois Woman's Alliance and its
         sister organization, the New York Working Women's So-
         ciety.   A chapter on the Socialist party focuses on its
         position on woman suffrage and concludes with a brief
         biography of Mother Jones.   Chapters on organization in
         the garment trade and the textile industry, 1909-1916, con-
         tain information on women activists and concise narratives
         of the major strikes of the era.

422.   Foner, Philip S.   Women and the American Labor Movement
from World War I to the Present.   New York: The Free
Press, 1980.
         Emphasizes the role Communist women played in labor
         organizations since World War I.   Takes a hard line against
         Socialists, in discussing the warfare in the garment unions
         during the 1920's, and underscores the contribution of Com-
         munists, especially to the formation of the CIO.   A later
         section reviews the Communist party's position on the pro-
         posed Equal Rights Amendment.

423.   Furio, Columba M.   "The Cultural Background of the Italian-
Immigrant Woman and Its Impact on Her Unionization in the
New York City Garment Industry, 1880-1919," in George E.
Pozzetta, ed., Pane e Lavoro: The Italian American Work-
ing Class (Toronto: The Multicultural History Society of
Ontario, 1980):   81-98.
         A sensitive, detailed portrait of the Italian immigrant wom-
         an's role in an expanding industrial America.   If women
         are to be viewed as part of the historical process and not
         simply as bystanders, the roles they played and the tensions
         that emerged in their roles as immigrants, workers, wives,
         and mothers must be examined.   These tensions, and their
         eventual resolution, are the key factors in the preservation
         or destruction of the prevailing social norms existing with-
         in a particular cultural group.   While these factors affect
         all women, they are especially important to Italian immi-
         grant women because of the intensity of the Itlaian family

structure and the strictly defined role that women played,
and often still play, within that structure. It therefore
becomes clear that any analysis of Italian women's behavior
patterns would be incomplete without an understanding of
the family. This is the first point to be analyzed in this
paper.

424.   Furio, Columba M.   "Immigrant Women and Industry: A
       Case Study. The Italian Immigrant Women and the Garment
       Industry, 1880-1950."   Unpublished Ph.D. dissertation, New
       York University, 1979.
       Examines four questions in American immigration and
       labor history: first, what was the impact of immigration
       on Italian women? second, what were the factors which
       determined whether or not Italian women joined and re-
       mained members of the garment unions at various time
       periods? third, how did the union affect Italian immigrant
       women? and fourth, what contributions did these women
       make to the American labor movement? Immigration was
       the answer to the economic necessities of the Italian peasants.
       While immigrant women experienced social and economic
       problems in their efforts to adapt to their new environ-
       ment, the longest, and often most wrenching adjustments
       had to be made in cultural transplantation and amalgmation;
       therein the crisis of immigration was truly evident. In
       southern Italian society, sociocultural forces and the person-
       alities of the individual members in that society, interacted
       with each other. Each made demands of the individual.
       The behavior of the Italian women was, in many ways, an
       expression of the sanctions which operated within that
       culture. Pre-industrial or peasant values persisted when
       the family unit emigrated to an industrial society. One of
       these values was familialism. Values of the dominant
       American culture entered into the social consciousness of
       these women, though at a slower rate than for the men.
       Factors which determined whether or not Italian women
       joined and remained union members varied according to
       time periods. Shows that unions were a tripartite force
       in the assimilation of Italian women to American society.
       Evidence has also shown that Italian women engaged in
       labor struggles through most of the twentieth century.
       "Italian-ness" and "rebel-ness" were not necessarily di-
       chotomous qualities, but often appeared side by side in
       women unionists.

425.   Ganz, Marie. Rebels: Into Anarchy and Out Again. New
       York: Dodd, Mead, 1920.
       Portrait vignettes of radical women reformers.

426.   Goldmark, Josephine C. "The Necessary Sequel of Child
       Labor Laws." The American Journal of Sociology, 11 (1905):
       312-325.

427. Griffen, Clyde. Natives and Newcomers: The Ordering of
      Opportunity in Mid-Nineteenth Century Poughkeepsie.   Cam-
      bridge, Mass.: Harvard University Press, 1978.
          Examines the relative occupational mobility of the native-
      born, blacks, immigrants, and women, and finds that
      Poughkeepsie generally conformed to current interpretation.
      Finds that changes in the scale of economic organization
      and in the division of labor significantly affected mobility
      patterns.

428. Groneman, Carole. " 'She Earns as a Child--She Pays as
      a Man': Women Workers in a Mid-Nineteenth Century New
      York Community," in Richard L. Ehrlich, ed., Immigrants
      in Industrial America 1850-1920 (Charlottesville: University
      Press of Virginia, 1977), pp. 33-46.

429. Groneman, Carole. "Working Class Immigrant Women in
      Mid-Nineteenth Century New York: The Irish Women's Ex-
      perience." Journal of Urban History, 4 (1978): 255-74.
          Examines the work, leisure patterns, and family life that
      constituted the cultural community of young, single, female,
      Irish immigrants of the era.

430. Haraven, Tamara. "Family Time and Industrial Time: Family
      and Work in a Planned Corporation Town, 1900-1924." Journal
      of Urban History, 1 (1975): 365-89.
          Contends that French-Canadian working-class families in
      Manchester, New Hampshire, were not passive recipients
      of social and economic change, but rather made the town's
      factories adjust their work schedules to accommodate family
      behavior. Considers the families as the major buffer be-
      tween the members and the dehumanizing effects of indus-
      trialization.   .

431. Haraven, Tamara. "The Laborers of Manchester, New Hamp-
      shire, 1912-1922: The Role of Family and Ethnicity in Ad-
      justment of Industrial Life." Labor History, 16 (1975): 249-
      65.
          Claims that Manchester's new immigrant laborers were
      not the passive victims of urbanization and modernization,
      but rather active agents who tried to shape the system to
      their own needs and who exercised great collective strength.

432. Henry, Alice. The Trade Union Woman. New York: D.
      Appleton, 1915.
          Describes the trade union movement for women, the woman
      organizer, immigrant women, vocational training for wom-
      en, and the working woman and marriage.

433. Henry, Alice. Women and the Labor Movement. New York:
      George H. Doran, 1923. Reprint. New York: Arno Press,
      1971.
          For many years, the author was editor of the publication

of the Women's Trade Union League which was founded,
with President Gompers' blessing, at the 1903 convention
of the A. F. of L.   For a quarter of a century the WTUL
championed the working women on the job and in the union.
In this volume, the author inventoried the strength and
position of women workers in the early twenties.   She
surveyed the variety of union policies for the female worker,
her position in the ranks of union leadership, and pointed
out the indications of discrimination.   Fascinating chapters
trace the work of women in primitive, colonial and machine
age times.   Other chapters focus on protective legislation
for women and the minimum wage.

434.   Herron, Belva M.   The Place of Labor Organization Among
Women,   Together with Some Considerations Concerning Their
Place in Industry.   Urbana: University of Illinois Press,
[1906].

435.   Hill, Joseph A.   Women in Gainful Occupations, 1870-1920.
Washington: Government Printing Office, 1929.

436.   Holmes, Lizzie Swank.   "Women Workers of Chicago."
American Federationist, 12 (1905):   506-10.

437.   Hughes, Gwendolyn.   Mothers in Industry: Wage Earning by
Mothers in Philadelphia.   New York: New Republic, 1925.

438.   Hundley, Norris C., Jr.   "Katherine Philips Edson and the
Fight for the Minimum Wage, 1912-1923."   Pacific Historical
Review, 29 (1960):   271-85.
       Describes the role of Katherine Edson as a special agent
       for the Bureau of Labor Statistics for southern California
       and her lobbying efforts on behalf of minimum wages for
       women and children, which led to the creation in 1913 of
       the state's first industrial Welfare Commission.

439.   Hutchinson, Emilie J.   Women's Wages: A Study of the Wages
of Industrial Women and Measures Suggested to Increase Them.
New York: Columbia University Press, 1919.   Reprint.   New
York: AMS Press, 1968.
       Studies various factors, including trade unionism and legis-
       lation affecting women's wages during World War I.

440.   Jacoby, Robin Miller.   "The Women's Trade Union League
and American Feminism."   Feminist Studies, 3 (1975):   126-
40.
       Defines the league as a coalition of female trade unionists,
       settlement house residents, and social reformers who con-
       stituted the women's branch of the labor movement and the
       industrial branch of the women's movement.   Concludes
       that the league did much more for the cause of women
       than the latter did for female workers.

441. Josephson, Hannah. The Golden Threads: New England's
      Mill Girls and Magnates. New York: Sloan & Pearce, 1949.
      Describes "showplace" cotton mills of Lowell, Massachu-
      setts. Companies provided room and board for girls
      (mostly Irish immigrants) who came to work in the mills.
      One company built a school, library, and church. Facto-
      ries were pleasant and well-ventilated. Conditions declined
      in the 1840's due to falling profits which led to speed-ups
      and cuts in benefits.

442. Julianelli, Jane. "Bessie Hillman: Up from the Sweatshop!"
      Ms., 1 (May 1973): 16-20.
      Bessie Abramowitz Hillman (1895-1970) played a leading
      role in the Chicago garment strike of 1910. Together with
      her husband, Sidney Hillman, she became a founder of the
      Amalgamated Clothing Workers of America and later, a
      prominent union organizer.

443. Karni, Michael G., and Douglas J. Ollila, Jr., eds. For
      the Common Good: Finnish Immigrants and the Radical Re-
      sponse to Industrial America. Superior, Wis.: Tyomies So-
      ciety, 1977.
      Includes eight original essays by American and Finnish
      scholars dealing with different aspects of the Finnish radi-
      cal labor movement, including its newspapers, attitudes
      towards women's rights, educational agencies, and attitudes
      toward the Finnish Civil War. Most essays deal entirely
      or partially with the Progressive era, with considerable
      attention to immigrant women and the Finnish family.

444. Karvonen, Hilja J. "Three Proponents of Women's Rights in
      the Finnish-American Labor Movement from 1910-1930: Selma
      Jokela McCone, Maiju Nurmi and Helmi Mattson." In For
      the Common Good: Finnish Immigrants and the Radical Re-
      sponse to Industrial America. Superior, Wis.: Tyomies So-
      ciety, [1977], pp. 195-216.
      Karvonen traces the development of the Toveritar, a Social-
      ist newspaper founded in 1909, edited by women and devoted
      primarily to women's issues. Its early editors, particularly
      Selma Jokela McCone, managed to keep the newspaper alive
      and to make it responsive to its female readers. With
      McCone's management, the Toveritar achieved a circulation
      of 5,000 in 1915 and became a women's newspaper, with
      household tips, advice columns, a children's department,
      and the usual literary and political articles. Toveritar's
      subsequent editors, Maiju Nurmi and Helmi Mattson, brought
      the newspaper through wartime censorship of radical period-
      icals into the 1920's. Karvonen provides important bio-
      graphical information.

445. Kelley, Florence. Our Toiling Children. Chicago: Woman's
      Temperance Publishing Association, 1889.
      Kelley (1859-1932) helped establish the United States Chil-

dren's Bureau. See also Kelley's "Child Labor," Frank
Leslie's Illustrated Weekly (February 1890); and "The
Sweating System," in Hull House Maps and Papers (1895).
Particulary important is her Modern Industry in Relation
to the Family, Health, Education, Morality (1914); and a
series of autobiographical sketches in The Survey: "My
Philadelphia," October 1, 1926; "When Co-education Was
Young," February 1, 1927; "My Novitiate," April 1, 1927;
and "I Go to Work," June 1, 1927.

446.   Kellogg, Paul U., et al.   The Pittsburgh Survey.   6 vols.
        New York: Russell Sage Foundation, 1909-1914.
        Includes studies on Women and the Trades by Elizabeth
        B. Butler; Work Accidents and the Law by Crystal East-
        man; The Steel Workers by J. A. Fitch; Homestead's House-
        holds by Margaret F. Byington; The Pittsburgh District
        Civic Frontage by Kellogg; and Wage-Earning Pittsburgh by
        Kellogg.   Contains a great deal of social and economic in-
        formation about the city, its ethnic working class, and
        working immigrant women.

447.   Kenneally, James M. "Woman and Trade Unions, 1870-1920:
        The Quandary of the Reformer." Labor History, 14 (1973):
        42-55.
        Claims that trade-union response to working women was
        severely handicapped by labor's mutually exclusive con-
        victions that women must be organized if they worked, al-
        though they really belonged at home.

448.   Kessler-Harris, Alice. "Organizing the Unorganizable: Three
        Jewish Women and Their Union." Labor History, 17 (Winter
        1976): 5-23.

449.   Kessler-Harris, Alice. "Where Are the Organized Women
        Workers." Feminist Studies 3 (1975): 95-104.

450.   Kessner, Thomas, and Betty Boyd Caroli. "New Immigrant
        Women at Work: Italians and Jews in New York City, 1880-
        1905." Journal of Ethnic Studies, 5 (1978): 19-32.
        Explores the ways that Italian and Jewish immigrant women
        reacted to an urban environment characterized by rapid
        change and new economic opportunities.   The different
        cultural and historical perspective of New York's Russian
        Jewish and Italian women led these two groups to divide
        paths in their occupational priorities and objectives.

451.   Kingsbury, Susan M., ed. Labor Laws and Their Enforce-
        ment with Special Reference to Massachusetts. [By] Charles
        E. Persons, Mabel Parton, Mabelle Moses and Three "Fellows".
        New York: Longmans, Green, 1911.
        Under the editorship of Kingsbury, seven experts discuss
        the history of legislation from 1825 to 1910 focusing upon
        the protection of working women and children.

452.   Klaczynska, Barbara.   "Why Women Work: A Comparison of
       Various Groups in Philadelphia, 1910-1930."   Labor History,
       17 (Winter 1976):   73-87.

453.   Kleinberg, Susan.   "Technology's Stepdaughters: The Impact
       of Industrialization upon Working-Class Women, Pittsburgh,
       1865-1890."   Unpublished Ph.D. dissertation, University of
       Pittsburgh, 1973.

454.   Kleinberg, Susan J.   "Technology and Women's Work: The
       Lives of Working Class Women in Pittsburgh, 1870-1900."
       Labor History, 17 (Winter 1976):   58-72.

455.   Knight, Charles, ed.   The Lowell Offering.   Mind Amongst
       the Spindles: A Selection from the Lowell Offering, A Mis-
       cellany Wholly Compiled by the Factory Girls of an American
       City.   London: C. Knight, 1844.

456.   Lahne, Herbert J.   The Cotton Mill Worker.   New York:
       Farrar and Rinehart, 1944.
           Describes the "all-embracing paternal system" in cotton
       mill villages which affected the lives of immigrant women
       and children.   Evaluates and compares New England and
       southern villages.   Describes a broad range of conditions
       from model villages to ramshackle slums.   Discusses the
       scrip payment system which tied employees to the mill by
       encouraging them to build a debt at the company store.
       Companies often required employees to live in mill housing
       as a condition of employment.   During strikes, workers
       were evicted and their credit at the store was cut.   Compa-
       nies supported churches and schools and thus controlled
       what was taught and preached.

457.   Lan, Dean.   "Chinatown Sweatshops," in Emma Gee, ed.,
       Counterpoint: Perspectives on Asian America.   Los Angeles:
       University of California (1976), pp. 347-358.

458.   Lauck, W. Jett.   "The Cotton-Mill Operatives of New England."
       Atlantic Monthly, 109 (1912):   706-713.

459.   Leiserson, William M.   Adjusting Immigrant and Industry.
       New York: Harper & Brothers, 1924.   Reprint.   Arno Press,
       1971.
           A comprehensive study of how industry can be used to help
       the immigrant assimilate into the American way of life.
       Using the common denominator of work and pay to cut
       across the ethnic, racial and national differences that set
       workers apart, shows how union and factory experiences
       function to give the newcomer his first taste of a free so-
       ciety.   It emphasizes the importance in industry and so-
       ciety of such matters as placement services, the relations
       between the employer and the immigrant, the working con-
       ditions, his management and his training, his relations with

labor organizations, and the government's responsibility.
Fully documented with statistical tables and actual case
histories.

460. Lerner, Gerda. "The Lady and the Mill Girl: Changes in
the Status of Women in the Age of Jackson." Midcontinent.
American Studies Journal, 10 (1969): 5-15.

461. Levine, Louis [Louis Lorin, pseud.]. The Women's Garment
Workers: A History of The International Ladies Garment
Workers' Union. New York: Huebsch, 1924. Reprint. New
York: Arno Press, 1971.
Drawing largely from union source materials and based on
actual interviews with the men and women who engaged in
the battle against the sweatshop, offers a complete history
of an industry of women and immigrants. At the turn of
the century the women's garment industry seemed the least
likely to develop a permanent union in its midst. Yet within the first decade garment workers engaged in two historic
strikes--the shirtwaist makers' walkout in 1909 and the
cloakmakers' revolt in 1910--that established the ILGWU
as a continuing union. Particular emphasis is placed on
the 1910 strike which helped to forge the first industry
agreement--the Protocol of Peace--whose provisions still
provide precedents in industrial relations.

462. McCreesh, Carolyn Daniel. "On the Picket Lines: Militant
Women Campaign to Organize Garment Workers, 1880-1917."
Unpublished Ph. D. dissertation, University of Maryland, 1975.
Focuses on the interaction between middle-class reformers
and immigrant wage earners in such organizations as the
Woman's Trade Union League. Analyzes the differences
in goals and perspectives which limited interactions but
did not prevent effective cooperation on many fronts.

463. McFarland, C. K. "Crusade for Child Laborers: 'Mother'
Jones and the March of the Mill Children." Pennsylvania
History, 38 (July 1971): 283-96.
In 1903 Mother Jones left the coal fields to take part in
the textile strike in the Kensington section of Philadelphia.
She discovered among the strikers over 10,000 children,
many under ten years of age. Describes the historic march
of 150 adults and 50 factory children from Philadelphia to
New York City, a march to call attention to the evils of
child labor.

464. McGill, Nettie P. The Welfare of Children in Bituminous
Coal Mining Communities in West Virginia. U.S. Department
of Labor, Bureau of Labor Statistics, Bulletin 117. Washington: Government Printing Office, 1923.
A survey of employer welfare programs affecting children
in 11 West Virginia mining villages. Based on visits to
every home with children under age 18, survey examined

such welfare benefits as company housing, schools, health
and medical care, recreation, and safety conditions for
children who worked in the mines.

465.   Manning, Caroline.   The Immigrant Woman and Her Job.
       Washington: Government Printing Office, 1930.   Reprint.
       Arno Press, 1970.
       The study was made in order to ascertain how and to what
       extent immigrant women are fitting into American industrial
       life, how necessary such employment was for the women,
       and what it meant to them and to their families, and how
       much of their time and strength were given to American
       industries.

466.   Marsh, Margaret S.   "The Anarchist-Feminist Response to
       the 'Woman Question' in Late Nineteenth-Century America."
       American Quarterly, 30 (Fall 1978):   533-47.
       Compares anarchist feminists with participants in the main-
       stream women's movement.   Contends that most American
       feminists emphasized differences between the sexes and
       asked for women's rights on a basis of feminine moral
       superiority.   Anarchists espoused an "equality based on a
       shared humanity" and chose the more radical course.
       Claims that anarchist feminism developed logically from
       anarchism's advocacy of the absolute liberty of the individual.
       Anarchist feminists criticized women's subordination in the
       family, aimed to reorder the household, advocated "free
       unions" in place of conventional marriage, and insisted on
       women's financial independence.

467.   Marsh, Margaret S.   Anarchist Women 1870-1920.   Phila-
       delphia: Temple University Press, 1981.
       Offers sociobiographical sketches of individual women.   In-
       cludes an appendix which compares ten anarchist women
       with a comparable sample of Socialist, mainstream suf-
       fragist, and labor activist women, on places of birth, ethnic
       backgrounds of parents, educational attainments, social
       class, occupations, and attitudes toward marriage and
       violence.

468.   Matthews, Lillian Ruth.   Women in Trade Unions in San
       Francisco.   Berkeley: University of California Press, 1943.

469.   Maupin, Joyce.   Labor Heroines: Ten Women Who Led the
       Struggle.   Berkeley, Calif.: Union W.A.G.E. Educational
       Committee, 1974.
       Biographical sketches of Leonora Barry, Elizabeth Gurley
       Flynn, Dolores Huerta, Clara Lemlich, Rose Schneiderman,
       and other immigrant and ethnic labor activists.

470.   Meltzer, Milton.   Bread and Roses: The Struggle of Ameri-
       can Labor, 1865-1915.   New York: Alfred A. Knopf, 1967.
       Illustrated with contemporary prints and photographs.

Immigrant women and children in the factories, with harrowing descriptions of working conditions.

471.   Miller, Sally. The Radical Immigrant. New York: Twayne Publishers, 1974.

472.   Miller, Sally M. "From Sweatshop Worker to Labor Leader: Theresa Malkiel, a Case Study." American Jewish History, 68 (December 1978): 189-205.
        Theresa Serber Malkiel (1874-1949) was an organizer in the Jewish labor movement in the 1890's and a prominent activist and propagandist in the New York Socialist party after the turn of the century. Born in Bar, Russia, Malkiel immigrated to the United States in 1891 and soon after entered the infant cloakmakers' industry.

473.   Mindiola, T. "The Cost of Being a Mexican Female Worker in the 1970 Houston Labor Market." Aztlan, 11 (Fall 1980): 231-247.
        Focuses on Mexican female worker discrimination in comparison to Anglo and black females and to Mexican and black males. Estimates the cost of being a Mexican female worker and discusses the occupations and industries in which Mexican females encountered the most discrimination.

474.   Montgomery, David. "The Working Classes of the Pre-Industrial American City, 1780-1830." Labor History, 9 (1968): 3-22.

475.   National Civic Federation. Woman's Department. Committee on Welfare Work for Industrial Employees. Examples of Welfare Work in the Cotton Industry. New York, 1910.
        Traces the development of welfare work in the textile industry. Describes a wide range of benefits, using examples from several companies. Benefits include schools, housing, recreational and athletic facilities, and medical care. Costs to companies are estimated.

476.   New York State Legislature. Report and Testimony Taken Before the Special Committee of the Assembly Appointed to Investigate the Condition of Female Labor in the City of New York. Transmitted to the Legislature, January 16, 1896. Albany, N.Y.: Wynkoop, Hallenbeck, Crawford Co., 1896.

477.   North, Simon Newton D. Statistics of Women at Work. Washington: Government Printing Office, 1907.

478.   Odencrantz, Louise C. Italian Women in Industry: A Study of Conditions in New York City. New York: Russell Sage Foundation, 1919. Reprint. Arno Press, 1979.
        Odencrantz's aim in Italian Women in Industry is "to give insight into the means of livelihood of a group of these

women, to show their incomes, their home life, the standards they are able to maintain, the effect of American
industrial and living conditions upon their native standards,
and conversely, the effect of their Italian standards of
life and work on the industries they engage in." The period
of the study is 1911-1913, and the area studied was "the
lower end of Manhattan, below Fourteenth Street, which
includes several Italian neighborhoods." Included in the
study were 1,095 Italian women wage earners, and information was gathered during visits to the homes of the workers
and their places of work.

479. O'Neill, William L., ed. Women at Work. Chicago: Quad-
      rangle Books, 1972.

480. Oppenheimer, Valerie Kincade. "Demographic Influence on
      Female Employment and the Status of Women." American
      Journal of Sociology, 58 (January 1973): 946-951.

481. Oppenheimer, Valerie Kincade. The Female Labor Force in
      the United States: Demographic and Economic Factors Govern-
      ing Its Growth and Changing Composition. Berkeley: Institute
      of International Studies, University of California, 1970.

482. O'Sullivan, Judith, and Rosemary Gallick. Workers and Allies:
      Female Participation in the American Trade Union Movement,
      1824-1976. Washington: Smithsonian Institution Press, 1975.

483. Parsons, Elsie C. "Women's Work and Wages in the United
      States." Quarterly Journal of Economics, 29 (1915): 201-34.

484. Pekin, H. "Migrant Women in Host Countries: The Situation
      of Migrant Women Workers." International Migration, 19
      (1981): 75-82.

485. Penny, Virginia. Employments of Women: Cyclopedia of
      Women's Work. Boston: Weller, Wise, 1863.
          Pioneer work. Lists 533 occupations for women as well
      as wages paid to men and women for same work, qualifi-
      cations, effects on health, occupations in the South and in
      Europe. Includes professional, industrial, and domestic
      categories as well as those in which no women were then
      employed.

486. Penny, Virginia. Think and Act: A Series of Articles Per-
      taining to Men and Women, Work and Wages. Philadelphia:
      Claxton, Remsen & Haffelfinger, 1869.
          A collection of Penny's shorter pieces in which she argues
      that woman's work role must be more than that of a do-
      mestic, schoolmarm, or mill hand.

487. Perry, Lorinda. The Millinery Trade in Boston and Phila-
      delphia: A Study of Women in Industry. Binghamton, N.Y.:
      Vail-Ballou, 1916.

488.   Phizacklea, Annie, ed. One Way Ticket: Migration and Fe-
        male Labour. Boston: Routledge & Kegan Paul, 1983.

489.   Plotkin, Sara. Full-Time Active: Sara Plotkin, An Oral
        History. Edited by Arthur Tobler. New York: Community
        Documentation Workshop, 1980.
            Born just before the turn of the century in White Russia,
            Plotkin remembers her youth in the shtetl--the poverty,
            the grind of daily life, the oppressive religious atmosphere--
            and her awakening socialist consciousness. After immi-
            grating to the United States in 1922, Plotkin became an
            organizer for the Communist party. During the Depression
            she helped unionize cafeteria workers in New York City
            and steel workers and coal miners in Pittsburgh and in
            Wheeling, West Virginia. She also rallied the unemployed
            and helped people obtain welfare.

490.   Poole, Ernest. The Streets. Its Child Workers. New York:
        University Settlement Society, [1903].

491.   Poole, Ernest. "Waifs of the Street." McClure's Magazine,
        21 (1903): 43-44.

492.   Price, George M. "Cloak, Suit, Skirt, Dress, and Waist
        Industries." The Modern Hospital, 7 (1916): 111-114.
            Summarizes work of the New York Joint Board of Sanita-
            tion Control, which policed sanitary, health, and safety
            standards in the garment industry (in which garment workers were
            overwhelmingly women immigrants). The Board provided
            physical examinations to workers and promoted industrial
            health programs, especially for the care of tuberculosis.
            It also educated workers on safety and health regulations
            and practices.

493.   Reisler, Mark. By the Sweat of Their Brow: Immigrant
        Labor in the United States, 1900-1940. Westport, Conn.:
        Greenwood Press, 1978.

494.   Richardson, Dorothy. "The Difficulties and Dangers Con-
        fronting the Working Woman." The Annals, 27 (1906): 624-
        26.

495.   Richardson, Dorothy. The Long Day. The Story of a New
        York Working Girl as Told by Herself. New York: The
        Century Company, 1906.

496.   Richardson, Dorothy. "Trades-Unions in Petticoats." Les-
        lie's Monthly Magazine, 57 (March 1904): 489-496.

497.   Ritter, Ellen M. "Elizabeth Morgan: Pioneer Female Labor
        Agitator." Central States Speech Journal, 22 (Winter 1971):
        242-51.
            Born in England, Elizabeth Morgan was a major figure in

the Chicago labor movement in the 1880's and 1890's. She
brought together trade unionists, Socialists, and women reformers in a campaign to improve the working conditions
of women (largely immigrant) and children.

498. Robinson, Harriet Jane. Loom and Spindle. New York:
     Boston, T. Y. Crowell and Company, 1898.
     Describes life among the mill girls of Lowell, Massa-
     chusetts. The companies kept watch over the girls' morals
     by requiring them to attend church, by supervising their
     living habits with boarding house mothers, and by requiring
     them to sign an oath of morality. The companies provided
     lodgings, food, and pleasant (?) working conditions. The
     Lowell Offering, a literary magazine, contained stories
     and articles written by the mill girls.

499. Scarpaci, Jean A. "Angela Bambace and the International
     Ladies Garment Workers Union: The Search for an Elusive
     Activist," in George E. Pozzetta, ed., Pane e Lavoro: The
     Italian American Working Class (Toronto: The Multicultural
     History Society of Ontario, 1980): 99-118.
     An overview of the career of Angela Bambace (1898-1975),
     labor activist, union officer, and community leader. Born
     of Italian immigrant parents in Brazil, Bambace and her
     family finally settled in East Harlem, New York City.
     Findings: "This account of her life relies heavily then on
     oral testimony, on conversations with Angela Bambace, her
     friends, and her relatives. Such sources obviously include
     only those who have survived, and so important opinions
     like those of her husband, Romolo Camponeschi, will never
     be recorded. Her friend and companion, the Italian Ameri-
     can anarchist, Luigi Quintilliano, her associates from the
     Italian anti-fascist and labor movement, Carlo Tresca,
     Luigi Antonini, and Frank Bellanca, knew her well but
     left almost no account of their shared struggle."

500. Scharnau, Ralph. "Elizabeth Morgan, Crusader for Labor
     Reform." Labor History, 14 (1973): 340-51.
     Portrays Morgan as the person who, more than any other,
     welded the rising discontent among Chicago's women work-
     ers into trade unionism and political action. Regards
     "revisionist socialism" as the wellspring of her motivation.

501. Schneiderman, Rose. All for One, with Lucy Goldthwaite.
     New York: Paul S. Ericksson, Inc., 1967.
     Rose Schneiderman (1882-1972), an immigrant from Russian
     Poland, was a labor activist throughout her adult life. In
     the mid-1890's, she found her first job in a New York de-
     partment store. Oppressed by the long working hours and
     poor pay, she took a better job in a cap factory. Here
     she began a career in trade unionism and gained her first
     contact with radical activists. In 1903, with two co-workers
     Schneiderman organized the first women's local of the Jewish

Socialist United Cloth Hat and Cap Makers' Union. She emerged a local leader, a delegate to the New York Central Labor Union, and a militant agitator during a capmakers' strike in 1905. After 1907 the Women's Trade Union League became her organizational home.

502.   Schuster, Eunice Minetta. "Native American Anarchism." Smith College. Studies in History, 17 (1932): 5-202.

503.   Seifer, Nancy. Absent from the Majority: Working Class Women in America. New York: National Project on Ethnic America, American Jewish Committee, 1973.

504.   Seifer, Nancy. Nobody Speaks for Me: Self-Portraits of American Working Class Women. New York: Simon & Schuster, 1976.

505.   Schulman, Alix Kates. "Emma Goldman--Feminist and Anarchist." Women: A Journal of Liberation, 1 (Spring 1970): 21-24.
        Relates standard biographical information about Goldman and offers a brief assessment of her anarchist beliefs. Focuses on Goldman's perspectives on sexual morality and women's oppression. Concludes that Goldman, in establishing her political distance from the women's rights and suffrage movements, cast herself into the role of philosophical forerunner of women's liberation.

506.   Shulman, Alix Kates. To the Barricades: The Anarchist Life of Emma Goldman. Lexington, Mass.: D. C. Heath, 1970. A sympathetic biography for young people. Contains an important chapter on the Woman Question that places Goldman's contribution within the context of the women's liberation movement of the late 1960's.

507.   Smuts, Robert W. Women and Work in America. New York: Schocken Books, 1971.

508.   Snyder, Robert E. "Women, Wobblies, and Workers' Rights: The 1912 Textile Strike in Little Falls, New York." New York History, 60 (January 1979): 29-57.
        The Little Falls textile strike, led by Socialists and Wobblies, was one in a series of strikes led by recent immigrants from southern and eastern Europe. Lasting for three months, from October 9, 1912, until January 4, 1913, the Little Falls strike involved over 1,300 unskilled workers, of which an estimated 70 percent were women. Although the strikers gained wage increases and forced a major investigation of labor conditions in their city, their IWW local soon collapsed, and many of its most active leaders faced imprisonment for their strike activities.

509.   Spadoni, Adriana. "The Italian Working Woman in New York." Collier's, 49 (March 23, 1912): 14-16.

Case histories of Italian immigrant women, their reluctance
(for complex reasons) to join the mascot union movement
in American labor, and their exploitation by employers.

510.   Steel, Edward.   "Mother Jones in the Fairmont Field, 1901."
Journal of American History, 57 (September 1970):   290-307.
A monographic account of the defeat suffered by the United
Mine Workers of America in the northern West Virginia
coal strikes at the turn of the century.   Focused on the
role of Mother Jones.   Although Jones succeeded in the
southern mining area, she found herself "badly outgeneralled"
by the management of the Fairmont Field, due in part,
Steel concludes, to her adherence to a simple socialistic
economic philosophy.

511.   Stein, Leon, ed.   Out of the Sweatshop: The Struggle for
Industrial Democracy.   New York: Quadrangle, 1977.
Contains over one hundred commentaries on sweatshop
conditions and the efforts of the International Ladies Garment Workers Union and state and federal governments to
correct abuses.   Includes sections on the shirtwaist workers' and cloakmakers' strikes of 1909 and 1910.   Poignant
accounts by immigrant women workers.

512.   Stein, Leon.   The Triangle Fire.   Philadelphia: J. B. Lipp-
incott Co., 1962.
A poignant account of a tragic loft fire (New York City)
on March 25, 1911, which claimed the lives of 148 immigrant women (Italian and Jewish, largely) shirtwaist trade
workers.   A fictionalized treatment is James Oppenheimer's
The Nine-Tenths (1911).

513.   Stigler, George Joseph.   Domestic Servants in the U.S., 1900-
1940.   New York: National Bureau of Economic Research,
1946.

514.   Sumner, Helen L.   History of Women in Industry in the United
States.   [Report on Conditions of Woman and Child Wage-
Earners in the United States, Volume IX; 61st Congress, 2nd
Session, Senate Document No. 645].   Washington, D.C.:
Government Printing Office, 1910.
An eminent labor historian presents a thorough summary
of working conditions for women from colonial times to
the beginning of the twentieth century.

515.   Tax, Meredith.   The Rising of the Woman: Feminist Soli-
darity and Class Conflict, 1880-1917.   New York: Monthly
Review Press, 1980.
Examines several cross-class alliances of women between
the late 1880's and World War I, and judges the political
success of each institution within its historical context.
The strongest section of this book centers on the Illinois
Woman's Alliance formed in Chicago in 1888.   Considers

in detail the New York shirtwaist makers' strike of 1909-
1910 and the Lawrence textile strike of 1912, and judges
the work of the various coalitions that offered support to
the strikers.

516.   U.S. Women's Bureau.   The Employment of Women in Hazard-
       dous Industries in the United States.   Bulletin No. 6.   Wash-
       ington: Government Printing Office, 1920.

517.   U.S. Women's Bureau.   Hours and Conditions of Work for
       Women in Industry in Virginia.   Bulletin No. 10.   Washing-
       ton: Government Printing Office, 1920.

518.   U.S. Women's Bureau.   The New Position of Women in Ameri-
       can Industry.   Bulletin No. 12.   Washington: Government
       Printing Office, 1920.

519.   U.S. Women's Bureau.   A Physiological Basis for the Shorter
       Working Day for Women.   By George W. Webster.   Bulletin
       No. 14.   Washington: Government Printing Office, 1921.

520.   U.S. Women's Bureau.   Domestic Workers and Their Employ-
       ment Relations: A Study Based on the Records of the Domes-
       tic Efficiency Association of Baltimore, Maryland.   By Mary
       V. Robinson.   Bulletin No. 39.   Washington: Government
       Printing Office, 1924.

521.   U.S. Women's Bureau.   Facts About Working Women: A
       Graphic Presentation Based on Census Statistics and Studies
       of the Women's Bureau.   Bulletin No. 46.   Washington: Gov-
       ernment Printing Office, 1925.

522.   U.S. Women's Bureau.   Industrial Accidents to Women in
       New Jersey, Ohio, and Wisconsin.   Bulletin No. 60.   Wash-
       ington: Government Printing Office, 1927.

523.   U.S. Women's Bureau.   The Development of Minimum-Wage
       Laws in the United States, 1912-1927.   By Mildred Larcom
       (Jones) Gordon.   Bulletin No. 61.   Washington: Government
       Printing Office, 1928.

524.   U.S. Women's Bureau.   Chronological Development of Labor
       Legislation for Women in the United States.   Bulletin No. 66-
       II.   Washington: Government Printing Office, 1929.

525.   U.S. Women's Bureau.   Activities of the Women's Bureau of
       the United States.   By Agnes Lydia Peterson.   Bulletin No.
       86.   Washington: Government Printing Office, 1931.

526.   U.S. Women's Bureau.   The Occupational Progress of Women,
       1910-1930.   By Mary V. Dempsey.   Bulletin No. 104.   Wash-
       ington: Government Printing Office, 1933.

527. U.S. Women's Bureau. The Commercialization of the Home Through Industrial Home Work. Bulletin No. 135. Washington: Government Printing Office, 1935.

528. U.S. Women's Bureau. Women at Work: A Century of Industrial Change. Bulletin No. 161. Washington: Government Printing Office, 1939.

529. U.S. Women's Bureau. Women of Spanish Origin in the U.S. Washington: Government Printing Office, 1976.

530. Van Kleeck, Mary. "Working Hours of Women in Factories." Charities and the Commons 17 (1906): 13-21.

531. Van Kleeck, Mary. Working Girls in Evening Schools: A Statistical Study. New York: Russell Sage Foundation, 1914.

532. Van Kleeck, Mary. "The Workers' Bill for Unemployment." The New Republic 81 (1934-35): 121-24.

533. Walkowitz, Daniel J. Worker City, Company Town: Iron and Cotton-Worker Protests in Troy and Cohoes, New York, 1855-1884. Urbana: University of Illinois Press, 1978.

534. Walkowitz, Daniel J. "Working-Class Women in the Gilded Age: Factory, Community and Family Life Among Cohoes, New York Cotton Workers." Journal of Social History, 5 (1972): 464-490.

535. Ware, Caroline F. The Early New England Cotton Manufacture. Boston: Houghton Mifflin Company, 1931.
   Includes descriptions of boarding houses provided by northern cotton mills to attract a labor supply of "respectable girls." Most boarding houses had matrons who looked after the girls' morals. Describes generally crowded but comfortable living conditions in typical boarding houses.

536. Ware, Norman. The Industrial Worker, 1840-1860: The Reaction of American Industrial Society to the Advance of the Industrial Revolution. Boston: Houghton Mifflin, 1924.

537. Wertheimer, Barbara M., and Anne H. Nelson. Trade Union Women: A Study of Their Participation in New York City Locals. New York: Praeger Publishers, 1978.

538. Wertheimer, Barbara M. We Were There: The Story of Working Women in America. New York: Pantheon Books, 1977.
   Designed for trade-union education courses, includes sections on Socialist women who were active in the labor movement. Chapters on the Women's Trade Union League and the garment unions with brief biographical sketches of Rose Schneiderman, Leonora O'Reilly, Clara Lemlich, and Dorothy Jacobs Bellanca, and information on Pauline Newman.

539.   Willett, Mabel H.   The Employment of Women in the Clothing
       Trade.   New York: Columbia University, 1902.   Reprint.
       New York: AMS Press, 1968.
              Includes historical background and information on factory
              conditions, immigrant women, labor legislation, and trade
              unions.

540.   Wolfson, Theresa.   The Woman Worker and the Trade Unions.
       New York: International Publishers Co., 1926.
              Early study of women's role in trade unions.   Appendix
              includes statistics on women workers from 1910 to 1925,
              as well as union policies toward women workers.

541.   Woolman, Mary.   "The Manhattan Trade School for Girls."
       Educational Review, 30 (September 1905):   178-188.

542.   Wright, Carroll D.   The Working Girls of Boston: From the
       Fifteenth Annual Report of the Massachusetts Bureau of Sta-
       tistics of Labor for 1884.   Boston: Wright & Potter, 1889.
       Reprint. New York: Arno Press, 1969.
              Pioneering work concerning itself with moral aspects of
              employment, with considerable information on the lives of
              immigrant (largely Irish) women workers.

543.   Wyman, Lillie B. Chance.   "Studies of Factory Life: Among
       the Women."   Atlantic Monthly, 62 (1881):   315-21.

544.   Yans-McLaughlin, Virginia.   "Italian Women and Work: Ex-
       perience and Perception" in Milton Cantor and Bruce Laurie,
       eds., Class, Sex, and the Woman Worker (Westport, Conn.:
       Greenwood Press, 1977), pp. 138-157.

IV. IMMIGRANT WOMEN AND PROGRESSIVE
REFORMERS

545. Abbott, Edith. Some American Pioneers in Social Welfare. Select Documents. Chicago: University of Chicago Press, 1937.
Includes materials on Samuel Gridley Howe (1801-1876);
Dorothea L. Dix (1802-1887); and Charles Loring Brace
(1826-1890); the texts of American poor relief documents
(1870-1885); and documents on the first public welfare association.

546. Abbott, Edith. "Ten Years' Work for Children." North
American Review, 218 (1923): 189-200.

547. Abbott, Edith. The Tenements of Chicago, 1908-1935 [1936].
New York: Arno Press, 1974.
For more than a quarter of a century the School of Social
Service Administration of the University of Chicago made
studies of housing conditions in the city. Collected here,
these reports provide one of the most detailed accounts of
housing conditions in the twentieth century. Special emphasis is given to housing conditions of different ethnic groups
--Jewish, Polish, Czech, German, Italian. Studies of
tenement house legislation, and of specific problems caused
by furnished rooms, overcrowding, and the breakdown of
relief payments for rent money during the Depression are
included. Edith Abbott, who was dean of the University
of Chicago's School of Social Service Administration at the
time, felt that neither private developers nor local government was equipped to handle the problems of tenement
housing and her reasoning led her to recommend Federal
intervention, thus anticipating by a quarter of a century
Federal aid for urban housing.

548. Abbott, Grace. "A Study of Greeks in Chicago." American
Journal of Sociology, 25 (November 1909): 349-393.
The Greek community and the problems of adjustment.
Greek immigrant women and children.

549. Addams, Jane. "The Chicago Settlements and Social Unrest."
Charities and the Commons, 20 (May 2, 1908): 155-166.

550. Addams, Jane. Democracy and Social Ethics. Edited by
Anne F. Scott. Cambridge, Mass.: Harvard University
Press, 1964.
Originally published in 1902. Includes notices of immi-
grant women and children in Chicago, 1902.

551.   Addams, Jane. Forty Years at Hull House: Being Twenty
        Years at Hull House and the Second Twenty at Hull House.
        New York: Macmillan, 1935.
               A consolidation of Twenty Years at Hull House with Auto-
               biographical Notes (1910; reprinted 1911; and 1923, edited
               by Eva Warner Case); and The Second Twenty Years at
               Hull House: September 1909 to September 1929, with a
               Record of a Growing World Consciousness (1930). Its
               publication (with an "Afterword" by Lillian Wald) was a
               memorial to Jane Addams who died in 1935. With the
               exception of an index for The Second Twenty Years, no
               changes were made in the reprinting of the two volumes.
               The "Afterword" by Lillian Wald was written for the me-
               morial volume and provided "the opportunity to tell the
               story of Jane Addams from the time of the conclusion of
               her Second Twenty Years at Hull House to her death."

552.   Addams, Jane. "A Function of the Social Settlement." An-
        nals (Academy of the Political and Social Sciences), 12 (May
        1899): 35-55.

553.   Addams, Jane. My Friend, Julia Lathrop. [1935]. New
        York: Arno Press, 1974.
               Covers Julia Lathrop's career before and after her ten
               years (1912-1921) as chief of the U.S. Children's Bureau.
               It contains much information about the early days at Hull
               House, the work of the Illinois State Board of Charities,
               the organization of the first juvenile court and Lathrop's
               associations with Florence Kelley and other reformers.

554.   Addams, Jane. The Second Twenty Years at Hull House,
        September 1909 to September 1929, with a Record of a Grow-
        ing World Consciousness. New York: Macmillan Co., 1930.
               Contains material on the Progressive Party, the women's
               movement between 1909 and 1929, peace efforts 1914-19,
               domestic and international postwar problems, prohibition,
               immigration, the courts, and the work at Hull House.

555.   Addams, Jane. "Social Education of the Industrial Democ-
        racy." Commons, 5 (June 30, 1900): 17-20.

556.   Addams, Jane. Twenty Years at Hull House. New York:
        Macmillan, 1910.
               An autobiography which covers the first twenty years of
               Jane Addams of Hull House, including influences on her
               work, the founding of Hull House, work on labor legislation
               in Illinois and efforts to help the immigrants and promote
               education.

557.   Aldrich, Mark, and Randy Albelda. "Determinants of Work-
        ing Women's Wages During the Progressive Era." Explora-
        tions in Economic History, 27 (1980): 323-341.

558.   Bainbridge, Lucy Seaman. Helping the Helpless in Lower
       New York. New York: Fleming H. Revell, 1917.
       Urban conditions described by the Superintendent of the
       Woman's Branch of the New York City Mission Society.

559.   Barrows, Esther G. Neighbors All: A Settlement Notebook.
       Boston: Houghton Mifflin, 1929.

560.   Batinich, Mary Ellen M. "The Interaction Between Italian
       Immigrant Women and the Chicago Commons Settlement House,
       1909-1944." In Betty Boyd Caroli, Richard F. Harney, and
       Lydio F. Tomasi, eds., The Italian Immigrant Women in
       North America (Toronto: The Multicultural History Society
       of Ontario, 1978), pp. 154-167.
       The lives of three women presented are based on data
       drawn from the papers of the Chicago Commons Settlement
       House. While these are not case histories, the character-
       izations are representative of the three periods of existence
       of the Italian Mothers Club (IMC): the late teens and twen-
       ties; the thirties and the Great Depression era; and the
       early forties, during the war years. While complete docu-
       mentation was not available for each of the years, there
       was sufficient information to portray women typical of
       those who frequented the Commons during these three periods.

561.   Beck, Robert H. "Progressive Education and American Pro-
       gressivism." Teachers College Record, 40 (1958-1959): 77-
       89; 129-137; 198-208.
       On leaders in the movement, e.g., Felix Adler, Caroline
       Pratt, Margaret Naumberg.

562.   Berger, Morris Isaiah. The Settlement. The Immigrant and
       the Public School: A Study of the Influence of the Settlement
       Movement and the New Migration Upon Public Education, 1890-
       1924. New York: Arno Press, 1980.
       The social settlement arose as a reaction to the evils of
       industrialism. It was born of an effort by socially con-
       scious reformers to combat the ugliness, the poverty, and
       the social disintegration of the urban slum. Its goal was
       nothing less than a total regeneration of the slum neighbor-
       hood. The settlement was to be the center of a new self-
       conscious community, and from this center the people were
       to draw their strength. Describes the transformation. Be-
       gins by briefly describing the early settlement movement,
       its activities and aspirations. An analysis is then made
       of the impact of the new migration upon American society
       and the close connection of the settlement movement with
       this migration. The history of the Educational Alliance,
       an institution that combined settlement work with immi-
       grant education, follows as a case study. The impact of
       the settlement movement and the new migration upon public
       education are subsequently considered. Finally, the study
       shows how settlement work and the activities of immigrant

institutions coalesced with other forces to support the movement to make the public school the center of community
life. Originally, Ph.D. dissertation, Columbia University,
1956.

563.   Berrol, S. "When Uptown Met Downtown: Julia Richman's
        Work in the Jewish Community of New York, 1880-1912."
        American Jewish History, 70 (1980): 35-51.

564.   Betts, Lillian. "The Child Out of School Hours." Outlook,
        75 (September 1903): 209-216.

565.   Betts, Lillian W. The Leaven in a Great City. New York:
        Dodd, Mead, 1903.

566.   Bliss, William D[wight] P[orter] and Rudolph M. Binder, eds.
        The New Encyclopedia of Social Reform: Including All Social-
        Reform Movements and Activities, and the Economic, Indus-
        trial, and Sociological Facts and Statistics of All Countries
        and All Social Subjects. 3rd ed. [1910]. New York: Arno
        Press, 1974.
            Provides an excellent starting point for any research on
        reform in the Progressive Era. Many of the most famous
        urban reformers contributed articles--Adna F. Weber on
        "The Eight Hour Day," Frank Giddings on "Sociology,"
        Owen Lovejoy on "Child Labor," and Frank Parsons on
        "Municipal Ownership." Notable articles on settlement
        houses, immigration, factory legislation, penology, with
        statistics--figures on commerce, strikes, wages, education,
        elections, crime, and many other similar subjects are
        included. The organization of the articles, biographies,
        charts, and statistical analyses is alphabetical by subject
        and The New Encyclopedia is an especially effective re-
        search tool.

567.   Blumberg, Dorothy R. Florence Kelley: The Making of a
        Social Pioneer. New York: Augustus M. Kelley, 1966.
            Florence Kelley (1859-1932), a major force in the cam-
        paigns against the evils of industrialism and especially
        against child labor. See also, Josephine Goldmark, Im-
        patient Crusader: The Life Story of Florence Kelley (1953).

568.   Bowers, C. A. "The Ideologies of Progressive Education."
        History of Education Quarterly, 7 (Winter 1967): 452-473.
            Interrelationships of educational theories and political move-
        ments in the first third of the twentieth century. See also
        Bowers, The Progressive Educator and the Depression:
        The Radical Years (1969).

569.   Brace, Charles Loring. Short Sermons to News Boys. With
        a History of the Formation of the News Boy's Lodging-House.
        New York: Charles Scribner, 1866.
            A rare early work by a founder of the Children's Aid So-

ciety on the life of the urban homeless boy. Vignettes of
urban street life and the immigrant Irish community with
detailed accounts of programs in social reform. Invaluable
for later Settlement House movement and efforts in child
labor legislation.

570.   Bradbury, Dorothy E. Five Decades of Action: A History
        of the Children's Bureau. Washington: Government Printing
        Office, 1962.
            See also Alice E. Padgett, "The History of the Establish-
        ment of the United States Children's Bureau." Unpublished
        M. A. thesis, University of Chicago, 1936.

571.   Brandeis, Louis D., and Josephine Goldmark. Women in
        Industry. [1907]. New York: Arno Press, 1971.
            Curt Muller who operated a modest laundry in Portland,
        Oregon bargained with several of his laundresses over the
        length of their work day and the amount of their pay. In
        so doing he violated a state law which limited the female
        work day to ten hours. He was subsequently arrested and
        brought to trial in a case which was carried to the Supreme
        Court. Louis Brandeis, later to become a member of that
        Court, defended the Oregon law in a precedent shattering
        brief that contained only two pages of law, but more than
        a hundred pages of citations gathered by a team of re-
        searchers who combed through libraries of books by bio-
        logists, sociologists, doctors, criminologists, and studied
        the impact of overwork on women and consequently society.
        By adding the logic of facts to the logic of law, Brandeis
        won the praise of the Court for his brief--both in this
        volume--and scored a breakthrough for a shorter work
        day.

572.   Brandt, Lilian. The Charity Organization Society of the City
        of New York, 1882-1907. History: Account of Present Ac-
        tivities. Twenty-Fifth Annual Report for the Year Ending
        September Thirtieth, Nineteen Hundred and Seven. New York:
        United Charities Building, 1907.

573.   Brandt, Lilian. Five Hundred and Seventy-Four Deserters
        and Their Families: A Descriptive Study of Their Character-
        istics and Circumstances. [1905]; and Baldwin, William H.
        Family Desertion and Non-Support Laws. [1904]. New York:
        Arno Press, 1972.
            Some of the most insightful studies of lower-class family
        life were made by Progressive reformers. Eager to
        strengthen family life among the poor, both for reasons of
        sentiment and for the general social stability, they care-
        fully investigated the phenomenon of family desertion, hop-
        ing to find clues to the larger problems of family cohesion,
        dislocation, and disintegration. The study by Brandt was
        one of the most successful of these efforts, clarifying the
        kinds of men who actually deserted, their motives, and

what happened to them and their families afterwards. The
statutes compiled by William Baldwin provide a thorough
account of state legislation in this field.

574.   Brandt, Lilian. Growth and Development of AICP and COS:
A Preliminary and Exploratory Review. Report to the Committee on the Institute of Welfare Research. New York:
Community Service Society of New York, 1942.
The Association for Improving the Condition of the Poor
(founded 1843), and the Charity Organization Society (founded
1882), interrelationships, and the union of the two organizations in 1939. Invaluable resource for information on
immigrant child, immigrant women, the immigrant poor,
and social interventions.

575.   [Breckinridge, Sophonisba P. ed.] The Child in the City: A
Series of Papers Presented at the Conferences Held During
the Chicago Child Welfare Exhibit. [1912]. New York: Arno
Press, 1974.
The Chicago Child Welfare Exhibit was held in May of 1911
and provided a forum for the exchange of information and
ideas among the major reformers of the Progressive era
on the problems of city children. Julia Lathrop, Lillian
Wald, Jane Addams, Florence Kelley, Charles Zeublin and
other prominent reformers spoke. This book is a collection of the papers presented by these reformers at the
Exhibit and they show the enormous scope and sensitivity
of the Progressives in the matters of child welfare and
the immigrant family. The papers favor a wide range of
changes and suggest solutions to a number of problems--
sex education, school breakfasts, improved recreational
facilities--in addition, several of the papers advocate in-
stituting juvenile and domestic relations courts.

576.   Breckinridge, Sophonisba P., and Edith Abbott. The Delinquent Child and the Home. [1912]. New York: Arno Press,
1974.
Using material gathered from court files, probation officers'
records, interviews with probation officers, and investigators'
visits, Sophonisba Breckinridge and Edith Abbott presented
one of the first studies of the causes of juvenile delinquency.
Their profiles of the wards of the Juvenile Court of Chicago
demonstrated that the delinquent child generally came from
a troubled home, largely immigrant, where poverty had
brutalized or degraded the parents. The histories of these
families proved so compelling that the authors included the
more illuminating of the biographies in the appendix. In
speaking of the study, and of the Juvenile Court system,
in her introduction Julia Lathrop remarks: "Never before
has the setting of the child in his family been made part
of the statement of his overt disobedience to law; never
before has this picture been submitted to a court of law,
instead of the facts technically recognized as legal evidence;

never before has the judge been free to dispose of the
child solely with a view to offering him the best chance of
wholesome life without regard to previous offenses."

577. Breckinridge, Sophonisba P. New Homes for Old. New
York: Harper & Brothers, 1921.
Deals with problems arising in immigrant families and of
means of dealing with them so as to insure effective adjustment to American society. Part of the "Americanization Studies: The Acculturation of Immigrant Groups into
American Society" commissioned by the Carnegie Corporation.

578. Breckinridge, Sophonsiba P. Women in the Twentieth Century:
A Study of Their Political Social and Economic Activities.
[1933]. New York: Arno Press, 1976.
A monograph, published under the direction of the President's Research Commission on Social Trends, which surveyed the changing and expanding role of women's clubs,
national organizations, occupational and professional groups.
It also recorded new occupations, wage comparisons and
voting experience as gleaned from official reports, convention proceedings and personal interviews.

579. Bremner, Robert H. "Scientific Philanthropy, 1873-1893."
Social Service Review, 30 (June 1956): 168-173.

580. Bruno, Frank J. Trends in Social Work, 1874-1956: A
History Based on the Proceedings of the National Conference
of Social Work. New York: Columbia University Press,
1957.
See also Nathan E. Cohen, Social Work in the American
Tradition (1958); and Kathleen Woodroofe, From Charity
to Social Work in England and the United States (1962).

581. Buenker, John D. "The Progressive Era: A Search for a
Synthesis." Mid-America, 51 (July 1969): 175-93.
A brief survey of Progressive historiography. Contends
that historians will not achieve a comprehensive explanation
of Progressive reform until they understand that the movement was caused by the interaction of industrialization,
immigration, and urbanization.

582. Byington, Margaret Frances. Homestead: The Households
of a Mill Town (Originally published as part of The Pittsburgh
Survey, edited by Paul Underwood Kellogg). [1910]. New
York: Arno Press, 1971.
A penetrating and compassionate portrait of life in an immigrant community dominated by a powerful industrial giant.
Based on interviews conducted by a trained field staff, the
book investigates family, social, and cultural existence in
a mill town where the wages are subsistence and the work
varies from 12 hours a day and 7 days a week to no work

at all. It encompasses the full spectrum of activities from
how "the family feeds and clothes itself and what it does
for enjoyment .... through the effect of social relations in
the plant versus those in the community ... to seeking out
a corner of life that escapes the shadow of the mill."

583.   Campbell, Helen S. Prisoners of Poverty: Women Wage
        Earners, Their Trades and Their Lives. Boston: Roberts
        Brothers, 1887. Reprint. New York: AMS Press, 1972.
        Sketches of individual working women including immigrant
        Irish domestics. Considers improving their lives through
        general and industrial education, and introduction of social-
        istic principles of management.

584.   Campbell, Helen. "Certain Convictions as to Poverty." The
        Arena, 1 (1889-90): 101-13.

585.   Campbell, Helen. "White Child Slavery." The Arena, 1
        (1889-90): 589-91.

586.   Campbell, Helen. "The Working Women of Today." The
        Arena, 4 (1891): 329-39.

587.   Campbell, Helen S., ed. Darkness and Daylight: Or Lights
        and Shadows of New York Life. A Woman's Narrative of
        Mission and Rescue Work in Tough Places, with Personal
        Experience Among the Poor in Regions of Poverty and Vice;
        An All-Night Missionary's Experience in Gospel Work in the
        Slums; A Journalist's Account of Little-Known Phases of
        Metropolitan Life; And a Detective's Experience and Observa-
        tions Among the Dangerous and Criminal Classes, The Whole
        Portraying Life in Darkest New York by Day and by Night.
        Hartford, Conn.: A. D. Worthington, 1899.

588.   Carey, John J., Jr. "Progressives and the Immigrant, 1885-
        1915." Unpublished Ph.D. dissertation, University of Con-
        necticut, 1968.

589.   Carlson, Robert A. The Quest for Conformity: Americaniza-
        tion Through Education. New York: John Wiley, 1975.
        "Americanization" process as a continuing long-term quest
        for conformity, with education used to homogenize Ameri-
        cans into a white, Protestant, middle class.

590.   Chambers, Clarke A. Seedtime of Reform: American Social
        Service and Social Action, 1918-1933. Minneapolis: Uni-
        versity of Minnesota Press, 1963.
        Focuses on the origins of such voluntary welfare agencies
        as the National Consumers League, Women's Trade Union
        League, American Association for Labor Legislation, and
        the National Child Labor Committee during the Progressive
        era and on their continued efforts at reform during the New
        Era. Sees the New Deal as a result of their combined and
        cumulative activities.

591. Chapin, Robert Coit. The Standard of Living Among Work-
      ingmen's Families in New York City. New York: Charities
      Publication Committee, 1909. Reprint. New York: Arno
      Press, 1971.
          Sponsored by the New York State Conference on Charities
          and Corrections, this study was one of the first thorough
          and statistical investigations of the style of life of immi-
          grant urban families. From these data, the conditions of
          an important segment of the labor force take on an unusual
          specificity and clarity.

592. [Chicago Vice Commission]. The Social Evil in Chicago: A
      Study of Existing Conditions with Recommendations by the Vice
      Commission of Chicago. Chicago: Gunthorp-Warren Printing
      Co., 1911.
          In its report, made during the Progressive Era, the Chicago
          Commission offered a number of recommendations to elimi-
          nate prostitution which were eventually adopted, not only
          in Chicago, but in many other cities.

593. [Children's Aid Society]. Children's Aid Society Annual Re-
      ports, 1-10. February 1854- February 1863. New York:
      Arno Press, 1971.
          Headed by the noted reformer, Charles Loring Brace, the
          Society set a new trend for child care in the middle dec-
          ades of the nineteenth century. The CAS was the first
          group to formulate an alternative to orphan asylums and
          reformatories for indigent children, and the story of their
          placing-out procedures is of crucial importance to social
          history.

594. [The Children's Aid Society]. The Crusade for Children: A
      Review of Child Life in New York During 75 Years, 1853-
      1928. New York: The Children's Aid Society, 1928.
          Founded in 1853, the Society was, from its beginnings, in-
          volved with the needs of immigrant children and the immi-
          grant family. See also The Children's Aid Society of New
          York: Its History, Plans and Results (1893).

595. [Citizens' Association of New York]. Report of the Council
      of Hygiene and Public Health of the Citizens' Association of
      New York upon the Sanitary Conditions of the City. [1866].
      New York: Arno Press, 1974.
          Provides one of the most detailed descriptions of the physi-
          cal condition of an American city in mid-nineteenth century.
          The Citizens' Association, a group of prominent New York-
          ers who aimed to work for "municipal reform and public
          improvement," conducted this study as a result of mob
          violence in slum and immigrant areas in the summer of
          1863. Results of the study indicated that New York City's
          high mortality rate (highest in the country and higher even
          than London's and Liverpool's) was related to overcrowding
          and lack of proper ventilation and sunshine in slum areas.

Topography, drainage and sewage, conditions of streets,
number and type of houses, courts and alleys, brothels,
saloons, stores and markets, stables, churches and schools,
the character of the population, the condition of sanitation
and amount of sickness in tenement houses, and the source
of preventable disease in each district of the city are detailed in the Report. The Report had its effect; shortly
after its publication, New York City organized a Board of
Health and passed a tenement house law.

596.   Clark, Sue A. , and Edith Wyatt. Making Both Ends Meet.
        The Income and Outlay of New York Working Girls. New
        York: Macmillan, 1911.
             Reports investigations made for the National Consumers'
             League of abysmal conditions of women workers, many of
             them immigrants, that resulted in remedial legislation.
             Discusses effect of "scientific management" on women in
             various industries.

597.   Cohen, Sol. Progressives and Urban School Reform: The
        Public Education Association of New York City, 1895-1954.
        New York: Teachers College Press, 1964.
             Examines the efforts of school reformers to deal with the
             social problems posed by immigrant children and the slums,
             and presents progressive education as part of a broader
             social reform effort. The Public Education Association of
             New York City as a case history in urban progressive edu-
             cation intended as "a contribution to American social and
             intellectual history." An invaluable history.

598.   Cohen, Sol. "The Industrial Education Movement, 1906-1917."
        American Quarterly, 20 (1968): 95-110.
             Shows that the industrial education movement sought not to
             add vocational courses to existing curricula but rather to
             transform the entire school system from traditional general
             education to industrial education. While passage of the
             Smith-Hughes Act marked its defeat, the movement still
             left many educators feeling that mass education along aca-
             demic lines was inappropriate for most public school chil-
             dren.

599.   [Community Service Society of New York]. Frontiers in
        Human Welfare. The Story of a Hundred Years of Service
        to the Community of New York, 1848-1948. New York: Com-
        munity Service Society of New York, 1948.

600.   Connelly, Mark T. The Response to Prostitution in the Pro-
        gressive Era. Chapel Hill: University of North Carolina
        Press, 1980.

601.   Conway, Jill. "Jane Addams: An American Herione."
        Daedalus 93 (1964): 761-80.
             Analyzes Jane Addams as a symbol to American women

during the Progressive era for her public life of social
activism and extreme individualism.

602.   Conway, Jill.   "American Reformers and American Culture,
       1870-1930."   Journal of Social History, 5 (1971-72):   164-77.
       Focuses upon Jane Addams and Florence Kelley as proto-
       types of two distinct feminist leaders of the period: the
       Victorian sage and the professional expert.   Feels that
       both rejected Victorian bourgeois and economic values
       while retaining the era's sexual stereotypes.

603.   Conyngton, Mary.   How to Help: A Manual of Practical
       Charity.   [1909].   New York: Arno Press, 1971.
       Intended as a practical handbook for volunteers and pro-
       fessional charity workers, the volume surveys the social
       agencies of the Progressive era, from the mammoth Charity
       Organization Society to settlement houses and fresh air
       funds.   The nervousness and suspicion as well as the con-
       cern and benevolence of the groups are evident in these
       pages.

604.   Cordasco, Francesco.   "Charles Loring Brace and the Dan-
       gerous Classes: Historical Analogues of the Urban Black
       Poor."   Journal of Human Relations, 20 (3rd Quarter, 1972):
       379-386.
       On Charles Loring Brace (1826-1890), one of the founders
       of the Children's Aid Society, and the author of The Dan-
       gerous Classes of New York and Twenty Years Work Among
       Them (1872).

605.   Cordasco, Francesco.   Jacob Riis Revisited: Poverty and
       the Slum in Another Era.   New York: Doubleday, 1968.
       Selections from three books by the Danish immigrant so-
       cial reformer, Jacob August Riis (1849-1914):   How the
       Other Half Lives (1890); The Children of the Poor (1892);
       and A Ten Years' War: An Account of the Battle with
       the Slums in New York (1900).   Includes considerable ma-
       terial on the immigrant family, particularly Irish and
       Italian.   See also Louise Ware, Jacob A. Riis (New York:
       D. Appleton-Century, 1939).   The Jacob A. Riis Collection,
       Museum of the City of New York is a rich collection of
       memorabilia of the era.

606.   Cordasco, Francesco.   "Street Arabs and Gutter Snipes."
       Journal of Human Relations, 20 (3rd Quarter, 1972):   387-
       390.
       On George C. Needham's Street Arabs and Gutter Snipes
       (1884), slum life in the late nineteenth-century American
       cities, the immigrant family, and neglected and destitute
       children.

607.   Cremin, Lawrence A.   The Transformation of the School:
       Progressivism in American Education, 1876-1957.   New York:
       Alfred A. Knopf, 1961.

"The story of the progressive education movement: of its
genesis in the decades immediately following the Civil War;
of its widespread appeal among the intellectuals at the turn
of the century; of its gathering political momentum during
the decade before World War I; of its conquest of the organized teaching profession; of its pervasive impact on
American schools and colleges, public and private; of its
fragmentation during the 1920's and 1930's; and of its
ultimate collapse after World War II; is the substance of
this volume" (Preface, ix).   The most comprehensive study
of the progressive education movement.

608.   Daniels, Doris Groshen.   "Lillian D. Wald: The Progressive
       Woman and Feminism." Unpublished Ph. D. dissertation, City
       University of New York, 1977.
            Examines Wald's involvement with an activist network of
       social reformers, labor organizers, revolutionaries, and
       settlement workers.   Focuses on her role as a bridge
       between middle-class feminists and immigrant workers
       attempting to foster both women's rights and social justice.

609.   Daniels, Harriet M.   The Girl and Her Chance.   A Study of
       Conditions Surrounding the Young Girl Between Fourteen and
       Eighteen Years of Age in New York City.   New York: Flem-
       ing H. Revell, 1914.
            A monograph prepared for the Association of Neighborhood
       Workers of New York City which centers on "The life of
       the industrial family, and especially ... the young girl who
       has suddenly emerged from the protection of a highly cen-
       tralized and authoritative family life into the confusion of
       modern industrialism."

610.   Davis, Allen F.   American Heroine: The Life and Legend
       of Jane Addams.   New York: Oxford University Press, 1973.
            Traces the influences and circumstances that led to Addams'
       founding of Hull House in 1889 and focuses on her reputa-
       tion and public image.   Uses Addams to illuminate the
       changing attitudes toward social reform between 1889 and
       1935.   Locates Addams' motivation in a quest for peace,
       justice, and community rather than in a search for order
       or a cult of efficiency.   Richly detailed biography drawn
       largely from primary manuscript collections (for which
       see bibliography, pp. 295-296).   See also, James W. Linn,
       Jane Addams: A Biography (1935); Daniel Levine, Jane
       Addams and the Liberal Tradition (1971); John C. Farrell,
       Beloved Lady: A History of Jane Addams' Ideas on Reform
       and Peace (1967).

611.   Davis, Allen F., and Mary L. McCree, eds.   Eighty Years
       at Hull House.   Chicago: Quadrangle Books, 1969.
            Selections about Hull House by women involved in its found-
       ing and programs.

612.   Davis, Allen F. Spearheads for Reform: The Social Settle-
       ments and the Progressive Movement, 1890-1914. New York:
       Oxford University Press, 1967.
              Presents material on Jane Addams, Lillian Wald, Mary
       Simkhovitch, Mary Kelley, and others in a broad social
       context.   Considerable material on working women and
       children.

613.   DeForest, Robert W., and Lawrence Veiller, eds. The Tene-
       ment House Problem: Including the Report of the New York
       State Tenement House Commission of 1900. New York: Mac-
       millan, 1903. 2 vols. Reprint. New York: Arno Press,
       1974.
              Prior to the passage in 1901 of the building law recom-
       mended in the report around which this book is centered,
       conditions in New York City's tenements (largely immi-
       grant) were the worst in the country.   The tenements were
       overcrowded, unventilated, unlighted, unsanitary, fire and
       health hazards.   The Report details the conditions found
       in the tenements and recommends a building law which set
       new standards for light, air, and sanitation in all new
       tenements and required landlord to make improvements in
       existing buildings.   Robert DeForest, who for many years
       was regarded as the "First Citizen of New York" for his
       humanitarian activities, was chairman of the New York
       State Tenement House Commission.   After passage of the
       new building law, DeForest was appointed the first com-
       missioner of the New York City Tenement House Depart-
       ment with responsibility for enforcing the new building law.
       The book includes, in addition to the Report, a brief history
       of tenement house legislation, and a chapter on the enforce-
       ment of the new law.

614.   Devine, Edward T. Misery and Its Causes. [1913]. New
       York: Arno Press, 1971.
              A classic statement of Progressive attitudes toward the im-
       migrant poor, the book reveals the growing conviction of
       many observers that social and economic arrangements are
       at the root of poverty.   In attacking such traditional forms
       of relief as the almshouse, Devine insists that the oppor-
       tunity for steady employment and decent wages, rather than
       moral uplift, would do most to eliminate the presence of
       poverty.

615.   Dewey, John. The School and Society. Chicago: University
       of Chicago Press, 1899.
              A vast literature exists on John Dewey.   See George Dyk-
       huizen, The Life and Mind of John Dewey (1973).   South-
       ern Illinois University Press is currently publishing John
       Dewey's collected works.   The ongoing project has pub-
       lished two useful guides: Jo Ann Boydston, ed., Guide to
       the Works of John Dewey (1970); and Jo Ann Boydston and
       Kathleen Poulos, Checklist of Writings About John Dewey,
       1887-1973 (1974).

616.   Dorr, Rheta L. C. What Eight Million Women Want. Boston:
        Small, Maynard, 1910.
        Discusses women's club movement, women and the law,
        women in industry, Maude Miner's efforts on behalf of
        delinquent women, female domestic servants (largely immi-
        grant), and suffrage.

617.   Dubovsky, Melvyn. When Workers Organize: New York City
        in the Progressive Era. Amherst: University of Massa-
        chusetts Press, 1968.
        A study of New York workers' attempts to organize during
        the period 1909 to 1916. Claims that while the workers
        sought the support of middle-class reformers, "organiza-
        tion and union recognition were always more important to
        the worker than reform legislation."

618.   Durand, Kelly, and Louis Seswin. "The Italian Invasion of
        the Ghetto." University Settlement Studies, 1, No. 4 (1908),
        [whole issue].
        The social milieu of the Italian immigrant family. See
        also Lillian Betts, "Italians in New York," University Settle-
        ment Studies, 1, No. 3 (1908), [whole issue].

619.   Eisele, J. Christopher. "John Dewey and the Immigrants."
        History of Education Quarterly, 15 (Spring 1975): 67-85.
        Dewey's views toward immigrants and schooling. See also
        Clarence J. Karier, "John Dewey and the New Liberalism:
        Some Reflections and Responses," History of Education
        Quarterly, 15 (Winter 1975): 417-443.

620.   [Ets, Marie Hall]. Rosa: The Life of an Italian Immigrant.
        Foreword by Rudolph J. Vecoli. Minneapolis: University of
        Minnesota Press, 1970.
        Narrative by a social worker at the Chicago Commons
        (World War I and after) of the life of an Italian immigrant
        peasant woman, assembled out of stories told by Rosa of
        her early life and experiences. See Review, F. X. Fem-
        minella, International Migration Review, 6 (Spring 1972):
        84-85.

621.   Feldman, Egal. "American Reformers and the Ethnic Factor."
        Cimarron Review, 15 (1971): 37-45.
        Maintains that in America, unlike other western countries,
        poverty was more than a social and economic problem. It
        was an ethnic, religious, and racial problem as well, and
        this was recognized by two groups which dealt most directly
        with poverty--reformers and organized labor.

622.   Feldman, Egal. "Prostitution: The Alien Woman and the
        Progressive Imagination, 1910-15." American Quarterly, 19
        (1967): 192-206.
        Contends that the attempt to eliminate prostitution focused
        on the immigrant girl whom investigations had revealed

was the prime victim of prostitution. The most important
leaders in this reform movement to protect the immigrant
were women who wanted to make modern urban America
safe not only for the defenseless immigrant, but for all
women.

623.   Folks, Homer. The Care of Destitute, Neglected, and De-
       linquent Children. New York: Macmillan, 1902.
           See Walter I. Trattner, Homer Folks: Pioneer in Social
       Welfare (New York: Columbia University Press, 1968).
       Folks served as Commissioner of Public Charities of the
       City of New York. Valuable as a source on abuse of im-
       migrant child. See also Folks, Changes and Trends in
       Child Labor and Its Control (New York: National Child
       Labor Committee, 1938).

624.   Glenn, John M. ; Lilian Brandt; and F. Emerson Andrews.
       The Russell Sage Foundation: 1907-1946. New York: Rus-
       sell Sage Foundation, 1947. 2 vols.
           A valuable chronicle of the Foundation's important role in
       socialized education and the movements for educational and
       social reform.

625.   Goldenweiser, E. A. "Immigrants in Cities." The Survey,
       25 (January 1911): 596-602.

626.   Greene, M. Louise. Among School Gardens. New York:
       Russell Sage Foundation, 1911.

627.   Harrison, Dennis Irven. "The Consumers' League of Ohio:
       Women and Reform, 1909-1937." Unpublished Ph.D. disser-
       tation, Case Western Reserve University, 1975.
           Maintains that the League progressed from voluntary, pri-
       vate efforts to political action in the fields of child and
       women's labor. Contends that the wartime emergency ac-
       tually furthered these causes in Ohio, and that the League
       continued to press for advances in these areas in the 1920's
       and 1930's.

628.   Hart, Hastings H. Preventive Treatment of Neglected Chil-
       dren. With Special Papers by Leading Authorities. [1910].
       New York: Arno Press, 1971.
           This well-organized statement of the Progressive viewpoint
       and programs, describes the new organization of reforma-
       tories, juvenile courts, settlement houses, and big brother
       clubs. An expert in the field of child care, Hart carefully
       analyzes the faults that he and his contemporaries found in
       earlier procedures, and the promise of their innovations.

629.   Henderson, Charles R. Introduction to the Study of the De-
       pendent, Defective and Delinquent Classes and of Their Social
       Treatment. Boston: Heath, 1901.
           A standard text of the period. See also Samuel G. Smith,
       Social Pathology (1911).

630. Henderson, Charles R. Social Settlements. New York:
      Lentilhon, 1899.
      A perceptive statement by Henderson (1848-1915), a major
      Baptist social reformer. See also his Major Methods of
      Charity (1904) and A Reasonable Social Policy (1909).

631. Hendrick, Burton J. "The Jewish Invasion of America."
      McClure's Magazine, 40 (March 1913): 125-165.

632. Horowitz, Helen L. "Varieties of Cultural Experience in Jane
      Addams' Chicago." History of Education Quarterly, 14 (Spring
      1974): 69-86.
      Hull House, culture and middle-class values, and the edu-
      cational mission to the immigrant community. See also
      the author's "Culture and the City: Cultural Philanthropy
      in Chicago, 1890-1917," unpublished Ph. D. dissertation,
      Harvard University, 1969.

633. Hunter, Robert. Poverty. New York: Macmillan, 1904.

634. Hunter, Robert. "The Relation Between Social Settlements
      and Charity Organization." Journal of Political Economy, 11
      (1902-3): 75-88.

635. Irwin, Elizabeth A. "The Story of a Transplanted Industry:
      Lace Workers of the Italian Quarter of New York." Crafts-
      man, 12 (1907): 404-409.

636. Juliani, Richard N. "The Settlement House and the Italian
      Family." In Betty Boyd Caroli, Richard F. Harney, and
      Lydio F. Tomasi, eds. The Italian Immigrant Woman in North
      America (Toronto: The Multicultural History Society of On-
      tario, 1978), pp. 103-123.
      Conclusions: The adjustment and integration of European
      immigrants into American society has been a historical
      process which was shaped by a number of different social
      institutions. For the Italians, as well as other groups,
      who came during the period of mass immigration in the
      last two decades of the nineteenth and early twentieth cen-
      turies to the northern cities of the United States, the set-
      tlement house was frequently a conspicuous part of their
      experience. The purpose of this paper is to re-examine
      the role of the settlement house in urban America and, in
      particular, its relationship to the immigrant family. The
      use of some original primary sources in the form of ar-
      chival materials has been brought to bear upon a revised
      view of the social settlement as an assimilating institution.

637. Karpf, Maurice J. Jewish Community Organization in the
      United States. [1938]. New York: Arno Press, 1971.
      A comprehensive yet brief description of organized Ameri-
      can Jewish life is provided in this thorough account of the
      charitable, educational, and social associations functioning

in the Jewish community in the 1930's. Described are the
tasks they attempted and the problems they faced.

638. Kellor, Frances A. Out of Work: A Study of Unemployment.
      New York: G. P. Putnam's Sons, 1915. Reprint. New York:
      Arno Press, 1971.
          One of the most complete surveys in the Progressive era
      of the problem of unemployment. The focus of the book
      is on the structure of the labor market, presenting a lucid
      picture of the economic and social problems of finding and
      keeping a job.

639. Kennedy, Albert J., ed. Social Settlements in New York
      City: Their Activities, Policies, and Administration. New
      York: Columbia University Press, 1935.

640. Koepplin, Leslie Wayne. "A Relationship of Reform Immi-
      grants and Progressives in the Far West." Unpublished Ph. D.
      dissertation, University of California, 1971.
          Challenges the traditional view that immigrants were hostile
      or indifferent to Progressive era reform efforts. Uses
      voting analysis and editorial comment, and also discusses
      the interaction between native-born reformers and immi-
      grant leadership. Sees reform as a two-way street which
      ultimately promoted the assimilation of immigrants through
      their participation in a changing society.

641. Kogut, Alvin B. "The Charity and Organization Societies,
      the Settlements and National Minorities in the Progressive
      Era." Unpublished Ph. D. dissertation, Columbia University,
      1970.

642. Kraus, Harry P. The Settlement House Movement in New
      York City, 1886-1914. New York: Arno Press, 1980.
          Profile sketches of New York City settlement workers re-
      veal a predominantly Protestant, college educated group
      of men and women. These settlement workers, of small
      town or rural background, were the first representatives
      of the middle class to voluntarily enter and live in the
      ghetto. Their purpose was to help improve the way of
      life of the slum residents whose condition, in this instance,
      was aggravated by their immigrant status. Settlement
      houses were the first to welcome the European immigrant
      without rejecting his Old World culture. In formulating
      programs for neighborhood reform, settlement workers
      found it necessary to influence state and national leaders.
      By 1910, these workers found that their influence in the
      neighborhood was beginning to be affected by changing popu-
      lation, institutional developments, the rise of the profes-
      sional social worker, and the competition of publicly admin-
      istered programs. On the eve of the first World War, the
      pace of the settlement growth in New York City had less-
      ened. Originally, Ph. D. dissertation, New York University
      1970.

643.   Lane, James B. "Bridge to the Other Half: The Life and
        Urban Work of Jacob Riis." Unpublished Ph. D. dissertation,
        University of Maryland, 1970.

644.   Lane, James B. "Unmasking Poverty: Jacob A. Riis and
        How the Other Half Lives." Maryland Historian, 2 (1971):
        27-29.
            Credits How the Other Half Lives (1890) with initiating a
            generation of examination and reform in the areas of
            poverty and related matters. Sees Riis's qualities of
            energy, moralism, sentimentality, chauvinism, and optimism
            as representative of the Progressive era mood.

645.   Lane, James B. "Jacob A. Riis and Scientific Philanthropy
        during the Progressive Era." Social Service Review, 47
        (1973): 32-48.
            Sees Riis as an unyielding advocate of neighborhood control
            and democratized urban planning who opposed the profes-
            sionalization of social work and urban planning on the
            grounds that their practitioners would form self-serving
            professional bureaucracies.

646.   Lasch, Christopher. The New Radicalism in America, 1889-
        1963: The Intellectual as a Social Type. New York: Alfred
        A. Knopf, 1965.
            Progressives and the reform of education, culture and sex-
            ual mores; the advancement of social reform and women's
            rights; the avoidance of war, and the exposure of corrup-
            tion.

647.   Lasch, Christopher, ed. The Social Thought of Jane Addams.
        Indianapolis: Bobbs-Merrill, 1965.
            Includes selections from Addams' writings on social settle-
            ments, cities and immigrants, and political and social re-
            form including suffrage, education, and peace activities.

648.   Lemons, J. Stanley. "The Sheppard-Towner Act: Progres-
        sivism in the 1920's." Journal of American History, 55
        (1969): 776-86.
            Maintains that the Sheppard-Towner Maternity and Infancy
            Protection Act of 1921 was an important link in the 1920's
            between old progressives and later New Dealers. It was
            also a product of the recent enfranchisement of women,
            who strongly supported the bill.

649.   Lemons, J. Stanley. "Social Feminism in the 1920's: Pro-
        gressive Women and Industrial Legislation." Labor History,
        14 (1973): 83-91.
            Argues that "social feminists" continued their involvement
            in efforts to protect working women and children during
            the 1920's, and that they achieved some important results
            through the mechanism of women's legislative councils
            which united working and middle-class women.

650. Lemons, J. Stanley. The Woman Citizen: Social Feminism
      in the 1920's. Urbana: University of Illinois, 1973.
            Urges that "social feminism," a major trend of the Pro-
      gressive era, continued in somewhat abated fashion during
      the 1920's. Feels that feminists advanced progressivism
      in social, political, and humanitarian areas, while pushing
      the cause of women's rights.

651. Leonard, Henry B. "The Immigrants' Protective League of
      Chicago, 1908-1921." Journal of the Illinois State Historical
      Society, 66 (1973): 271-84.
            Regards Jane Addams' and Grace Abbott's league a failure
      because it never attracted nearly enough support to achieve
      broad governmental programs for immigrants. Notes,
      nevertheless, that it was "a serious attempt to deal with
      the 'immigration problem' in an imaginative, enlightened
      and humane way."

652. Levine, Daniel. Jane Addams and the Liberal Tradition.
      Madison: State Historical Society of Wisconsin, 1971.
            Considers Addams' Hull House career and her involvement
      in a variety of reform efforts, including child labor, crime,
      poverty, immigration, labor relations, woman suffrage,
      pacifism, and the Progressive party. Presents Addams
      as a "window on the age" who asked the "right" questions
      and gave many of the "right" answers.

653. Lowell, Josephine Shaw. Public Relief and Private Charity.
      New York: G. P. Putnam's Sons, 1884. Reprint. New
      York: Arno Press, 1971.
            A leading statement of post-Civil War attitudes toward
      poverty, the book points in particular to the effects of
      social Darwinism on philanthropy, and in general to the
      thinking that promoted the Charity Organization Society.
      The appeal of these ideas was so widespread that not even
      the Progressive reformers could altogether escape them.

654. Lowell, Josephine Shaw. "Methods of Relief for the Unem-
      ployed." The Forum, 16 (1893-94): 655-62.

655. Lowell, Josephine Shaw. "The True Aim of Charity Organiza-
      tion Societies." The Forum, 21 (1896): 494-500.

656. Lubove, Roy. The Progressives and the Slums: Tenement
      House Reform in New York City, 1890-1917. Pittsburgh:
      University of Pittsburgh Press, 1962.
            Evaluates the issue of housing reform during the Progres-
      sive era, focusing particularly on the activities of Jacob
      Riis and Lawrence Veiller. Criticizes reformers for
      focusing on restrictive codes, rather than on constructing
      public housing and for failing to understand the connection
      between bad housing and general social conditions.

657.   Lubove, Roy. The Professional Altruist: The Emergence of
       Social Work as a Career, 1880-1930. Cambridge, Mass.:
       Harvard University Press, 1965.
            Analyzes the development of social work from the Charity
            Organization Society Movement in the 1880's through the
            gradual systematizing of social work at the hands of the
            experts with unique work skills necessitated by an in-
            creasingly urbanized society. Contends that the change
            fitted social workers to perform limited services to in-
            dividuals and groups, but not to mediate between social
            groups or mobilize resources.

658.   Lynd, Staughton. "Jane Addams and the Radical Impulse."
       Commentary 32 (July 1961): 54-59.

659.   MacLean, Annie M. Wage-Earning Women. New York:
       Macmillan, 1910.

660.   MacLean, Annie M. Women Workers and Society. Chicago:
       A. C. McClurg, 1916.

661.   Mann, Arthur. Yankee Reformers in the Urban Age: Social
       Reform in Boston, 1880-1900. New York: Harper & Row,
       1954.

662.   More, Louise Bolard. Wage Earners' Budgets: A Study of
       Standards and Cost of Living in New York City. [1907].
       New York: Arno Press, 1971.
            Completing the picture drawn by such investigators as
            Robert Chapin, the study provides a quantitative account
            of the standard of living among Blue Collar workers and
            their families in New York City. Although these families
            could cover daily expenses, they were unable to meet
            emergencies of illness or unemployment. A recognition
            of these facts was essential to the Progressive program of
            economic reform.

663.   Nassau, Mabel Louise. Old Age Poverty in Greenwich Village:
       A Neighborhood Study. New York: Fleming H. Revell, 1915.
            An important monograph on the indigent aged done as a
            community study, with a discussion of various plans pro-
            posed for caring for the aged poor, largely immigrant; a
            significant precursor of social legislation and relevant to
            continuing current concerns.

664.   [New York Association for Improving the Conditions of the
       Poor]. AICP Annual Reports Investigating Poverty, Nos. 1-
       10. [1845-1853]. New York: Arno Press, 1971.
            Perhaps the most influential charitable organization in the
            middle of the nineteenth century, the AICP set the tone for
            private relief practices for the next fifty years. Its annual
            reports describe not only the workings of the Association
            but the attitudes that underlay their program, and the
            reasons for their popularity.

665.   [New York Association for Improving the Condition of the
        Poor]. Fighting Poverty. What the A. I. C. P. Does to Elimi-
        nate the Causes of Distress and to Prevent Their Recurrence.
        New York: New York Association for Improving the Condition
        of the Poor, 1912.

666.   [New York Child Labor Committee]. A Five Years Fight for
        New York's Children, 1903-1908. New York: The Committee,
        1908.
            Child labor and the compulsory education movement. See
            also "Child Labor Reform in New York," Survey, vol. 10
            (January 10, 1903): 52-56; and Fred S. Hall, Forty Years,
            1902-1942: The Work of the New York Child Labor Com-
            mittee (1942). Also, Felix Adler, "Child Labor in the
            United States and Its Great Attendant Evils," Annals, 25
            (May 1905): 417-29; Samuel McLindsay, "Child Labor and
            the Public Schools," Annals, 29 (January 1907): 104-109;
            and Lewis M. Parker, "Compulsory Education, The Solu-
            tion of the Child Labor Problem," Annals, 32 (July 1908):
            40-56.

667.   [New York State Commission on Relief for Widowed Mothers].
        Report of the New York State Commission on Relief of Widowed
        Mothers. [Albany, 1914].
            Prepared at the request of the New York State Legislature,
            this report is a comprehensive study of aid to dependent,
            fatherless children before the Social Security Act of 1935
            expanded earlier attempts at "Mothers' pension" laws.

668.   O'Grady, John. Catholic Charities in the United States: His-
        tory and Problems. [1930]. New York: Arno Press, 1971.
            This survey of Catholic organizations traces their develop-
            ment from small parish bodies to national associations.
            The elaborate network of welfare institutions reflects both
            the special concerns of American Catholics and the in-
            fluence of the broader society.

669.   Orenstein, Marie S. "The Servo-Croats of Manhattan."
        Survey 29 (December 7, 1912): 278-280.

670.   Richmond, Mary E. Friendly Visiting Among the Poor: A
        Handbook for Charity Workers. New York: Macmillan, 1899.
        Rev. 1914.
            Also, the author's Social Diagnosis (New York: Russell
            Sage Foundation, 1917); and "What Is Charity Organization?"
            The Charities Review, 9 (1899-1900): 490-500; and What
            Is Social Case Work? (1922).

671.   Richmond, Mary E., and Fred S. Hall. A Study of Nine
        Hundred and Eighty-Five Widows Known to Certain Charity
        Organization Societies in 1910. New York: Russell Sage
        Foundation, 1913.
            A landmark investigation led by a devoted social worker,

Mary E. Richmond (1861-1928), considers the families,
working conditions, and social welfare of immigrant women
who were unfortunate enough to lose their husbands and as
a result were forced to depend on charity.

672.   Riis, Jacob A. How the Other Half Lives: Studies Among
the Tenements of New York. New York: Charles Scribner's
Sons, 1890.
A panorama of urban destitution and the social world of
the immigrant child by the Danish immigrant social reformer, Jacob August Riis (1859-1914). An edition of How
the Other Half Lives (New York: Dover Press, 1971) includes 100 photographs (taken by Riis) from the Jacob A.
Riis Collection of the Museum of the City of New York,
and should be consulted. Since printers had not yet per-
fected the halftone process of reproducing photographs in
1890, Riis's photography included in How the Other Half
Lives and in his other books were redrawn by artists.

673.   Riis, Jacob A. The Children of the Poor. New York:
Charles Scribner's Sons, 1892. Reprint. With an introduction by Francesco Cordasco, New York: Garrett Press, 1970.

674.   Riis, Jacob A. "The Children of the Poor." Scribner's
Magazine, 11 (1892): 531-56.

675.   Riis, Jacob A. "Special Needs of the Poor in New York."
The Forum, 14 (1892-93): 492-502.

676.   Riis, Jacob A. "The Tenement House Exhibition." Harper's
Weekly, 64 (1900): 104.

677.   Riis, Jacob A. A Ten Years' War. An Account of the Battle
with the Slum in New York. Boston: Houghton Mifflin, 1900.

678.   Riis, Jacob A. The Making of an American. New York:
Macmillan, 1903.

679.   Rousmaniere, John P. "Cultural Hybrid in the Slums: The
College Woman and the Settlement House, 1889-1894." American Quarterly, 32 (1970): 45-66.

680.   Scott, Anne Firor. "Jane Addams and the City." Virginia
Quarterly Review, 43 (1967): 53-62.
Considers Addams one of the earliest and most perceptive
of urban theorists, based largely upon her Hull House
experiences. Sketches the outline of her theories and the
reforms that she supported as a result.

681.   Shelton, Brenda K. Reformers in Search of Yesterday: Buf-
falo in the 1890's. Buffalo: State University of New York
Press, 1976.
Evaluates the efforts of upper-middle-class citizens to

deal with the problems of poverty, housing, public health,
education, immigration, and organized labor. Faults them
for harboring moralistic and condescending attitudes toward
minority groups and for failing to understand the real cause
of the problems they sought to solve.

682.   Simkhovitch, Mary Kingsbury.   The City Worker's World in
        America. [1917]. New York: Arno Press, 1971.
            The director of New York's Greenwich House portrays the
        urban environment at the start of the century. The per-
        vasive influence of poverty on the one hand and opportunity
        on the other are skillfully traced. She discusses the con-
        ditions in the work shop as well as in the home, the street
        and the neighborhood club. How workers contend with
        rises in the cost-of-living, language problems, generation
        gaps, Americanization, and ethnic group competition are
        carefully spelled out. There are also sections on sickness,
        child labor, immigrant women, and the lung-blocks in the
        tenement neighborhoods.

683.   Simkhovitch, Mary Kingsbury, and Elizabeth Ogg.   Quick-
        sand, the Way of Life in the Slums. Evanston, Ill.: Row,
        Peterson, 1942.

684.   Smith, Mary Gove. "Raphael in the Background: A Picture
        for Teachers of Aliens." Education, 39 (January 1919): 270-
        79.

685.   Spargo, John. The Bitter Cry of the Children. With an
        Introduction by Walter I. Trattner. Chicago: Quadrangle
        Books, 1968.
            A reprint of the 1906 edition which included an Introduction
        by Robert Hunter. See particularly, Chapter II: "The
        School Child," pp. 57-124.

686.   Speakman, Joseph M. "Unwillingly to School: Child Labor
        and Its Reform in Pennsylvania in the Progressive Era."
        Unpublished Ph.D. dissertation, Temple University, 1976.
            On the efforts of educators and social reformers to regulate
        child labor over the objections of the glass, textile, and
        mining industries. Portrays the reformers as motivated
        by a variety of concerns, and as eventually succumbing to
        the notion of making the child an efficient and well-trained
        worker.

687.   Spencer, Anna G. Woman's Share in Social Culture. New
        York: M. Kennerly, 1913. Reprint. New York: Arno
        Press, 1972.
            Collected articles by a woman preacher involved with
        problems of child labor, women and the work place, and
        prostitution.

688.   Stevens, Edward W., Jr. "Social Centers, Politics, and

Social Efficiency in the Progressive Era." History of Education Quarterly, 12 (Spring 1972): 16-33.
    Establishment of social centers ("schoolhouse social centers')
    as "an agency of adjustment--an organizational response
    to the threat of instability, uncontrolled change, and the
    loss of traditional values faced by an industrial society."
    Discusses the following: Edward J. Ward, The Social
    Center (1913); Clarence A. Perry, How to Start a Social
    Center (1914); Irving King, Education for Social Efficiency
    (1913); and David Snedden, Sociological Determination of
    Objectives in Education (1921).

689. Taylor, Graham. Religion in Social Action. With an Intro-
      duction by Jane Addams. New York: Dodd, Mead, 1913.
      An important early work in the "social gospel" movement
      which brought the churches into the battle against urban
      social ills. The author lived for twenty years at the Chi-
      cago Commons, a social settlement which he founded in
      "one of those shifting city districts in which people of a
      score of nationalities are drawn from all parts of the world
      in response to industrial opportunities . . . that too often
      exploit them but seldom unite them. . . . This book will
      doubtless be of value to men and women of all faiths who
      are eager that the current of their religion should pour
      itself into broader channels of social purpose" (Jane Addams).

690. Taylor, Mary Argyle. "Italian Industries for Women." At-
      lantic Monthly, 100 (1907): 547-552.

691. Tolman, William H., and Charles Hemstreet. The Better
      New York. New York: Baker and Taylor, 1904.
      A handbook and guide to the "many-handed philanthropies,
      as various as human needs" of New York City presented
      in a series of vignettes and informational digests on all
      of the charitable and philanthropic efforts in New York
      City at the turn of the century.

692. Tomasi, Lydio, ed. The Italian in America: The Progressive
      View, 1891-1914. New York: Center for Migration Studies,
      1972.
      Brings together out of the progressive journal Charities a
      significant corpus of materials on the milieu of the immi-
      grant child: materials on immigration, assimilation, labor
      abuses, crime and criminality, health and the scourge of
      tuberculosis. Reviewed (with other works), F. Cordasco,
      Contemporary Sociology, 3 (March 1974): 164-166.

693. Trattner, Walter I. Crusade for the Children: A History of
      the National Child Labor Committee and Child Labor Reform
      in America. Chicago: Quadrangle, 1970.
      A sociopolitical history of the crusade to abolish child
      labor with the role of the NCLC as a point of focus. See
      review by Joseph F. Kett, History of Education Quarterly,
      13 (Summer 1973): 191-194.

694. True, Ruth S. The Neglected Girl. New York: Survey Associates, 1914.

695. Tuckerman, Joseph. On the Elevation of the Poor: A Selection from His Reports as Minister at Large in Boston. [1874]. New York: Arno Press, 1971.
    A collection of sermons by one of the first ministers to leave the fixed bounds of his parish and preach to the poor wherever they could be found. Tuckerman's Boston experience was emulated in other growing cities in the Jacksonian period, and his message, sensitive to the plight of the needy, helped to awaken middle and upper class Americans to the problem.

696. Turner, George K. "The Daughters of the Poor." McClure's Magazine, 34 (1909-1910): 45-61.

697. Van Kleeck, Mary. "Child Labor in New York City Tenements." Charities, 19 (January 1908): 1405-1420.

698. Van Kleeck, Mary. Artificial Flower Makers. New York: Survey Associates, 1913.
    Sponsored by the Russell Sage Foundation for a study of largely immigrant women workers. Material on wages, working conditions, unemployment, training, and relevant legislation. Appendix includes text of state laws pertaining to women's employment.

699. Van Kleeck, Mary. Women in the Bookbinding Trades. New York: Survey Associates, 1913.

700. Van Kleeck, Mary. A Seasonal Industry: A Study of the Millinery Trade in New York. New York: Russell Sage Foundation, 1917.

701. Van Kleeck, Mary. "Women and Machines." Atlantic Monthly, 120 (February 1921): 250-60.

702. Van Vorst, Bessie, and Marie Van Vorst. The Woman Who Toils, Being the Experiences of Two Ladies as Factory Girls. New York: Doubleday, Page, 1903.
    Two upper-class women report their experiences in a Pittsburgh factory, a New York shirt factory, a Chicago theatrical costume factory, a Lynn, Massachusetts shoe factory, and a Southern cotton mill.

703. Veiller, Lawrence. Tenement House Legislation in New York, 1852-1900. Prepared for the Tenement House Commission of 1900. New York: The Commission, 1900.
    An indispensable register of legislative efforts in urban tenement reform by a leading social reformer of the Progressive Era: "Veiller, America's first professional housing reformer, not only changed the course of New York City's housing development, but influenced the housing

history of states and cities throughout the nation in the
two decades after 1900." (Lubove, The Progressives and
the Slums, p. 148).

704.   Wade, Louise C. "The Educational Dimension of the Early
Chicago Settlements." Adult Education, 17 (Spring 1967):
166-178.
See also Wade's "The Heritage from Chicago's Early Settlement Houses," Journal of the Illinois State Historical Society, 60 (1967): 42-57.

705.   Wald, Lillian D. The House on Henry Street. New York:
Henry Holt, 1915.
Lillian D. Wald (1867-1940), organizer of public health
nursing at the Henry Street Settlement in New York City.
Much of the materials in the book had appeared in the
Atlantic Monthly (March through August, 1915). A major
source on the immigrant child and his community. Lillian
Wald, Windows on Henry Street (1934). Also, the Lillian
Wald Papers are in the New York Public Library and are an
invaluable collection for study of the settlement movement
and all aspects of social reform.

706.   Walling, William E. "What the People of the East Side Do."
University Settlement Studies Quarterly, 1 (July 1903): 79-85.

707.   Ward, Edward J. The Social Center. New York: D. Apple-
ton, 1915.
Making the school a center of community life to promote
Americanization of the immigrant poor.

708.   Warner, Amos. American Charities: A Study in Philanthropy
and Economics. New York: Thomas Y. Crowell, 1894. Revised 1908, 1919. Reprint. New York: Arno Press, 1971.
A standard text of the period on poverty and charity which
emphasized hereditary weakness. Important for understanding attitudes toward poverty and the immigrant child and
woman.

709.   Watson, Frank D. The Charity Organization Movement in the
United States: A Study in American Philanthropy. New York:
Macmillan, 1922. Reprint. New York: Arno Press, 1971.
A comprehensive history of the charity organization movement dealing with foreign antecedents; antecedents in the
United States; functions, principles and methods; beginnings;
extension of the movement (1883-1895); movements for the
prevention of poverty (1896-1904); nationalization of the
movement (1905-1921); social case work; tests of efficiency;
prejudices, criticisms, and philosophy. Includes a valuable
bibliography.

710.   Weinstein, Gregory. The Ardent Eighties. With a Foreword
by Lillian D. Wald. New York: International Press, 1928.
An intimate portrayal of life in the urban ethnic subcom-

munity; the world of work in late nineteenth century urban America; with biographical and critical accounts of social reformers, e.g., Stanton Coit, Henry George, Felix Adler, Lillian Wald, Josephine Shaw Lowell.

711. Weller, Charles Frederick. Neglected Neighbors. Stories of Life in the Alleys, Tenements and Shanties of the National Capital. Philadelphia: John C. Winston, 1908.

712. White, G. C. "Social Settlements and Immigrant Neighbors, 1886-1914." Social Service Review, 33 (March 1959): 55-66.

713. Wilson, Otto, in collaboration with Robert South Barrett. Fifty Years' Work with Girls, 1883-1933: A Story of the Florence Crittenton Homes. [1933]. New York: Arno Press, 1974.
      In 1883 Charles Crittenton founded the first Florence Crittenton Mission in New York City for the rescue of prostitutes and wayward girls. Under the leadership of Kate Waller Barrett (1858-1925), Crittenton's assistant and successor as president of the National Mission, the homes became refuges for expectant unwed mothers. By 1933 there were 65 Florence Crittenton Homes located across the country. Contains histories of the national organization and the individual homes, along with biographical sketches of Crittenton and Mrs. Barrett.

714. Woods, Robert A. Americans in Progress: A Settlement Study of Residents and Associates of the South End House. New York: Riverside Press, 1903.

715. Woods, Robert A., ed. The City Wilderness: A Settlement Study by Residents and Associates of the South End House. Boston: Houghton Mifflin, 1898. Reprint. New York: Arno Press, 1972.
      The South End district of Boston was a working class neighborhood of Irish, Jews, Germans, Italians, as well as white American born citizens. There was no such desperate poverty as in Charles Booth's London slums or in the worst areas of New York City; only about 10 percent of the people in the South End were very poor. Nevertheless, as these essays show, there were serious problems of unemployment, unsanitary conditions, dilapidated and unhealthy housing with inadequate facilities. More detrimental than helpful was the political machine, and in a particularly perceptive essay, "The Roots of Political Power," the relationship of the machine to the saloon, boys' gangs, and various other social groups is made vividly clear. Among the many suggestions put forth for the improvement of the neighborhood are the extension of educational opportunities for talented children, destruction of the worst tenements, a full-scale attack on prostitution and the saloons, and the federation and cooperation of

charitable organizations, other settlement agencies, and
churches of all faiths.

716.   Woods, Robert A., and Albert J. Kennedy, eds. Handbook
of Settlements. New York: Charities Publication Committee,
1911. Reprint. New York: Arno Press, 1974.
Compiled at the height of the settlement house movement
by one of the movement's most effective members and
organizers, this book offers the most comprehensive listing
available of settlement houses throughout the United States.
It also enumerates the activities of each settlement house.
An important reference, it illustrates the size and scope
of the settlement house movement and leads to a realization
of the enormous influence Progressive era reformers had
on the neighborhoods of the nation.

717.   Woods, Robert A. The Neighborhood in Nation-Building: The
Running Comment of Thirty Years at the South End House.
[1923]. New York: Arno Press, 1974.
Robert Woods had a long and rich experience in neighborhood settlement service. He trained at Toynbee Hall in
London and was instrumental in the development of South
End House in Boston. Includes articles and addresses
written and delivered over a period of thirty years; deals
chiefly with the methods and results in city settlements,
especially with those of South End House, and is a record
of the milestones in his career. In The University Settlement Idea (1892) he argues that a college or university has
an obligation to work for social improvement. Another
essay argues that recreational, health, educational, and
infant welfare services ought to be provided for the community. An important source for an understanding of the
aims and achievements of settlement houses.

718.   Woods, Robert A., et al. The Poor in Great Cities: Their
Problems and What Is Doing to Solve Them. New York:
Charles Scribner's Sons, 1895. Reprint. With a New Foreword by Sol Cohen. New York: Garrett Press, 1970.
Casting new light on the transformation of American attitudes toward the poor, this noted collection of essays
contains some of the earliest and freshest reactions of
Progressive reformers to poverty. The scope is wide,
ranging from descriptions of the poor in Chicago and Boston
to developments in Naples and London, from tenements to
the fresh air fund, from settlement houses to boys' clubs.

719.   Woods, Robert A., and Albert J. Kennedy. The Settlement
Horizon: A National Estimate. [1922]. New York: Arno
Press, 1974.
This book is a comprehensive account of the work of the
settlement houses from their inception in England in the
1880's through to 1922. Settlement houses dealt with a
variety of problems caused by the industrial revolution,

the mass influx of immigrants, and the congestion of the
cities.   Classes in English, courses in industrial trades,
summer camps and kindergartens were offered by the
settlement house.   Settlements also undertook to organize
consumer cooperatives, establish pure milk depots, infant
welfare centers, and a visiting nurse service.   In politics
the settlement worked for improved public schools, cleaner
streets, more efficient garbage removal, public baths, more
branch libraries, and the elimination of prostitution and
the saloon.   Reviews the history of the settlement house,
evaluates its accomplishments, and surveys the social
problems as yet untackled by the settlement house.

720.   Woods, Robert A., and Albert J. Kennedy, eds.   Young
       Working Girls.   A Summary of Evidence from Two Thousand
       Social Workers.   With an Introduction by Jane Addams.   Bos-
       ton and New York: Houghton Mifflin, 1913.
       An inquiry undertaken upon the formation of the National
       Federation of Settlements in 1911.   "It is possible in
       keeping with the multiple object of the study, that it records
       the experiences of more than two thousand people who are
       daily concerned with the welfare of young girls, and that
       these experiences gathered from a score of cities fall so
       easily into a composite impression" (Jane Addams).

721.   Woolf, Michael Angelo.   Sketches of Lowly Life in a Great
       City.   New York: G. P. Putnam's Sons, 1899.

722.   Wright, Carroll D.   The Working Girls of Boston.   [1889].
       New Introduction by Leon Stein and Philip Taft.   New York:
       Arno Press, 1971.
       The Bureau of Labor was created in the Department of
       the Interior in 1884 at which time Carroll Wright was
       named as the first Commissioner.   His book is an actual
       case study which fully outlines the working situations of
       girls in Boston, detailing their occupations, income, and
       financial difficulties, and consequently destroying the widely
       held view that loose behavior is characteristic of working
       women.   For example, he found that of the 39,000 women
       employed in Boston in 1880, some 20,000 were in occupa-
       tions other than domestic service, and of those, 69 percent
       lived at home.

V. THE FAMILY, IMMIGRANT CHILD, AND EDUCATIONAL INFLUENCES

723. Abbott, Clarence. "On the Education of the Immigrant." American Leader, 3 (June 1913): 698-701.

724. Abbott, Edith, and Sophonisba Breckinridge. Truancy and Non-Attendance in the Chicago Schools. Chicago: University of Chicago Press, 1917. Reprint. New York: Arno Press, 1974.

"If compulsory education laws were needed for the education of the native American, they are doubly needed for the immigrant who today needs to learn not only our language, but also the principles of our democracy, if these principles are to endure and the promise of American life is not to be obscured." See also The Delinquent Child and the Home: A Study of the Delinquent Wards of the Juvenile Courts of Chicago (New York: Russell Sage Foundation, 1912). One of the greatest achievements of Progressive Era reformers was the passage of strong compulsory education legislation in many states. Their principle problem though, especially in the cities, was to get the law enforced and accepted by the people. In Chicago and its suburbs, as in most other large cities, the poverty and immigrant background of the population were major obstacles to acceptance, immigrants often did not understand that education in Chicago was free and that compulsory education meant regular and not merely occasional attendance. This excellent study by two famous members of the University of Chicago faculty describes how the appropriate legislation was passed, how it worked, and what additional legislation was needed. Among their more concrete suggestions, Abbott and Breckinridge recommended that the minimum working age for children be raised from fourteen to sixteen, that a reform school for girls be established, and that all illiterate minors be forced to attend continuation school until the age of twenty-one.

725. [Abbott, Grace]. The Educational Needs of Immigrants in Illinois. Bulletin of the Immigration Commission. Springfield, Ill.: The Immigration Commission, 1920.

726. Abbott, Grace. The Immigrant and the Community. New York: Century Publishing, 1917.

727. Ade, Lester K. Home Classes for Foreign Born Mothers.

Harrisburg: Commonwealth of Pennsylvania Department of
Public Instruction Bulletin 295, 1939.

728.   [American Association for the Study and Prevention of Infant
Mortality].   Transactions of the First Annual Meeting of the
American Association for the Study and Prevention of Infant
Mortality. [1910].   New York: Arno Press, 1974.
The Association, formed as a result of a conference held
at New Haven in 1909, chose J. H. Mason Knox as its
first President.   Knox, who taught at Johns Hopkins University and directed Maryland's child health program, was
one of the pioneers in the child health movement.   At the
meeting important addresses and papers were presented
by such notables as Irving Fisher (Yale University), William
Welch (Johns Hopkins), Abraham Jacobi, and John Fulton
(then at Johns Hopkins, subsequently at Yale).   There was
a significant discussion of "Municipal, State and Federal
Prevention of Infant Mortality."   The Association advocated
establishment of a Federal Department of Health, within
which there would be a Department of Child Hygiene.   It
issued an attack on the "League for Medical Freedom"
which opposed public medical programs.

729.   Atzmon, Ezri.   "The Educational Programs for Immigrants
in the United States."   History of Education Journal 9 (September 1958):   75-80.

730.   Bahr, Ingeborg.   Generational Conflict in Immigrant Families
in Five Norwegian-American Novels.   M. A. thesis presented
to the Department of English, University of Oslo, Fall Term
1981.
Surveys the relationships between first-generation Norwegian
immigrant parents and their children in five novels: Ole
Rölvaag's Peder Victorious and Their Father's God and
three novels written by second-generation immigrant women;
Borghild Margarethe Dahl's Homecoming, Kathryn Forbes'
Mama's Bank Account, and Margarethe Erdahl Shank's
The Coffee Train.   The relationship between immigrant
mothers and their sons is contrasted with that of mothers
and their daughters.

731.   Ballard, Walter.   "Adult Education in New York City."   Journal of Education, 68 (November 1908):   540-541.

732.   Banfield, Edward C.   The Moral Basis of a Backward Society.
New York: Free Press, 1958.
A study of southern Italian society and family life which
advances a theory of "amoral familism," that is, an ethos
"which has been produced by three factors acting in combination: a high death rate, certain land tenure conditions,
and the absence of the institution of the extended family."
Reference should be made to Charlotte G. Chapman, Milocca:
A Sicilian Village (1971), a study undertaken in 1928, written
in 1935, and published in 1971 which does not use Banfield's

conceptual approach; and to Feliks Gross, Il Paese: Values and Social Change in an Italian Village (1973).

733. Barron, Milton L. People Who Intermarry: Intermarriage in a New England Industrial Community. Syracuse, N.Y.: Syracuse University Press, 1946.
A sociological study, based on official records, questionnaires, interviews, and correspondence of marriages involving different ethnic and religious groups in Derby, Conn., during 1929-1930 and 1940. The Jews, "one of the most endogamous religious groups," had no instance of intermarriage in 1929-1930 and only one in 1940. During 1900-1935, with few exceptions, "all rates of Jewish intermarriage were found to be low, most of them ranging from one per cent to ten per cent. Almost everywhere Jewish men intermarry more than Jewish women" (p. 341). Annotated bibliography.

734. Bayer, Alan E. The Assimilation of American Family Patterns by European Immigrants and Their Children. New York: Arno Press, 1980.
Attempts to establish the degree of assimilation of American family life by second generation European immigrants and specify some conditions and factors that affect the degree of assimilation. Data from the U.S. Bureau of the Census one in 1,000 sample of the 1960 population of the United States are used to compare four family variables (marital status, nuclear-extended family membership, age at first marriage, and number of children) of white native Americans with native parents to those of second generation European immigrants, and those of foreign-born European immigrants. Age, sex, rural-urban residence, socioeconomic score, and region of European origin are controlled in all analyses. Conclusions: The second generation immigrants have most readily adopted the American family value system regarding family size, followed by family membership status, marital status, and, finally, age at first marriage. However, the distribution of all of these family patterns in the foreign stock is different from that of the natives, indicating that the assimilation of basic American institutional patterns is not completed by the second generation and that several more generations may be necessary to completely eradicate any differences. Originally, Ph.D. dissertation, Florida State University, 1965.

735. Beecher, Catharine. Letters to Persons Who Are Engaged in Domestic Service. New York: Leavitt & Trow, 1842.

736. Berkson, Isaac B. Theories of Americanization: A Critical Study with Special Reference to the Jewish Group. New York: Teachers College, Columbia University, 1920. Reprint. New York: Arno Press, 1970.

Published as No. 109 in Teachers College Contributions to Education. A classic statement of the case for cultural pluralism in American Education.

737.   Berman, Louis A. Jews and Intermarriage: A Study in Personality and Culture. New York: Thomas Yoseloff, 1968. A detailed study of the various problems and issues of Jewish-Christian marriages in the United States in the light of researches in the behavioral sciences. The author's viewpoint is that "intermarriage per se is not a threat to Jewish survival."

738.   Bernard, William S., ed. Americanization Studies: The Acculturation of Immigrant Groups into American Society. Montclair, N.J.: Patterson Smith, 1971. 10 vols. Vol. I: Schooling of the Immigrant. By Frank V. Thompson, with a general introduction to the republished studies by William S. Bernard, and a new introduction by Clarence Senior; Vol. II: America via the Neighborhood. By John Daniels, with a new introduction by Florence G. Cassidy; Vol. III: Old World Traits Transplanted. By William I. Thomas, together with Robert E. Park and Herbert A. Miller, with a new introduction by Donald R. Young; Vol. IV: A Stake in the Land. By Peter A. Speek, with a new introduction by Rabel J. Burdge and Everett M. Rogers; Vol. V: Immigrant Health and the Community. By Michael M. Davis, Jr., with a new introduction by Raymond F. O'Dowd; Vol. VI: New Homes for Old. By Sophonisba P. Breckinridge, with a new introduction by William S. Bernard; Vol. VII: The Immigrant Press and Its Control. By Robert E. Park, with a new introduction by Read Lewis; Vol. VIII: Americans by Choice. By John Palmer Gavit, with a new introduction by William S. Bernard; Vol. IX: The Immigrant's Day in Court. By Kate Holladay Claghorn, with a new introduction by Ann S. Petluck; Vol. X: Adjusting Immigrant and Industry. By William M. Leiserson, with a new introduction by Gerd Korman. See review of series, Milton Gordon, Social Forces, 54 (December 1975): 470-474.

739.   Berrol, Selma C. "Education and the Italian and Jewish Community Experience." In Jean Scarpaci, ed., The Interaction Between Italians and Jews in America. (New York: American Italian Historical Association, 1975), pp. 31-41.

740.   Berrol, Selma C. Immigrants at School: New York City, 1898-1914. New York: Arno Press, 1978. In this study of immigrant Jewish and Italian children in New York City schools, Berrol provides invaluable historical backgrounds on the responses of American schools to the culturally different and language-minority child. The objectives of the study were to find out what changes were made in the educational structure of the city under the

pressure of the Italian and Jewish immigrant groups, and
to determine "if there were any clues to the viability of
the New York City schools of today ascertainable in the
developments of sixty years ago." Among the many new
educational programs initiated during the period (intended
largely to assimilate the immigrant child), discusses the
"Grade C" classes, rudimentary beginnings of bilingual
education, intended for the non-English speaking child.
Originally, Ph.D. dissertation, City University of New
York, 1967.

741.   Berrol, Selma C. "Immigrants at School: New York City,
        1900-1910." Urban Education, 4 (October 1969): 220-230.

742.   Berrol, Selma C. "Education in New York City: 1900-1920."
        Illinois Quarterly, 35 (1973): 20-30.
        Contends that during the period of heavy immigration into
        New York City, the public schools served an important
        role in the behavioral assimilation of immigrant children,
        thus minimizing social disorder, crime, and ethnic con-
        flict, and, therefore, preserving the stability of the hetero-
        geneous city.

743.   Bierstadt, Edward H. Aspects of Americanization. Cincin-
        nati: National Americanization Committee, 1922.
        A critic of the Americanization movement. See also his
        "Pseudo-Americanization," The New Republic, 26 (May 25,
        1921): 371-373, and 27 (June 1, 1921): 19-23.

744.   Blegen, Theodore C. "Immigrant Women and the American
        Frontier." Norwegian-American Studies and Records, 5 (1930):
        26-29.

745.   Bloch, Harriet. "Changing Domestic Roles Among Polish
        Immigrant Women." Anthropological Quarterly, 49 (Jan. 1976):
        3-10.
        Argues that while immigration did not diminish the economic
        importance of Polish women in the family, it may have
        had a negative effect on the quality of women's lives by
        interfering with community solidarity and limiting their
        opportunities for interaction with other women and even
        with their own children.

746.   Bogue, Mary. Administration of Mothers Aid in Ten Locali-
        ties: With Special Reference to Health, Housing, Education,
        and Recreation. United States Department of Labor Children's
        Bureau Publication No. 184. Washington, D.C.: Government
        Printing Office, 1928.

747.   Boulette-Ramirez, T. Determining Needs and Appropriate
        Counseling Approaches for Mexican-American Women: A Com-
        parison of Therapeutic Listening and Behavioral Research.
        San Francisco: R. & E. Research Associates, 1976.

748.   Breckinridge, Sophonisba P. The Family and the State: Select Documents. [1934]. New York: Arno Press, 1972.
A collection of documents tracing the changing legal and social relationship between the family and the broader society. Compiled by one of the leading scholars of social work, this volume treats such subjects as marriage and divorce, the legal position of the child, adoption, illegitimacy, desertion, and the legal rights of women. An invaluable introduction to the study of the family in American society.

749.   Breed, R. L. "Italians Fight Tuberculosis." Survey, 23 (February 12, 1910): 702-3.

750.   Bremner, Robert H. , ed. Care of Dependent Children in the Late Nineteenth and Early Twentieth Centuries. New York: Arno Press, 1974.
Includes the following:
(a) John C. Ferris, Child Helping in Tennessee (Reprinted from Proceedings of the National Conference of Charities and Corrections, 1883), Boston, 1883;
(b) Elbridge T. Gerry, The Relation of Societies for the Prevention of Cruelty to Children to Child-Saving Work (Reprinted from Proceedings of the National Conference of Charities and Corrections, 1882), Madison, Wisconsin, 1883;
(c) Hastings H. Hart, Placing Out Children in the West (Reprinted from Proceedings of the National Conference of Charities and Corrections, 1884), Boston, 1884;
(d) Lyman P. Alden, The Shady Side of the "Placing-Out System" (Reprinted from Proceedings of the National Conference of Charities and Corrections, 1885), Boston, 1885;
(e) Josephine Shaw Lowell, Report on the Institutions for the Care of Destitute Children of the City of New York (Reprinted from New York State Board of Charities Annual Report for the Year 1885), Albany, New York, 1886;
(f) C. D. Randall, Michigan: The Child; The State (Reprinted from Proceedings of the National Conference of Charities and Corrections, 1888), Boston, 1888;
(g) S. J. Hathaway, Children's Homes in Ohio (Reprinted from Proceedings of the National Conference of Charities and Corrections, 1890), Boston, 1890).
(h) Homer Folks, The Child and the Family (Reprinted from Proceedings of the National Conference of Charities and Corrections, 1892), Boston, 1892;
(i) Homer Folks, The Removal of Children from Almshouses (Reprinted from Proceedings of the National Conference of Charities and Corrections, 1894), Boston, 1894;
(j) William Pryor Letchworth, Dependent Children and Family Homes (Reprinted from Proceedings of the National Conference of Charities and Corrections, 1897), Boston, 1897;

(k) John G. Shortall, Child-Saving Work of the Humane
Societies (Reprinted from Proceedings of the National Conference of Charities and Corrections, 1897), Boston, 1897;
(l) Robert W. Hebberd, Placing out Children: Dangers
of Careless Methods (Reprinted from Proceedings of the
National Conference of Charities and Corrections, 1899),
Boston, 1899;
(m) Charles Richmond Henderson, The Relief and Care
of Dependent Children (Reprinted from Introduction to the
Study of the Dependent, Defective, and Delinquent Classes),
Boston, 1901;
(n) Mrs. Glendower Evans, What Do You Know of the
Children After They Leave Your Home or Institution: Do
You Supervise Them? (Reprinted from Proceedings of the
National Conference of Charities and Corrections, 1907),
Boston, 1907;
(o) Hastings H. Hart, The Care of the Dependent Child
in the Family (Reprinted from The Pedagogical Seminary,
Vol. XVI, 1909), Worcester, Mass., 1909.
The collection contains fifteen articles, many of them
originally presented as papers at annual meetings of the
National Conference of Charities and Corrections. The
period covered is the quarter of a century before the first
(1909) White House Conference on Dependent Children. The
authors include H. H. Hart, Homer Folks, William Pryor
Letchworth, Josephine Shaw Lowell and other leading figures
in child-saving movements. The articles discuss methods
of care in use in different states and communities, progress
in removal of children from almshouses, and the need for
better procedures and more care in child placement. Lowell's
report on care of destitute children in New York City,
prepared for the New York State Board of Charities, is a
graphic account of living conditions, daily routine, and educational training programs in institutional "homes."

751.   Bremner, Robert H., ed. Children's Bureau Studies. New
        York: Arno Press, 1974. With an Introduction by William
        M. Schmidt.
        Includes the following:
        (a) Emma Duke, Infant Mortality: Results of a Field
        Study in Johnstown, Pa., Based on Births in One Calendar
        Year (Reprinted from Children's Bureau Publication No. 9),
        Washington, D. C., 1915;
        (b) Grace L. Meigs, Maternal Mortality from All Con-
        ditions Connected with Childbirth in the United States and
        Certain Other Countries (Reprinted from Miscellaneous
        Series No. 6, Children's Bureau Publication No. 19), Wash-
        ington, D. C., 1917;
        (c) Lydia Roberts, The Nutrition and Care of Children
        in a Mountain County of Kentucky (Reprinted from U.S.
        Children's Bureau Publication No. 110), Washington, D. C.,
        1922;
        (d) U. S. Children's Bureau, Maternal Deaths: A Brief

Report of a Study Made in Fifteen States (Reprinted from Children's Bureau Publication No. 221), Washington, D.C., 1933;

(e) D[ouglas] A. Thom, Habit Clinics for Child Guidance (Reprinted from Children's Bureau Publication No. 135), Washington, D.C., 1939.

This collection contains the first scientific study of infant mortality by the Children's Bureau; two major investigations of maternal mortality which concluded that "infancy cannot be protected without the protection of maternity"; a landmark nutrition survey vividly written and spiced with comments from the mountain people whom it concerns; and a report, with many case illustrations, on the organization, work and value of child guidance clinics by an early worker in the child mental health movement.

752.   Bremner, Robert H., ed. The United States Children's Bureau, 1912-1972. New York: Arno Press, 1974.
Includes the following:

(a) Julia C. Lathrop, The Children's Bureau (Reprinted from Proceedings of the National Conference of Charities and Correction, 1912), Fort Wayne, Indiana, 1912;

(b) Grace Abbott, Ten Years Work for Children (Reprinted from U.S. Children's Bureau, 1923), Washington, D.C., 1923;

(c) Dorothy E. Bradbury, Five Decades of Action for Children: A History of the Children's Bureau, Washington, D.C., 1962;

(d) Frederick Green, et al., Anniversary Issue: Sixty Years of Service to Children: Children's Bureau 1912-1972 (Reprinted from Children Today March-April 1972), Washington, D.C., 1972.

The Children's Bureau was established by an act of Congress in 1912 and charged with responsibility to "investigate and report . . . upon all matters pertaining to the welfare of children and child life among all classes of our people . . . ." Under the brilliant leadership of Julia Lathrop, Grace Abbott, Katharine Lenroot, and Martha Eliot, the Bureau was the most important federal agency promoting the health and welfare of children and young people. These concise and informative summaries of the Bureau's activities are the work of women and men who were prominently associated with the Bureau in the first sixty years of its history.

753.   Briggs, John W. An Italian Passage: Immigrants to Three American Cities, 1890-1930. New Haven, Conn.: Yale University Press, 1978.
Considerable attention to the Italian immigrant family and the patterns of adjustment. See review, F. Cordasco, American Historical Review, 84 (February 1979): 267-268.

754.   Brindisi, Rocco. "The Italian and Public Health." Charities, 12 (May 7, 1904): 483-86.

755.   Brudno, Ezra S. "The Russia Jew Americanized." World's
        Work, 8 (March 1904): 4555-4567.

756.   Butler, Fred C. Community Americanization. Bureau of
        Education. Bulletin, 1919, No. 76. Washington: Govern-
        ment Printing Office, 1920.

757.   Butler, Fred C. State Americanization: The Part of the State
        in the Education and Assimilation of the Immigrant. Bureau
        of Education, Bulletin, 1919, No. 77. Washington: Govern-
        ment Printing Office, 1920.

758.   Buxbaum, Edwin C. The Greek American Group of Tarpon
        Springs, Florida: A Study of Ethnic Identification and Ac-
        culturation. New York: Arno Press, 1980.
            The study of the acculturation process of a Greek-American
        group and those factors affecting Greek ethnic identity. The
        main objective of the study is to examine basic assumptions
        of the social structure from the viewpoint of social inter-
        action and cultural equilibrium. A synchronic and dia-
        chronic presentation is used in applying a model of "organic"
        similarity and for the testing of a hypothesis on social
        stability and cultural continuity. Hypothesis postulates that
        in the United States, the identity of an ethnic group will
        be maintained only as long as it practices group endogamy,
        uses an ethnic language, and is affiliated with an ethnic
        church. In order to make use of the organic model, the
        ethnic group is treated as a simple organism. The his-
        torical background of Tarpon Springs is presented only as
        an aid in understanding the Greeks and their way of life
        in America. Aspects of geography, biology, demography,
        sponge fishing, technology, and economic, social, and re-
        ligious activities are central categories for the ethnographic
        description. Strong emphasis is placed on the economic
        practices, and the decline of sponge marketing because (1)
        it contributed to the economic decline of the group, (2) it
        has affected their ethnic identity, and (3) it has radically
        changed the third generation. Internal social factionalism
        supported by strong island loyalties and stereotypes of each
        other have been responsible for internal disunity and change.
        Originally, Ph.D. dissertation, University of Pennsylvania,
        1967.

759.   Caliandro, Gloria. "The Visiting Nurse Movement in the
        Borough of Manhattan, 1877-1917." Unpublished Ph.D. dis-
        sertation, Columbia University, 1970.
            Valuable materials on Health needs of immigrant women
        and children.

760.   Campisi, Paul J. "Ethnic Family Patterns: The Italian
        Family in the United States." American Journal of Sociology,
        53 (1948): 444-446.

761. Carillo-Beron, C. Traditional Family Idealogy in Relation to
      Chicano and Anglo Women. San Francisco: R and E Research
      Associates, 1974.

762. Carlson, Robert A. "Americanization as an Early Twentieth-
      Century Adult Education Movement." History of Education
      Quarterly, 10 (Winter 1970): 440-464.

763. Cellini, Leo. "Emigration, the Italian Family, and Changing
      Roles." In Betty Boyd Caroli, Richard F. Harney, and Lydio
      F. Tomasi, eds. The Italian Immigrant Woman in North
      America (Toronto: The Multicultural History Society, 1978),
      pp. 273-287.
          Presents a discussion of the role of emigration in the shap-
      ing of Italian kinship in North America and in Italy. This
      paper maintains that the Italian family is best represented
      by a dynamic model, not a static one, as a result of the
      role of the Italian family in emigration and the consequential
      social, economic, and political change. Suggests that the
      substantiation of western theory with Italian-based data is
      a result of a tautological approach which stems from ob-
      servations of the Italo-American experience and then of
      the Italian experience with the exclusion of the relationship
      between them. Such an approach is a narrow one which
      results in a limited geographic view of Italian kinship, there-
      by excluding the existent social, political, and economic
      ties which transcend geographical boundaries. Articulates
      the Italian family within a diachronic methodological frame-
      work in the context of such Italian regional differences as
      land fertility and land tenure systems.

764. Chang, L. L. "Acculturation and Emotional Adjustment of
      Chinese Women Immigrants." Unpublished Ph. D. dissertation,
      Columbia University, 1980.

765. Chin, A. S. "Adaptive Role of Chinese Women in the United
      States." Chinese Society of America Bulletin, 14 (January
      1979): 183-196.

766. Clopper, Edward N. Child Labor in City Streets. New York:
      Macmillan, 1912. Reprint. With an Introduction by Louis
      A. Romano. New York: Garrett Press, 1970.
          Regulation of child labor in the street trades--newspaper
      selling, shoe shining, peddling, messenger and delivery
      work--was one of the most controversial aspects of child
      labor reform. Clopper (1879-1953), secretary of the Na-
      tional Child Labor Committee for the Mississippi Valley,
      draws parallels between children's street work and other
      problems, compares the extent of children's street labor
      in the United States to comparable work in Europe, and
      discusses the regulation of street trading here and abroad.

767. Cody, F. "Americanization Courses in the Public Schools."
      English Journal, 7 (December 1918): 615-622.

126   The Immigrant Woman

768.   Cohen, David K. "Immigrants and the Schools." Review of
       Educational Research, 40 (1970): 13-27.
       Not really a "review" of the research, but, rather, an
       overview of the immigrant child and the IQ retardation,
       and measures of cognitive progress.

769.   Cohen, Fannia. "Twelve Years of Educational Activities of
       the International Ladies Garment Workers Union." American
       Federationist, 36 (1929): 105-111.

770.   Cohen, Fannia. "Educational and Social Activities of the Inter-
       national Ladies Garment Workers Union." American Feder-
       ationist, 36 (1929): 1446-1452.

771.   Cohen, Helen L. "Americanization by Classroom Practice."
       Teachers College Record, 20 (1919): 238-249.

772.   Cohen, Miriam. "Italian-American Women in New York City,
       1900-1950," in Milton Cantor and Bruce Laurie, eds. Class,
       Sex, and the Women Worker (Westport, Conn.: Greenwood
       Press, 1977), pp. 132-151.

773.   Cohen, Miriam. "From Workshop to Office: Italian Women
       and Family Strategies in New York City: 1900-1950." Un-
       published Ph.D. dissertation, University of Michigan, 1978.

774.   Concistrè, Marie J. "Adult Education in a Local Area: A
       Study of a Decade in the Life and Education of the Adult Im-
       migrant in East Harlem, New York City." Unpublished Ph.D.
       dissertation, New York University, 1943.
       Describes the full "round-of-life" of the Italian subcom-
       munity in East Harlem. Provides detailed vignettes of
       Italian traditions and heritages, the Italian family, language
       difficulties of immigrant groups, Italians and politics, eco-
       nomic status and housing, mobility and social effects, and
       the multiplicity of religious institutions which flourished.

775.   [Conference on the Care of Dependent Children]. Proceedings
       of the Conference on the Care of Dependent Children, Held at
       Washington, D.C., January 25, 1909. (60th Congress, 2nd
       Session, Senate Document No. 721). New York: Arno Press,
       1971.
       Convened by Theodore Roosevelt, this conference brought
       together practically every leading social reformer of the
       Progressive period. Their proposals for treating an esti-
       mated 168,000 needy and institutionalized children helped
       to revolutionize practices, and indicated, that for the first
       time, poverty would not be reason enough to break up a
       family.

776.   Cordasco, Francesco. "The Children of Immigrants in
       Schools: Historical Analogues of Educational Deprivation."
       Journal of Negro Education, 42 (Winter 1973): 44-53.

Limits itself to the experience in New York City, and largely to the period 1890-1915.

777. Cordasco, Francesco, ed. Italians in the City: Health and Related Social Needs. New York: Arno Press, 1975.
Includes Antonio Mangano, The Italian Colonies of New York City (1903); Antonio Stella, The Effects of Urban Congestion on Italian Women and Children (1908); John C. Gebhart, The Growth and Development of Italian Children in New York City (1924); and Some Health Problems of Italians in New York City: A Preliminary Survey (1934).

778. Cordasco, Francesco, and Eugene Bucchioni. The Puerto Rican Community and Its Children on the Mainland: A Source Book for Teachers, Social Workers and Other Professionals. 3rd ed. Metuchen, N.J.: Scarecrow Press, 1982.

779. Cordasco, Francesco. "Summer Camp Education for Underprivileged Children." School & Society, 93 (Summer 1965): 299-300.
On the Edgewater Creche (founded 1890) "to provide summer season Fresh Air day resorts near the City of New York for . . . poor children." See (New York) Evening Post, June 7, 1907.

780. Costantakos, Chrysie Mamalakis. The American-Greek Subculture: Processes of Continuity. New York: Arno Press, 1980.
An investigation into the American-Greek subculture that stresses "hypothesis generation" rather than "hypothesis testing" among both migrants and native-born Greek Americans of the second and third generations. Areas of subcultural continuity explored include factors in the current setting such as ethnic identification in its various manifestations, ethnic language preservation, church adherence, endogamy, community involvement, and family and kin; and origin factors such as region from Greece, or urban or rural residence prior to migration to the United States. Study took place in a metropolitan Greek community and resulted in several hypotheses concerning acculturation processes; values, attitudes, and antagonisms between native-born Greek Americans and recent migrants; and the typology of the subculture family. Originally, Ph.D. dissertation, Columbia University, 1971.

781. Covello, Leonard. "A High School and Its Immigrant Community." Journal of Educational Sociology, 9 (February 1936): 333-346.
Benjamin Franklin High School, East Harlem, New York City.

782. Covello, Leonard. The Social Background of the Italo-American School Child. A Study of the Southern Italian Family Mores

<u>and Their Effect on the School Situation in Italy and America</u>.
Edited and with an Introduction by F. Cordasco. Leiden:
E. J. Brill, 1967; Totowa, N.J.: Rowman and Littlefield,
1972.

A major study of ethnicity, of the school and the context
of poverty, of a minority's children, and of the challenges
to the American school. Part I: Social Background in
Italy; Part II: The Family as the Social World of the
Southern Italian <u>Contadino</u> Society; Part III: Italian Family
Mores and their Educational Implications; Part IV: Summary and Conclusions. "In view of the economic significance of the wife which is found in the general attitude of
the husband, and partly in the survival of ancient customs,
one may seriously hesitate to accept the position of the
southern Italian wife as one of utter subservience to the
husband. It must be admitted that the priority of the male
was so strongly imprinted in the communal mores that no
doubt exists in regard to the position of women. But just
as a line was drawn between the dominance of the male
parent because of his being the oldest male and his dominance because of his fatherhood, so there is reason to con-
jecture that the wife's subordination as a female and as a
mother are two different aspects of one and the same
function. In other words, despite the many signs to the
contrary, the traditional patterns provided for the mother
of a southern Italian <u>contadino</u> family a great deal of auth-
ority, much more than has been commonly attributed to
her. The assumed subservience of the mother seems all
too often to have been derived from observing the general
status of women; the real position of the mother acquires
proportions which are contrary to this assumption" (p.206).

783.   Covotsos, Louis John. "Child Welfare and Social Progress:
        A History of the United States Children's Bureau, 1912-1935."
        Unpublished Ph.D. dissertation, University of Chicago, 1976.
        Presents the bureau as a complex series of interrelated
        publicly and privately conducted activities in such areas
        as health, labor, dependency, delinquency, neglect, physical
        and mental handicap, recreation, and education. Evaluates
        the interactions among women reformers, social workers,
        and government bureaucrats.

784.   Crandall, J. A., et al. "Existing Programs for Orientation
        of Women Refugees and Migrants." <u>Migration Today</u>, 10
        (1982): 33-42.

785.   Crispino, James. <u>The Assimilation of Ethnic Groups: The
        Italian Case</u>. New York: Center for Migration Studies, 1980.
        A study of the assimilation process as it applies to Italian
        Americans. Its purpose is to determine whether and to
        what extent the Italian ethnic group has lost its corporate
        identity, has become acculturated to the larger society's
        cultural and value system and has assimilated into its social

structure. It is intended to specify the areas of social
life and the degree to which Italians have become less
"Italian." The research is basically a study of intra-ethnic
cultural and social structure, with emphasis on cultural
traditions and social participation in the neighborhood, in
friendship groups, and in marriage partner selection. Originally, Ph. D. dissertation, Columbia University, 1977.

786.   D'Andrea, Vaneeta-Marie. "The Social Role Identity of Italian-
American Women: An Analysis and Comparison of Familial
and Religious Expectations." In Richard N. Juliani, ed.,
The Family and Community Life of Italian Americans (Staten
Island, N. Y.: The Italian American Historical Association,
1983), pp. 61-68.
Conclusions: Stereotypical images of the Italian-American
woman commonly picture her as culture-bound to a life
defined by la via vecchia (the old way). Her role choices
within this context seem limited to those firmly established
by the Italian-American ethnic-social milieu. These influences are portrayed as converging most dramatically on
the roles she plays as wife and mother. In effect, the
mamma mia of the popular media. Consequently it would
seem that Italian-American women would be significantly
limited in their self development. In order to determine
the validity of this proposition this paper begins an assess-
ment of its basic assumptions. Some questions considered
include: What are the social role expectations of Italian-
American women? Within the structure of la via vecchia,
how do the major agents of socialization, the family and
religion, influence the role expectations of these women?
On the basis of their gender role expectations, how do
Anglo and Italo-American women compare in their opportunity for self development?

787.   Daniels, John. America via the Neighborhood. New York:
Harper & Brothers, 1920.
An examination of the "indigenous neighborhood activities
of the immigrants" that serve as "training classes" for
taking a larger self-governing part in America's life. Included are social settlements, community centers, neighborhood associations, ethnic organizations, charity and health
groups, labor unions and cooperatives, and political clubs.
Part of the "Americanization Studies: The Acculturation
of Immigrant Groups into American Society," commissioned
by the Carnegie Corporation.

788.   Dann, Martin E. "Little Citizens: Working Class and Immigrant Childhood in New York City, 1890-1915." Unpublished
Ph. D. dissertation, City University of New York, 1978.
An examination of ideological, experiential, and institutional
aspects of immigrant and working class childhood in urban
America, with specific emphasis on New York City in the
period from 1890 to 1915. This includes the ways in which

children were perceived, their changing role and function
in the labor force and the family, and their social organization, particularly in schools and settlement houses. A
fundamental concern is to understand the ways in which
childhood was transformed and how this transformation affected the processes of assimilation and social change.
Industrialization and immigration fostered new conceptions
of childhood and the family. The status of children was
enhanced, if not idealized. There were major cultural conflicts between parents and children over issues of assimilation, and the content and context of experiences which con-
stituted childhood changed substantially.

789.   Davis, Michael M. Immigrant Health and the Community.
        New York: Harper & Brothers, 1920.
        Davis was Director of the Boston Dispensary. The health
        problems of immigrants in urban environments with recom-
        mendations for improving health standards as an important
        element in effective Americanization. Part of the "Ameri-
        canization Studies: The Acculturation of Immigrant Groups
        into American Society," commissioned by the Carnegie
        Corporation.

790.   Di Blasi, F. "Migrant Women: The Bitter Taste of Earning
        A Crust." Conoscere, 1 (July 1979): 8-10.

791.   Drachsler, Julius. Democracy and Assimilation: The Blend-
        ing of Immigrant Heritages in America. New York: Mac-
        millan, 1920.

792.   Drachsler, Julius. Intermarriage in New York City: A
        Statistical Study of the Amalgamation of European Peoples.
        New York: [The Author], 1921.
        A statistical analysis of intermarriage of first and second
        generation immigrants. Fusion of nationality groups is
        most rapid where barriers of religion and color are not
        marked. The lower the ratio of intermarriage in the first
        generation, the greater the ratio in the second, and there-
        fore, the greater the relative increase. The ratio of inter-
        marriage for women is slightly lower than for men. The
        largest proportion of intermarriage takes place among
        persons of the middle culture plane rather than on the high
        or low cultural level.

793.   Dublin, Louis I. "Infant Mortality in Fall River, Massachu-
        setts." American Statistical Association Journal, 14 (June
        1915): 516-517.
        The rate of mortality for infants of mothers from Portugal
        and the Azores was a frightening 299 per thousand, as
        compared with 172 and 153 per thousand for infants of
        French-Canadian and native American mothers, respectively.
        More than twice as many of these Portuguese women worked
        in the mills during pregnancy than expectant mothers of any
        other ethnicity.

794.   Duffus, R[obert] L[uther], and L. Emmett Holt, Jr. L.
        Emmett Holt: Pioneer of a Children's Century. [1940]. New
        York: Arno Press, 1974.
            The biography of Dr. Holt, superintendent of the Babies
            Hospital of New York and professor of diseases of children
            at the College of Physicians and Surgeons, New York City.
            A pioneer in the children's health field, he was the author
            of some of the most widely read literature on pediatrics
            during his lifetime. Published in 1894, his book, The
            Care and Feeding of Children, was known virtually through-
            out the world. It was translated into Spanish, Russian and
            Chinese. In the foreword to this volume, one of his students
            recalled: ". . . his word was law, not only to physicians,
            but to countless parents faced with the responsibility of
            bringing up children. He dominated pediatrics."

795.   Dysart, J. "Mexican Women in San Antonio, 1830-1860:
        The Assimilation Process." The Western Historical Quarterly,
        7 (October 1976): 365-484.
            A historical analysis of the assimilation process of the
            Anglo-Americans with the Mexicans through an examination
            of the role played by the Mexican women. Examines the
            manner in which the Anglo-American attitude of cultural
            or racial superiority inhibited the incorporation of the two
            groups into a common culture.

796.   Earle, Alice Morse. Colonial Days in Old New York. New
        York: Charles Scribner's Sons, 1897. Reprint. Detroit:
        Singing Tree Press, 1968.
            Presents a detailed picture of the life and customs during
            the days when New York was under Dutch rule and was
            called New Netherland. Maintains that the Dutch influence,
            traits, customs, and language can still be found in the New
            York of her time. The chapters include descriptions of
            the work and activities in the typical daily life of these
            transplanted Dutchmen, their educational and child-rearing
            endeavors, courtship and wedding customs, town homes
            and life-styles, farm life, food preferences, wardrobe,
            holidays, sports, amusements, religious practices, burial
            customs, activities and responsibilities of the women, and
            their criminal laws and punishments.

797.   Ellis, Pearl Idelia. Americanization Through Homemaking.
        Los Angeles: Wetzel Publishing Company, 1929.
            The use of home economics classes to impose behavior
            acceptable to middle-class Anglo-Americans on Mexican-
            American girls.

798.   Farrington, Frederic E. Public Facilities for Educating the
        Alien. Bureau of Education, Bulletin, 1916, No. 18. Wash-
        ington: Government Printing Office, 1916.

799.   Femminella, Francis X., and Jill S. Quadagno. "The Italian

American Family." In Charles H. Mindel and Robert W.
Haberstein, eds., Ethnic Families in America: Patterns and
Variations (New York: Elsevier, 1976), pp. 61-88.

800.   Fernandez, Alice B.   The Problem of Adult Education in
        Passaic, New Jersey.   Bureau of Education, Bulletin, 1920,
        No. 4.   Washington: Government Printing Office, 1920.

801.   Flynn, Judith Z.   "Dress of Older Italian-American Women:
        Documentation of Dress and the Influence of Socio-Cultural
        Factors."   Unpublished Ph.D. dissertation, Ohio State Uni-
        versity, 1979.
            The purpose was to investigate everyday dress of older
        Italian-American women in relation to sociocultural factors.
        The theoretical basis for the sociocultural factors was based
        on Tonnies' (1890) ideal types of Gemeinschaft and Gesel-
        lschaft, often discussed as the change of culture from a
        rural community to an urban society.   Dress was viewed
        in relation to a Gemeinschaft/Gesellschaft continuum with
        three features of change selected to be analyzed: (1) the
        movement from family life to individuality, (2) the move-
        ment from neighborhood to city, and (3) the movement
        from religion to rationalities.   Methodology was based on
        field research from an ethno-methodological perspective.

802.   Folks, Homer.   The Care of Destitute, Neglected, and De-
        linquent Children.   New York: Macmillan, 1902.   Reprint.
        New York: Arno Press, 1971.
            Written by a famous pioneer social worker, the book is
        an excellent introduction to the study of child care institu-
        tions from the colonial period to the progressive era.
        Folks carefully enumerates and describes the different
        organizations treating needy children, and the major public
        legislation affecting them.

803.   Garcia-Castro, M.   "Women in Migration.   Colombian Voices
        in the Big Apple."   Migration Today, 10 (1982):   22-32.

804.   Gaus, John M.   "A Municipal Program for Educating Immi-
        grants in Citizenship."   National Municipal Review, 7 (May
        1918):   237-244.

805.   Gavit, John P.   Americans by Choice.   New York: Harper
        & Brothers, 1922.
            The process and problems of immigrant acquisition of
        citizenship.   Naturalization and Americanization.   Part of
        the "Americanization Studies: The Acculturation of Immi-
        grant Groups into American Society" commissioned by the
        Carnegie Corporation.

806.   Gebhart, John C.   The Growth and Development of Italian
        Children in New York City.   New York: New York Associa-
        tion for Improving the Condition of the Poor, 1924.

An interesting study reflecting the interests of the period which collects anthropometrical, medical, and social data on Italian children and immigrant families in a congested district in New York City.

807.   Gebhart, John C. The Health of a Neighborhood: A Social Study of the Mulberry District. New York: Association for Improving the Condition of the Poor, 1924.
       The social milieu of the Italian immigrant child and family. See also Gwendolyn H. Berry, Idleness and the Health of a Neighborhood. A Social Study of the Mulberry District (New York: AICP, 1933). Both of these pamphlets are in the Russell Sage Collection, City College of New York.

808.   Glanz, Rudolf. Jew and Italian: Historic Group Relations and the New Immigration (1881-1924). New York: [The Author], 1970.
       An informative monograph on the unusual theme of inter-action of two religious-ethnic-linguistic immigrant groups in New York City. Documentation in English, Italian, and Yiddish. See review, R. J. Vecoli, International Migration Review, 7 (Summer 1973): 208-209.

809.   Glasco, Lawrence A. Ethnicity and Social Structure: Irish, Germans and Native-born of Buffalo, N.Y., 1850-1860. New York: Arno Press, 1980.
       A study of the ethnic structure of Buffalo, New York, based primarily on an analysis of the 71,850 residents listed in the manuscript schedules of the 1855 New York State census. It focuses on the Irish, Germans, and native-born whites-- who together comprised four-fifths of the city's population-- compares their demographic, economic, and family struc-tures, and concludes that the dynamics underlying those structures pointed less in the direction of social pathology and conflict than in the direction of accommodation and stability. Demographic and family patterns aided ethnic adjustment and accommodation. Foreign-born family heads were not younger than their native-born counterparts, nor did they have a preponderance of either men or women. They were newcomers to the city in a limited sense. Native-born residents were recent arrivals also, and had been present on the average only five years longer than the im-migrants. Most residents lived in a family situation. Large boarding houses were rare and the city's boarders generally lived with a family. The family structure showed signs of stability. The nuclear family predominated and "broken" or female-headed families were exceptional. Foreign-born immigrants had a much higher birth rate than the native-born, but no group was overly burdened with children. Particularly for the immigrants, domestic service for their adolescent daughters functioned both to regulate their family size and also to introduce a sizable part of their population to native-born households, and to native-born values and

language. Originally, Ph.D. dissertation, State University
of New York (Buffalo), 1973.

810.   Glasco, Lawrence A. "The Life Cycles and Household Struc-
ture of American Ethnic Groups: Irish, Germans, and Native-
Born Whites in Buffalo, New York, 1855." Journal of Urban
History, 1 (1975): 339-364.

811.   Gobetz, Giles Edward. Adjustment and Assimilation of Slovenian Refugees. New York: Arno Press, 1980.
Slovenes, the smallest, westernmost Slavic people with a
population of only a million and a half, have successfully
resisted Germanization, Italianization, and Hungarianization.
Since they had no legal or military resources, forced assimilation was resisted on moral grounds alone. This
successful millennial resistance makes the study of the
adjustment and assimilation processes of Slovenian immigrants in America of special interest. The dissertation
consists of three parts: (1) conceptual analysis of adjustment and assimilation; (2) a sample of refugee correspondence (1945-1955); (3) analysis of 115 questionnaires completed by Slovenian refugees who have settled in the United
States and Canada since 1947. After an extensive examination of various definitions of and assumptions about assimilation, the conclusion is reached that its final test is
the development of reciprocal identifications between minority
and majority group members. An immigrant is assimilated
when he habitually and unreservedly identifies with the
majority group and when members of the majority group
reciprocate by identifying him with themselves. Various
commonly used indicators of assimilation are critically
examined and some oversimplifications exposed. Originally,
Ph.D. dissertation, Ohio State University, 1962.

812.   Gray, Robert F. "Americanism and Americanization Movement." Sierra Educational News, 16 (October 1920): 488-489.

813.   Griel, Cecile L. I Problemi Della Madre in un Paese Nuovo.
New York: National Board of the Young Women's Christian
Associations. [1919].
A series of advisements to immigrant Italian women on
the care and raising of their children, on work outside the
home, and on the family's adaptation to America.

814.   Griffen, Clyde, and Sally Griffen. "Family and Business in
a Small City: Poughkeepsie, New York: 1850-1880." Journal
of Urban History, 1 (1975): 316-38.
Maintains that the extended family, with its kinship networks
and self-help patterns, played an important role in business
entrepreneurship in the city of that era. Rejects the view
that the rise of largely immigrant business enterprise led
to the nuclear family.

815. Harney, Robert F., and J. V. Scarpaci, eds. Little Italies
      in North America. Toronto: The Multicultural History So-
      ciety of Ontario, 1981.
          The essays in this volume were originally prepared for a
      conference that took place in the spring of 1979 under the
      auspices of the University of Toronto's Ethnic and Immi-
      gration Studies Program and the Multicultural History So-
      ciety of Ontario. The American Little Italies discussed
      were those of Chicago, New York, Philadelphia, Baltimore,
      the canal town of Oswego in upstate New York, Tampa,
      New Orleans and St. Louis. For Canada, Little Italies in
      Toronto, Montreal and Thunder Bay were described. The
      cities were chosen to show some of the variety of settle-
      ment in the United States and Canada as well as to con-
      trast the Italian-Canadian and Italian-American experiences.
      The editors were interested in seeing if they "could limn
      more precisely the ways in which such variables as the
      size of each Italian colony, the predominant paesi of origin
      of the settlers in each, and the magnitude and nature--in
      terms of occupational possibilities and the presence of other
      ethnic groups--and the attitude toward immigrants of the
      host city or regional ecosystem, affected immigrant settle-
      ments and the subsequent Italian ethnoculture."

816. Hartmann, Edward. The Americanization of the Immigrant.
      New York: Columbia University Press, 1948.
          A study of the "Americanization Crusade" initiated at the
      opening of World War I and continuing into the post-war
      era which drew its leadership from the intelligentsia, the
      educators and social workers, the industrialists, and from
      business and civic groups generally. Invaluable data on
      urban immigrant subcommunities. Massive bibliography
      and documentation.

817. Hill, Robert. "Ethnic Status, Culture, and Community: The
      Polish-American Underclass in the Roman Catholic School
      System." [Paper presented at the Ethnicity and Education
      Symposium in the Department of Anthropology, University of
      Pittsburgh, 1971, ERIC document ED U58 372].
          Suggests that the German and Irish staff of the high school
      studied worked with the Polish immigrant home to dis-
      courage lower-class Polish girls from the pursuit of higher
      education.

818. Hill, R. T. "From Americanization to Adult Education."
      Survey, 62 (June 1929): 366-367.
          See also the author's "Contributions of Americanization to
      Education in the United States," School & Society, 33 (Janu-
      ary 1931); and "Letting Johnny Do It: Educating Parents
      Through Their Children," Survey, 61 (January 1929).

819. Houghton, Frederick. Immigrant Education: A Handbook
      Prepared for the Board of Education. New York: Board of
      Education, 1927.

820.   Ianni, Francis A. "Familialism in the South of Italy and in
        the United States." In S. M. Tomasi, ed., Perspectives of
        Italian Immigration and Ethnicity (New York: Center for
        Migration Studies, 1977), pp. 103-107.

821.   Johnson, E. S. "Role Expectations and Role Realities of
        Older Italian Mothers and Their Daughters." International
        Journal of Aging and Human Development, 14 (1982): 271.

822.   Kallen, Horace M. Culture and Democracy in the United
        States. New York: Boni and Liveright, 1924.
            One of the major critics of the Americanization movement,
            and an advocate of the philosophy of cultural pluralism.
            See also Kallen's "Democracy versus the Melting Pot,"
            The Nation, 100 (February 18 and 25, 1915): 190-194,
            217-220.

823.   Kallen, Horace M. "The Meaning of Americanism." Immi-
        grants in America Review, 1 (January 1916): 12-19.

824.   Kelly, Gail P. "The Schooling of Vietnamese Immigrants:
        Internal Colonialism and Its Impact on Women." In Beverly
        Lindsay, ed., Comparative Perspectives of Third World Wom-
        en: The Impact of Sex, Race and Class (New York: Praeger
        Publishers, 1980), pp. 276-296.

825.   Kendall, Glenn. "Educational Activities of the United States
        Immigration and Naturalization Service." Journal of Edu-
        cational Sociology, 17 (September 1943): 36-41.
            Cooperation with public schools for coordination of the in-
            structional program and the naturalization examination.

826.   Keppel, Ruth. Trees to Tulips; Authentic Tales of the Pioneers
        of Holland, Michigan. Holland, Michigan: [n. p.], 1947.
            The "tales" gathered together originated during the early
            days of the Dutch settlement in Michigan and are intended
            to illustrate the conditions and experiences of the early
            Dutch immigrant-pioneers of western Michigan. The author
            relates the story of the arrival of the Keppel family, the
            role of Dutch pioneer women, the methods of transportation
            available, and some outstanding pioneers.

827.   Kim, S. D. "Interracially Married Korean Women Immigrants:
        A Study in Marginality." Unpublished Ph.D. dissertation,
        University of Washington, 1979.

828.   Kitano, Harry. "Differential Child Rearing Attitudes Between
        First and Second Generation Japanese in the United States."
        Journal of Social Psychology, 53 (1961): 13-19.

829.   Kleinberg, Susan J. "Technology and Women's Work: The
        Lives of Working Class Women in Pittsburgh, 1870-1900."
        Labor History, 17 (1976): 58-72.

Focuses upon those women who worked in their own homes
and finds that the unequal distribution of municipal and
domestic technology made them work long hours and rein-
forced their isolation. Contends that their unpaid labor
helped sustain the entire urban-industrial system.

830. Krause, Corinne Azen. "Italian, Jewish, and Slavic Grandmothers in Pittsburgh: Their Economic Roles." Frontiers,
2 (Summer 1977): 18-28.
Oral histories of working grandmothers of Italian, Jewish
and Slavic backgrounds illustrate the active economic roles
of the older women included in the sample of Krause's
Pittsburgh study of ethnicity, mental health and continuity.
Document a wide variety of work done by married women
that is absent from the census data. Differences between
the ethnic groups were primarily in attitudes toward work
and values placed upon work, rather than in the nature of
the jobs performed. The primary motivation for work in
any breadwinning capacity was concern for the family.
Women of all three ethnic groups exhibit characteristics of
dignity, pragmatism, a sense of responsibility, and enhanced self-esteem from contributing to the welfare of
their families.

831. Krause, Corinne Azen. "Urbanization Without Breakdown:
Italian, Jewish, and Slavic Immigrant Women in Pittsburgh,
1900 to 1945." Journal of Urban History, 4 (1978): 291-306.
Maintains that immigrant women in Pittsburgh were able
to adjust to the rigors of urban life with very few traumatic
results, despite the culture shock and sense of alienation
engendered by life in a major manufacturing center.

832. Lane, Francis E. American Charities and the Child of the
Immigrant: A Study of Typical Child Caring Institutions in
New York and Massachusetts Between the Years 1845 and
1880. [1932]. New York: Arno Press, 1974.
A thorough study of Protestant and Roman Catholic child-
caring institutions in Massachusetts and New York during
the period 1845-1880. Approaches the history of child
care with the hypothesis that the huge influx of immigrants
and their offspring is directly related to the beginnings of
American charities. Makes continuing distinctions between
the methods of operation of the Catholic and Protestant
organizations.

833. Leder, Hans Howard. Cultural Persistence in a Portuguese-
American Community. New York: Arno Press, 1980.
Beginning with the assumption that the retention by a subcultural group of traditional cultural patterns will affect
the manner in which its members adjust, both socially and
psychologically, to acculturation-induced change, this study
analyzes not only the processes of cultural persistence, but
also its presumed effects. Selected for study in the San

Francisco Bay area of Northern California was a "colony"
of some 12,500 Portuguese-Americans, who were enclaved
in a fast-growing ethnically heterogeneous but predominantly
white, Anglo-Saxon, Protestant city of over 200,000 inhabitants. A major conclusion is that although the Portu-
guese-American subculture has remained marginal, it has
also maintained coherence, in contrast with the general
culture of the "receiving society." Also suggests that "in
future studies of acculturating groups, existing theoretical
approaches should be extended to include the following
postulates: (1) acculturation does not inevitably result in
disorganization but, on the contrary, may even have a
benign effect upon the social and psychological health of
a group; (2) in terms of these alternatives, the one actually
produced in a particular contact situation will be primarily
a function of: a) the coherence and consistency of the
acculturating group's core cultural patterns; and b) the
real nature, on all levels, of the opposition between the
patterns of the groups involved." Originally, Ph.D. dissertation, Stanford University, 1968.

834. Leonetti, I., and L. Newel-Morris. "Lifetime Patterns of
Childbearing and Employment: A Study of Second-Generation
Japanese American Women." Journal of Biosocial Science,
14 (January 1982): 81-97.

835. Letchworth, William P[ryor]. Homes of Homeless Children:
A Report on Orphan Asylums and Other Institutions for the
Care of Children. [1903]. New York: Arno Press, 1974.
Letchworth (1823-1910) was commissioner of the New York
State Board of Charities. Consists of three reports on
the care of destitute and pauper children first printed in
the Eighth (1875) and Ninth (1876) Annual Reports of the
New York State Board of Charities. The reports are based
on Letchworth's official inspections and contain invaluable
data on the history, administration, and physical conditions
in late nineteenth-century institutions for children.

836. Lewin, Ellen. Mothers and Children: Latin American Immigrants in San Francisco. New York: Arno Press, 1980.
The vital role of the mother in the adaptation of the Latin
American immigrant family to life in the United States is
described in this revealing portrait. The author provides
an examination of the experiences of 15 lower-class Mexican
and Central American immigrant women in the heavily
Latino Mission District of San Francisco. Based on her
observations and interviews, the author concludes that,
generally, these women have made excellent, rational de-
cisions in the face of relatively adverse circumstances.
Originally, Ph.D. dissertation, Stanford University, 1974.

837. Loomis, Frank D. Americanization in Chicago. Chicago:
The Chicago Community Trust, 1920.

838.   Lundberg, Emma O[ctavia], and Katharine F. Lenroot. Il-
        legitimacy as a Child-Welfare Problem, Parts I and II. [Re-
        printed from Children's Bureau Publications Nos. 66 and 75].
        [1920-1921]. New York: Arno Press, 1974.
            Part 1 of this report estimates the prevalence of illegiti-
        macy in the U.S. and foreign countries, survival of il-
        legitimate as compared to legitimate infants, and the needs
        for child care. The outstanding feature of this report is
        its focus on the child. Part 2 contains an overall historical
        review of the provisions the Commonwealth of Massachusetts
        has made for delinquent, physically and mentally defective,
        or otherwise needy children. Lundberg and Lenroot ana-
        lyzed numerous records to obtain statistics regarding the
        birth rate, mortality rate, and "something of the histories"
        of illegitimate infants. All the relevant material used in
        this study was compiled and correlated without benefit of
        computers or any of the modern data processing equipment
        now available. The resulting report, which took five years
        to complete, is impressive not only for its extensive ana-
        lyses, but for the quality of the data--which was used some
        fifty years later in conjunction with similar studies.

839.   MacKenzie, Kyle; Yvonne Tixier y Vigil; and Nan Elsasser.
        "Grandmothers' Stories." Frontiers, 2 (Summer 1977): 56-
        58.
            At age 85, Grandma Vigil gives her granddaughter the first
        threads to be woven with the lives of other Grandmas,
        madres and hijas into a Hispanic story of mothering.

840.   McLean, Annie M. "Life in the Pennsylvania Coal Fields,
        with Particular Reference to Women." American Journal of
        Sociology, 14 (November 1908): 329-51.
            Social life of Slavic immigrants. Tabulation of material
        on amusements, clubs and centers, and church efforts to
        ameliorate women's lives and with special attention to the
        Young Women's Christian Association.

841.   Mahoney, John J. Americanization in the United States.
        Bureau of Education, Bulletin, 1923, No. 31. Washington:
        Government Printing Office, 1923.

842.   Mahoney, John J., ed. Training Teachers for Americaniza-
        tion. Bureau of Education, Bulletin, 1920. No. 12. Wash-
        ington: Government Printing Office, 1920.

843.   Mancuso, Arlene. "Women of Old Town." In Betty Boyd
        Caroli, Richard F. Harney, and Lydio F. Tomasi, eds. The
        Italian Immigrant Woman in North America. (Toronto: Multi-
        cultural History Society of Ontario, 1978), pp. 312-323.
            A description of the family and community life of a small
        number of Italian-American women living in an ethnic en-
        clave of a large urban eastern city, an enclave referred
        to here as Old Town. The identity of the locale and its

inhabitants have been withheld. Using a variety of ethno-
graphic techniques, such as those used in anthropological
research, the study, done over a period of eighteen months,
attempts to describe a particular group through the examination of the social roles women play within the group.

844.   Mancuso, Arlene. "Women of Old Town." Unpublished Ph. D.
        dissertation, Columbia University, 1977.
        A description of the family life of a small number of Italian-
        American women living in an ethnic enclave of a large
        eastern city. The study, using a variety of ethnographic
        research techniques, is based on day-to-day observation of
        behavior in the community over a period of eighteen months.
        The major theoretical perspectives which inform this work
        are ethnicity, social role, and sex role identity as an as-
        pect of social role. Concepts are examined primarily as
        they relate to the female, within the framework of a de-
        scriptive study of family life. The bulk of the data was
        gathered from second generation Italian women, married
        and raising children. Yet the data were not limited to
        this group. The researcher sought out and interviewed
        women in the first, third, and fourth generations, and
        had access to husbands and male kin of these women across
        generations. Shows that the Old Town woman today stands
        at the center of a family system which stresses family
        solidarity and pragmatism. She is the core of the family
        and the nurturer and transmitter of those values. As the
        manager of internal affairs, she handles the purse strings
        and has a great deal of decision-making power in the family
        unit. Her role in the emotional, economic, and social
        functioning of the unit is essential to its continuance.

845.   Markham, Edwin, et al. Children in Bondage: A Complete
        and Careful Presentation of the Anxious Problem of Child
        Labor--Its Causes, Its Crimes, and Its Cures. [1914]. New
        York: Arno Press, 1971.
        Prior to World War I, child labor was rampant throughout
        the U. S. Not merely confined to street trades, children
        had become part of the heartless industrial discipline that
        used any source of labor, the cheaper the better. In an
        effort to transform a growing awareness into constructive
        action, a famous poet, a noted judge and an outstanding
        publicist launched an educational drive in the form of a
        series of magazine articles which depicted in unforgettable
        terms the evil and horror of child labor in country and
        city. This book is a record of their passionate pleas,
        sound arguments, and brutal facts.

846.   Martinelli, Phylis Cancilla. "Italian Immigrant Women in the
        Southwest." In Betty Boyd Caroli, Richard F. Harney, and
        Lydio F. Tomasi, eds. The Italian Immigrant Woman in
        North America (Toronto: Multicultural History Society of
        Ontario, 1978), pp. 324-336.

Italian men depicted in Andrew Rolle's book The Immigrant
Upraised were cattle barons riding herd along the Rio
Grande, missionaries pacifying Indians, homesteaders on
the Great Plains, miners, fur traders, businessmen--living
lives far different from their counterparts in the East.
Were Italian women riding the range beside their men,
working with Indians, exploring, and homesteading, or
were their lives in the more traditional Italian mode?
Were they withdrawn from the larger world, letting their
husbands, children, and relatives form the scope of their
lives? The answer is complex. To explore these com-
plexities this paper concentrates on the Southwest, namely,
the states of Colorado, Utah, New Mexico, and Arizona.
The lives of the women within the home in traditional roles,
and outside of the home in less typical roles, are considered.

847.   Mason, Gregory. "An Americanization Factory: An Account
of What the Public Schools of Rochester Are Doing to Make
Americans of Foreigners." The Outlook, 112 (February 23,
1916): 430-448.

848.   Maxson, Charles Hartshorn. Citizenship. New York: Oxford
University Press, 1930.
Naturalization, citizenship, and suffrage. Attention to im-
migrant women. (Chapter 9).

849.   Mayer, John E. Jewish-Gentile Courtships: An Exploratory
Study of a Social Process. New York: Free Press, 1961.
A sociological analysis, with frequent quotations of the
subjects' opinions, of the processes and problems of inter-
faith relationships which led to intermarriage.

850.   Melloh, Ardith K. "Life in Early New Sweden, Iowa," The
Swedish Pioneer Historical Quarterly, 32 (April 1981): 124-
146.
Describes the settlement of New Sweden, Iowa (Jefferson
County), by Swedish immigrants in 1849 and the years
following. Of particular interest is his analysis of special
problems encountered by Swedish immigrants and the kinds
of adaptations they had to make to succeed in America.

851.   Melville, Margarita B. "Mexican Women Adapt to Migration."
International Migration Review, 12 (Summer 1978): 225-236.
A study of recent Mexican female migrants to Houston,
Texas, which seeks to determine the strategies used by
these migrants to cope with the stress of migration.

852.   Meyer, Annie N., ed. Woman's Work in America. With an
Introduction by Julia Ward Howe. New York: Henry Holt,
1891.
Eighteen articles by such notables as Julia Ward Howe,
Mary Putnam Jacobi, Mary Livermore, Josephine Shaw

Lowell, Frances Willard, and Clara Barton describe the
period when many professions were beginning to open up
to women.

853.   Miaso, J.   The History of the Education of Polish Immigrants
        in the United States.   New York: Kosciuszko Foundation,
        1977.
        Examines the beginnings, development and the function of
        the Polish American school system over a one-hundred-
        year history.   Also covered is the participation of these
        newcomers in many different cultural and educational ac-
        tivities.   Included are parochial schools, vocational and
        technical schools as well as universities.   Includes notices
        of religious teaching orders (nuns) in the schools.

854.   Mindel, Charles H., and Robert W. Habenstein, eds.   Ethnic
        Families in America: Patterns and Variations.   New York:
        Elsevier Scientific Publishing, 1976.
        This collection is designed to fill a gap in the literature
        on ethnic and other minority group family styles in Ameri-
        ca.   Most of the contributors are members of the group
        about which they are writing.   In addition to brief intro-
        ductory and concluding chapters by the editors, consists
        of fifteen original essays, of which only two appear in
        other books.   Of the four sections of the book, the first,
        "early ethnic minorities," contains essays by Helena Z.
        Lopata on the Polish; Harry H. L. Kitano and Akemi
        Kikumura on the Japanese; Francis X. Femminella and
        Jill S. Quanagno on the Italians; Ellen Horgan Biddle on
        Irish-Catholics; and Lucy Jen Huang on the Chinese.   The
        second section, "recent and continuing ethnic minorities,"
        contains essays by Abdo A. Elkholy on the Arabs; George
        A. Kourvetaris on the Greeks; and Joseph P. Fitzpatrick
        on Puerto Ricans.   The third section, "historically sub-
        jugated but volatile ethnic minorities," includes essays by
        Robert Staples on Blacks; John N. Price on North American
        Indians, and David Alverez and Frank Bean on Mexicans.
        The concluding section, "socioreligious ethnic minorities,"
        is comprised of essays by Gertrude Enders Huntington on
        the Amish; Laurence French on the French; Bernard Farber,
        Charles H. Mindel, and Bernard Lazerwitz on the Jews;
        and Bruce L. Campbell and Eugene E. Campbell on the
        Mormons.

855.   Moore, Margaret D.   Citizenship Training of Adult Immigrants
        in the United States: Its Status in Relation to the Census of
        1920.   Washington: Government Printing Office, 1925.

856.   Morgan, Myfanwy, and Hilda H. Golden.   "Immigrant Families
        in an Industrial City: A Study of Households in Holyoke,
        1880."   Journal of Family History, 4 (1979):   56-67.
        Uses 1880 census data to derive a sample to investigate
        household size and composition, the characteristics of heads

of household, the presence of nonrelatives, and family
types. Finds significant variations between foreign-born
and native-born households.

857.   Moss, Leonard W. "The Family in Southern Italy: Yesterday
        and Today." In Humbert Nelli, ed., The United States and
        Italy: The First Two Hundred Years. (New York: The
        American Italian Historical Association, 1977), pp. 185-191.

858.   Myres, Sandra L. Westering Women and the Frontier Ex-
        perience 1800-1915. Albuquerque: University of New Mexico
        Press, 1982.
            Focuses on the lives of women on the United States frontier.
            Discusses the experiences of Indian, Mexican, French, and
            black women, as well as the experiences of Anglo-American
            women. Examines, among other topics, images of frontier
            women, women's views of the Indians and the frontier, wom-
            en's journeys westward, female frontier homemaking and
            women's participation in community building on the frontier.
            Women's experiences on the prairies and plains are parts
            of this history.

859.   Nichols, D. J. "Migration and Fertility in the United States:
        An Examination of the Roles of Origin and Destination on the
        Cumulative Fertility of American Women." Unpublished Ph. D.
        dissertation, Duke University, 1980.

860.   Obidinski, Eugene Edward. Ethnic to Status Group: A Study
        of Polish Americans in Buffalo. New York: Arno Press,
        1980.
            A distinct Polish American subcommunity has existed in
            Buffalo for almost a century despite continual assimilation
            of immigrants and their descendants. This study examined
            variables relevant to the continued existence of the sub-
            community and the transformation or change in subcom-
            munity patterns. Includes a brief history of the subcom-
            munity, an analysis of differences in attitudes and activities
            of second and third generation Polish Americans, an ex-
            amination of familial, religious, political, and economic
            practices, and characteristics of upper, middle, and work-
            ing class respondents. With the continued existence of a
            distinct subcommunity and its adjustment to conditions of
            the surrounding society, descendants of immigrants identi-
            fied less with each other in terms of common social status
            characteristics, such as political preference or involvement
            in church activities. Findings suggested several general
            conclusions regarding subcommunity persistence and change.
            First, traditional subcommunity practices and influences
            were strongest in familial and religious practices. Second,
            traditions and values of the ethnic subcommunity varies
            with generation. Members of third and successive genera-
            tions were less involved in subcommunity activities and
            show less response to traditional cultural patterns. Finally,
            such patterns survived among working class respondents

to a greater degree than among upper class respondents.
Originally, Ph. D. dissertation, State University of New
York (Buffalo), 1968.

861.   Olson, Audrey L. St. Louis Germans, 1850-1920: The
Nature of an Immigrant Community and Its Relation to the
Assimilation Process. New York: Arno Press, 1980.
Historians of German immigration to the United States have
recorded the deeds and contributions of that ethnic group
to American life. They have studied the German community with relation to its assimilation into the host society,
arriving at various conclusions: that the German ethnic
group was progressing toward assimilation until the First
World War forced them into a self-awareness of their
nationality; that the ethnic community was not becoming
assimilated until the First World War broke the hyphen
in German-American and that the wealthy German Americans abandoned the community, resulting in a resurgence
of ethnic self-consciousness on the part of the less economically and socially mobile members of the group.
These conclusions were based on the predication of the
existence of a close-knit German ethnic community. This
study investigates a German community in an urban setting,
St. Louis, Missouri, in order to determine the nature of
that community and its relation to the process of assimilation. Originally, Ph. D. dissertation, University of Kansas,
1970.

862.   Overton, Jacqueline [Marion]. "Dutch and English Colonial
Life on Long Island." New York History, 14 (October 1933):
331-45.
Attempts to show the contrast between and describes the
life-styles of the Dutch and the English who occupied sections of Long Island in 1650. Each group occupied its own
sections of the Island and maintained its own characteristics,
life-style, customs, and language. Overton talks of houses,
educational and religious practices, occupations, family
meals, status of women, holidays, and so forth. This
essay includes no documentation.

863.   Pedo, Antonio. "A Cross Cultural Change of Gender Roles:
The Case of Philipino Women Immigrants in Midwest City,
U. S. A." [Paper presented at the 6th Annual Conference on
Ethnic and Minority Studies, University of Wisconsin, La
Crosse, April 19-22, 1978. ERIC document ED 159 244.]

864.   Perry, Harriet. "The Metonymic Definition of the Female
and the Concept of Honour Among Italian Immigrant Families
in Toronto." In Betty Boyd Caroli, Robert F. Harney, and
Lydio F. Tomasi, eds. The Italian Immigrant Woman in
North America (Toronto: Multicultural History Society of
Ontario, 1978), pp. 222-231.
Considers the way that Italian immigrant females in Toronto

see themselves and the parts they might play in their life
here, and how they are seen by others in their immediate
environment of family, friends, and acquaintances. It is
based on fieldwork in Toronto during 1976-77 among 227
nuclear families. Informants were married couples (and
their children) in which both the husband and wife had been
born in Italy and had migrated from Italy directly to Canada
after they were at least 16 years of age. These families
represented a great diversity of area of origin within Italy
(each region was represented by at least eight families,
although there were none from the two northern border
areas) as well as a wide range of socioeconomic and educational levels, since none of these considerations were
made a criterion for participation in the interviews from
which this material was drawn.

865. Polowy, Hannah. "The Role of Pioneer Women in Family
Life." Ukrainian Canadian, 3 [March 1972]: 20-21.
Ukrainian pioneer women in the new world, and their role
in the preservation of Ukrainian culture.

866. Pozzetta, George E. "Immigrants and Craft Arts: Scuola
d'Industrie Italiane." In Betty Boyd Caroli, Richard F. Harney,
and Lydio F. Tomasi, eds. The Italian Immigrant Woman
in North America (Toronto: The Multicultural History of
Ontario, 1978), pp. 138-153.
Conclusions: Many scholars have noted that settlement
houses underwrote a significant revival of immigrant handi-
crafts in America's urban centers during the years sur-
rounding the turn of the present century. . . . The chance
to focus on a complete history of one of these ventures
has rarely presented itself. Usually, the settlement crafts
school was only one of many activities taking place in the
house, and its story was often buried within the larger
entity. Records do exist, however, which permit a close
look at one such institution, the Scuola d'Industrie Italiane,
a lace and embroidery crafts school founded for Italian
women in New York City. The Scuola was an unusually
ambitious and long-lived educational experiment in the field
of artistic handiwork. An examination of its history can
give us some insight into the nature of philanthropy and
social reform work among Italian immigrants, the character
of the ethnic community, and the condition of Italian immigrant women.

867. Proceedings of the National Conference on Americanization in
Industry. Nantucket Beach, Massachusetts, June 22-24, [1919].

868. Radzialowski, Thaddeus C. "Reflections on the History of
the Felicians in America." Polish American Studies, 23
(Spring 1975): 19-28.
Describes Polish parochial schools that Americanized without sacrificing ethnic identity and that offered young women
who became teaching nuns an opportunity for higher education.

869.   Ragsdale, Crystal S. "The German Woman in Frontier Texas."
        In Glen E. Lich and Dona B. Reeves, eds. German Culture
        in Texas: A Free Earth; Essays from the 1978 Southwest
        Symposium (Boston: Twayne Publishers, 1980), pp. 144-156.

870.   Ragucci, Antoinette T. "Generational Continuity and Change
        in Concepts of Health, Curing Practices, and Ritual Expres-
        sions of the Women of an Italian-American Enclave." Un-
        published Ph. D. dissertation, Boston University, 1971.
           Utilizing the method of participant-observer, delineates the
        convergence and divergence of folk concepts of health and
        healing practices. Continuities and discontinuities along
        a three-generation dimension are indicated. The women
        of the first or immigrant generation (i. e., emigrants of
        Italy five to six decades previously) comprise the baseline
        for the study. The recurring themes associated with folk
        or laymen's health and healing practices, and the manner
        in which these are expressed and reinterpreted within an
        urban milieu are identified.

871.   Ramkhalawansingh, C. "Language and Employment Training
        for Immigrant Women." Canadian Ethnic Studies, 13 (1981):
        91-96.
           Examines three aspects of the social and economic functions
        of landscape as it affects immigrants: 1) the role of lan-
        guage in social integration; 2) its implication for immigrant
        women; and 3) a program aimed at combining language and
        employment training for immigrant women.

872.   Reed, Dorothy. "Leisure Time of Girls in a 'Little Italy':
        A Comparative Study of the Leisure Interests of Adolescent
        Girls of Foreign Parentage, Living in a Metropolitan Com-
        munity, to Determine the Presence or Absence of Interest
        Differences in Relation to Behavior." Unpublished Ph. D. dis-
        sertation, Columbia University, 1932.

873.   Reed, Ruth. The Illegitimate Family in New York City: Its
        Treatment by Social and Health Agencies. [1934]. New York:
        Arno Press, 1972.
           A unique volume, providing some of the only historical in-
        formation available on illegitimacy. Among the first to
        examine this problem, Reed diligently explored such basic
        questions as the social origins of parents of illegitimate
        children (their education, religion, and occupations), the
        frequency with which they later married, and the amount
        of recourse to the courts. She also investigated the fate
        of the child, to learn how effectively social and health
        agencies responded to its needs.

874.   Rempson, Joe L. "Urban Minorities: Education of Immi-
        grants." In Lee C. Deighton, ed. The Encyclopedia of Edu-
        cation (New York: Macmillan, 1971, 10 vols.), IX, pp. 391-
        399.

875. Richmond, Marie L. "Beyond Resource Theory: Another
      Look at Factors Enabling Women to Affect Family Interaction."
      Journal of Marriage and the Family, 38 (May 1976): 257-265.
      The changing roles of Cuban women in immigrant families.

876. Richmond, Marie L. Immigrant Adaptation and Family Struc-
      ture Among Cubans in Miami, Florida. New York: Arno
      Press, 1980.
      Modifications in the structure of Cuban exile families have
      occurred as a result of adaptation to life in Miami. This
      study explores the special impact of two factors--the pres-
      ence of Americans as a new reference group and the con-
      siderable employment of Cuban exile women. Particular
      emphasis is placed on the resulting socialization of children
      and the changing role and status of women. Originally,
      doctoral dissertation, Florida State University, 1973.

877. Roberts, Peter. The Problem of Americanization. New York:
      Macmillan, 1920.

878. Rosenwaike, I. "Two Generations of Italians in America:
      Their Fertility Experience." International Migration Review,
      7 (Fall 1973): 271-280.

879. Rothman, David J., ed. The Family and Social Service in
      the 1920's. New York: Arno Press, 1972.
      Includes: Eddith Abbott and Sophonisba P. Breckinridge,
      The Administration of the Aid-to-Mothers Law in Illinois,
      Children's Bureau Publication, No. 82 (Washington, D.C.,
      1921); and Mary F. Bogue, Administration of Mother's Aid
      in Ten Localities. With Special Reference to Health, Hous-
      ing, Education, and Recreation (Washington, D.C., 1928).
      The most innovative family welfare legislation in the Pro-
      gressive era was the effort to give state pensions to needy
      widows with children--in effect, the earliest version of a
      modern Aid to Dependent Children program. Rather than
      dispatch the mother to the almshouse and her youngsters
      to an orphan asylum, the state would now support them
      together at home. These two studies demonstrate the fate
      of this program in the 1920's, and thereby offer a pene-
      trating look at both public relief practices and the experi-
      ences confronting families in need.

880. Ruddy, Anna C. (Christian McLeod, pseud.). The Heart of
      the Stranger: A Story of Little Italy. New York: Fleming
      H. Revell, 1908. Reprint. New York: Arno Press, 1975.
      Anna C. Ruddy came to East Harlem (New York City) from
      Canada in 1890 in the very early days of Italian immigra-
      tion. She devoted her life to working with Italian immi-
      grant families, and particularly with Italian young people.
      She learned Italian so she could communicate. In 1901
      she established "The Home Garden" as a meeting place
      for young Italians in East Harlem. In 1919, "The Home

Garden" was renamed "Haarlem House" and in 1957 its
name was changed to "La Guardia Memorial House." The
Heart of the Stranger, which is a distillation of Ruddy's
experience among the Italian poor of East Harlem, is a
series of fictionalized vignettes. It offers some of the
most sensitive portraits of immigrant urban life ever
sketched.

881.   Rutter, M., et al. "Children of West Indian Immigrants."
Journal of Child Psychology and Psychiarty, 16 (April 1975):
105-124.

882.   Ryan, Dennis P. "Beyond the Ballot Box. A Social History
of the Boston Irish, 1845-1917." Unpublished Ph.D. dissertation, University of Massachusetts, 1979.
Focuses on a variety of topics including the Irish's institutional response to poverty, parochial school experiences,
career patterns, relations with other ethnic and racial
groups, women's roles and associational and leisure activities.

883.   Salmon, Lucy M. Domestic Service. New York: Macmillan,
1897.

884.   Scanni, Giuseppina. "L'emigrazione delle donne e dei fanciulli
dalla Provincia di Caserta." Bollettino dell 'Emigrazione, 13
(1913): 3-23.
The emigration of Italian women and children to America.

885.   Scelsa, Joseph V. "Italian-American Women: Their Families
and American Education, Systems in Conflict." In Richard
N. Juliani, ed. The Family and Community Life of Italian
Americans (Staten Island, N.Y.: The Italian American Historical Association, 1983), pp. 169-171.
Conclusions: This paper examines through the use of case
studies some of the difficulties experienced by second and
third generation Italian-American women in attaining an
education and how in part this is due to the cultural legacy
of the southern Italian society which existed in the last
decades of the nineteenth and the first decade of the twentieth century. Specifically it has been the persistence of
this ethnic group's old world values and attitudes which
has become the source of conflicts for Italian-American
women today. She is caught in the middle between com-
peting systems each with their own values. These two
systems being the Italian-American family and the American educational system.

886.   Schneider, Florence H. Patterns of Workers Education: The
Story of the Bryn Mawr Summer School. Washington: American Council on Public Affairs, 1941.
Describes the educational activities provided by unions in
the early decades of the century.

887.   Schuster, S. T. "What the Evening School Is Doing for the
        Alien." Journal of Education, 79 (March 1914): 261-262.

888.   Seller, Maxine. "The Education of Immigrant Children in
        Buffalo, New York, 1890-1916." New York History, 57 (1976):
        183-200.
        Explores the educational aspirations of Polish, Italians,
        and Jewish immigrants in Buffalo and the motives of that
        city's educational reformers. Stresses that the native-
        born reformers established programs which reflected their
        own vision of America, basically one of middle-class values
        and patriotism, rather than the needs of the immigrants.

889.   Seller, Maxine. "The Education of the Immigrant Woman:
        1900 to 1975." Journal of Urban History, 4 (1978): 307-30.
        Finds that many urban, immigrant women were able to
        achieve a good education and even to organize their own
        educational programs, despite the common belief that edu-
        cation for women was superfluous or, at most, ought to
        be restricted to utilitarian subjects.

890.   Seller, Maxine. "Ethnicity as a Factor in the School Per-
        formance of Immigrant Children 1890-1930." Foundation
        Studies, 8 (1974): 2, 3-26, 42-53.

891.   Seller, Maxine S. "Protestant Evangelism and the Italian Im-
        migrant Woman." In Betty Boyd Caroli, Richard F. Harney,
        and Lydio F. Tomasi, eds. The Italian Immigrant Woman
        in North America (Toronto: The Multicultural History Society
        of Ontario, 1978), pp. 124-136.
        Conclusions: In the closing decades of the nineteenth cen-
        tury the home mission societies of the major Protestant
        denominations in the United States turned their attention
        from the evangelization of the frontier to the evangelization
        of the cities. Between 1890 and 1920 Baptists, Methodists,
        Presbyterians, Congregationalists, Episcopalians, and
        Lutherans invested increasing amounts of time, money,
        and energy in religious work among urban populations. One
        of their primary targets was the Italian immigrant, who
        was increasingly conspicuous in American urban life at the
        turn of the century. This paper has explored the motives
        and methods of Protestant missionary work among Italians
        with particular emphasis upon its impact on Italian women.
        It concludes with some explanations for the very meager
        results of this missionary work.

892.   Sharlip, William, and Albert A. Owens. Adult Immigration
        Education: Its Scope, Content, and Methods. New York:
        Macmillan, 1925.

893.   Smith, Judith E. "Italian Mothers, American Daughters:
        Changes in Work and Family Roles." In The Italian Immi-
        grant Woman in North America. Ed. by Betty Boyd Caroli,

Robert F. Harney, and Lydio F. Tomasi. Toronto: The
Multicultural History Society of Ontario, 1978, pp. 206-221.
Conclusions: "My speculations on mother-daughter relationships in America are based on an analysis of residence
and work histories of 160 Southern Italian immigrant families
sampled from an Italian neighborhood in Providence, Rhode
Island. I identified the families in the 1915 Rhode Island
state census, and then traced them back to their arrival
in Providence and forward to 1940, using state censuses,
city directories, and marriage, birth, and death records.
I used the vital records to determine kinship, and I also
traced whatever parents, sisters, brothers, and married
children I could find in Providence. One hundred and
forty-four of the family histories extend for at least 10
years, and 113 of them extend for 25 to 40 years, long
enough in most cases to see the second generation married
and situated with their husbands and wives" (pp. 206-207).

894.   Speek, Peter A. A Stake in the Land. New York: Harper
         & Brothers, 1921.
         Progress and problems of Americanization of immigrants
         in rural areas. Deals with immigrant land "colonization, "
         rural educational agencies, immigrant churches. Part of
         the "Americanization Studies: The Acculturation of Immi-
         grant Groups into American Society" commissioned by the
         Carnegie Corporation.

895.   Spencer, Anna Garlin, and Charles Wesley Birtwell, eds.
         The Care of Dependent, Neglected and Wayward Children:
         Being a Report of the Second Section of the International
         Congress of Charities, Correction and Philanthropy. Chicago:
         June, 1893. New York: Arno Press, 1974.
         This is the report of Section II of the International Congress
         of Charities, Correction, and Philanthropy held in Chicago
         in 1893. It contains papers by Anna Garlin Spencer ("So-
         cial Responsibility towards Child-Life"); Homer Folks
         ("Family Life for Dependent and Wayward Children"); and
         Charles W. Birtwell ("The Protection of Neglected and
         Abused Children"); and transcripts of the delegates' dis-
         cussion of issues raised by these and other papers.

896.   Stein, Howard T. An Ethno-Historic Study of Slovak-American
         Identity. New York: Arno Press, 1980.
         Ethnohistoric and psychoanalytic frames of reference are
         used to analyze the Slovak-American experience and explore
         the relation between personal and group identity process
         both in traditional feudal Slovakia and for the period from
         1880 to the present in the urban-industrial region of north-
         eastern, middle Atlantic, and midwestern United States.
         Dynamics of Americanization are explored along the dimen-
         sions of status denigration; cultural role continuity and
         discontinuity, and of rebellion against dependency and auth-
         ority. Explores traditional Slovak society and the Slovak-

American experience at several levels, and attempts to integrate these levels into an ethnohistoric and psychohistoric whole: baseline feudal Slovakia; postserfdom peasantry (1848 through the great migration of 1880-1914); changes in the economy, kinship structure, and family dynamics, and the process of migration, centers of immigration in the United States focusing on the three-rivers area of western Pennsylvania, and finally narrowing down to a study of a Monongahela River mill town, McKeesport. Emphasizes that self-reference (Slovak, Slovak American, American, etc.) must be conceptually distinguished from and psychodynamically integrated with, unconscious Slovak psychocultural "traits" such that a third-generation descendant who no longer identifies with "Slovakness" may, in fact, be "very" Slovak in his or her values, roles, conflicts, and interpersonal relations. Originally, Ph.D. dissertation, University of Pittsburgh, 1972.

897. Stella, Antonio. The Effects of Urban Congestion on Italian Women and Children. New York: Willian Wood, 1908.
"Studying the mortality of Italian women (and Italian adults in general) we are confronted with a peculiar contrast; the official statistics show a small death rate, especially in regard to pulmonary tuberculosis, yet we know--as all medical men, settlement workers, and others conversant with the situation know--that tuberculosis is very prevalent among them. The explanation of this discrepancy lies in the well-known fact that all adult Italians once affected by a serious disease, and so informed, board the first steamer and go back to Italy to die among the vines and orange groves. We cannot, therefore, gauge the mortality of Italian women from the tables of the Health Department, where they contribute only a small percentage (deaths from the very acute diseases, surgical operations, puerperal infection, etc.), but should count the wan-faced women that crowd the steerage of departing ships, or we should search the Bureaus of Vital Statistics of the little towns in Calabria or Sicily, where they swell the local death rate, and import from America tuberculosis where first it was unknown. The vast number of returning consumptives --both men and women--has taken such proportions of late that the Italian Government is considering special measures of quarantine both on board the ships and the point of debarkation" (pp. 25-26).

898. Stella, Antonio. "Tuberculosis and the Italians in the United States." Charities, 12 (1904): 486-489.
"Still worse is the condition where the sweat-shop system flourishes at home, either as extra work, done late in the night, by young men and women already exhausted by ten hours of work in a crowded factory, or as a regular practice, by poor housewives, desirous of adding to their husbands' earnings. Words can hardly describe the pathetic

misery of these Italian women, compelled to sew two or
three dozen of pants for forty cents, using up their last
spark of energy to make life better, when in fact they only
accomplish their self-destruction. For their health is
usually already drained by a too-productive maternity and
periods of prolonged lactation; they live on a deficient, if
not actually insufficient, diet; they sleep in dark, damp
holes, without sunshine or light, and have already had
enough to exhaust them, with the raising of a large family
and the strain of hard housework" (p. 488).

899.   Stokes, J. G. Phelps. "Public Schools as Social Centers."
        Annals of the American Academy of Political and Social Sci-
        ence, 23 (June 1904):   457-463.

900.   Strasser, Susan. Never Done: A History of American House-
        work. New York: Pantheon, 1982.
        Presents a theoretically informed, detailed, and generously
        illustrated history of housework in American society. Uses
        both Marxist and feminist perspectives to interpret a wide
        variety of evidence concerning changes in domestic labor
        over the past two centuries. The historical narrative is
        structured by theoretical insights; central among them is
        the idea that housework has been continually transformed
        with other economic changes. From a center of production
        during much of the nineteenth century, the household became
        a site for the reproduction of labor-power by the end of
        that century. Throughout the twentieth century, the house-
        hold has been transformed into a locus of consumption as
        commodity production has replaced more and more of the
        labor traditionally performed in the household. From this
        historicized vantage point, argues that the cultural ideology
        of separate spheres has always obscured important con-
        nections between the household and the larger economy and
        society, although it had a certain material validity as a
        description of men's and women's work in the nineteenth
        century that has largely disappeared in the twentieth.

901.   Straubenmuller, Gustave. "The Work of the New York Schools
        for the Immigrant Class." Journal of Social Science, 44
        (September 1906):   175-182.

902.   Strom, Sharon Hartman. "Italian-American Women and Their
        Daughters in Rhode Island: The Adolescence of Two Genera-
        tions, 1900-1950." In Betty Boyd Caroli, Richard F. Harney,
        and Lydio F. Tomasi, eds. The Italian Immigrant Woman in
        North America (Toronto: The Multicultural History Society
        of Toronto, 1978), pp. 191-204.
        Conclusions: "In 1974 I developed an undergraduate course
        at the University of Rhode Island on Women in American
        History and was searching for a paper assignment which
        would involve my students directly in the process of doing
        history. I decided to have them interview their mothers

and grandmothers. I asked them to use a questionnaire
some graduate students and I had developed in a research
seminar on women's history. We expected students to use
our questions as a guide and to omit or add questions
suited to their subjects' experiences. This paper is based
on the results of some of my students' interviews. It does
not represent a measurable sample of Italian-American
women. For one thing, the respondents probably come
from upwardly mobile families, since their offspring are
in college. Rather, this paper is an impressionistic analysis of growing up in Rhode Island, as this experience
was remembered and shared with daughters and granddaughters" (p. 191).

903.   Sturino, Franc. "Family and Kin Cohesion Among South
       Italian Immigrants in Toronto." In Betty Boyd Caroli, Robert
       F. Harney, and Lydio F. Tomasi, eds. The Italian Immi-
       grant Woman in North America (Toronto: Multicultural History
       Society of Ontario, 1978), pp. 288-311.
          This paper explores some of the ways that Italians who
       immigrated to Toronto after World War II through kinship
       chains have been able to preserve family and kindred co-
       hesiveness in the face of a New World environment while
       at the same time adjusting to it. The argument presented
       herein was derived from material collected as part of a
       wider study on the social history of South Italian immi-
       gration to Canada from the turn of the century to 1967.
       In this endeavor a case study approach is used, the focus
       being on half a dozen chosen villages located in the west-
       central part of the province of Cosenza. The province
       lies within the region of Calabria, the southernmost part
       of the Italian peninsula. In this study, in addition to
       utilizing standard historical sources such as archival and
       government material, recorded oral interviews are employed
       as a source of information.

904.   Tait, Joseph. Some Aspects of the Effect of the Dominant
       American Culture Upon Children of Italian-Born Parents.
       With a new Preface by Francesco Cordasco. Clifton, N.J.:
       Augustus M. Kelley, 1972.
          Originally a Ph.D. dissertation, Columbia University, 1942.
       The study explores the character traits of Italian children
       and undertakes to determine in what direction and to what
       extent children of Italian-born parents were affected by
       different degrees of contact with the dominant American
       culture.

905.   Talbot, Winthrop. Americanization. New York: H. W.
       Wilson, 1917.

906.   Tentler, Leslie. Wage-earning Women: Industrial Work and
       Family Life in the United States, 1900-1930. New York: Ox-
       ford University Press, 1979.

907.   Thomas, Alan M.   "American Education and the Immigrant."
        Teachers College Record, 55 (1953-54):   253-267.

908.   Thompson, Frank.   The Schooling of the Immigrant.   New
        York: Harper & Brothers, 1920.
            Thompson was Boston superintendent of schools.   Part of
            the "Americanization Studies: The Acculturation of Immi-
            grant Groups into American Society" commissioned by the
            Carnegie Corporation.   Deals with school administration,
            teaching of English, schooling in citizenship and the train-
            ing of teachers for the Americanization of the immigrant.
            "America is looking with anxious hope to the school as the
            chief instrument of Americanization."

909.   Thomson, Gladys Scott.   A Pioneer Family: The Birkbecks
        in Illinois 1818-1827.   London: Jonathan Cape, 1953.
            The letters of Morris Birkbeck and his daughters describe
            the activities and goals of an upper-middle-class Quaker
            family from Surrey, England, as they established a utopian
            colony forty-five miles from Shawneetown, Illinois.   Eliza-
            beth and Prudence Birkbeck record their early impressions
            of the growing community, of their acquaintances and re-
            lationships, of the social life that they value.

910.   Thurston, Henry W.   The Dependent Child: A Story of Chang-
        ing Aims and Methods in the Care of Dependent Children.
        [1930].   New York: Arno Press, 1974.
            Thurston was a leading authority on dependency and de-
            linquency.   This volume, published shortly before he re-
            tired as head of the children's department of the New York
            School of Social Work, traces methods of care for dependent
            and neglected children from the late medieval period to the
            1920's.   The treatment especially details the period after
            1850.   Thurston's discussions of binding out, almshouse
            care, orphan asylums, and placement in foster families
            are enlivened by quotations from contemporary sources
            including numerous statements by children about their ex-
            periences in institutions and foster homes.

911.   Tilly, Louise A., and Joan W. Scott.   Women, Work and
        Family.   New York: Holt, Rinehart, and Winston, 1978.

912.   Tomasi, Lydio F.   The Italian American Family: The South-
        ern Italian Family's Process of Adjustment to an Urban America.
        New York: Center for Migration Studies, 1972.
            Describes in detail the social world and family structure
            of the southern Italian (in which mother and wife was the
            central figure) and concludes that in the South the two
            systems coincide.   The unity of society is the family.   The
            values inherent in this system, born in response to a so-
            cially stagnant and economically impoverished and uncertain
            environment, were challenged by an individualistic urban
            society.   Through the generations conflict and adjustments

have occurred, but Tomasi doubts that class has replaced ethnicity as the cause of the cohesive structure of the middle-class Italian-American nuclear family.

913. "Trapped from Dawn to Dark: Exploited Immigrant Women in Canada." Migration Today, 28 (1981): 21-22.

914. Trattner, Walter I. "Homer Folks, the 'Boodle Board' and Section 647." Journal of American History, 52 (1965): 89-100.
    Presents Folks, a New York social reformer, as one of the foremost founders of the welfare state and a pioneer in urban housing, public health, and social work. Focuses on the struggle over tenement house reform in New York at the turn of the century.

915. Trattner, Walter I. "The First Federal Child Labor Law (1916)." Social Science Quarterly, 50 (1969): 507-24.
    Focuses upon the efforts of settlement house workers and organizations such as the National Child Labor Committee for labor legislation over the opposition of southern textile manufacturers.

916. Trattner, Walter I. Crusade for the Children: A History of the National Child Labor Committee and Child Labor Reform in America. Chicago: Quadrangle Books, 1970.
    Focuses on the efforts of the Child Labor Committee to achieve child labor reform, but places it within the context of a broad child welfare movement and of the many socio-economic, technological, political, and intellectual forces that combined to produce child labor legislation.

917. U.S. Department of Labor. Bureau of Naturalization. The Work of Public Schools with the Bureau of Naturalization. Washington: Government Printing Office, 1917.

918. U.S. Department of Labor. Bureau of Naturalization. Suggestions for Americanization Work Among Foreign-Born Women. Washington: Government Printing Office, 1921.

919. U.S. Department of Labor. Bureau of Naturalization. Suggestions for Securing and Holding Attendance of Foreign-Born Adults upon Public School English and Citizenship Classes. Washington: Government Printing Office, 1923.

920. U.S. Women's Bureau. Health Problems of Women in Industry. Bulletin No. 18. Washington: Government Printing Office, 1921.

921. U.S. Women's Bureau. The Family Status of Breadwinning Women: A Study of Material in the Census Schedules of a Selected Locality. Bulletin No. 23. Washington: Government Printing Office, 1922.

922.   U.S. Women's Bureau. Married Women in Industry, by Mary
        Nelson Winslow. Bulletin No. 38. Washington: Government
        Printing Office, 1924.

923.   Valletta, Clement Lawrence. A Study of Americanization in
        Carneta: Italian American Identity Through Three Generations.
        New York: Arno Press, 1975.
            Deals with the cultural adaptation and identity formation of
            three generations of an Italian-American group. This group,
            mainly of peasant origin, settled in a rural and industrial
            area in eastern Pennsylvania and established the borough
            of Carneta (a pseudonym). The study, covering the years
            1890-1965, offered an opportunity to evaluate the American-
            ization of "new" immigrants in an environment that was
            both rural and industrialized. Approach used was cultural/
            anthropological, with participant-observer techniques, and
            with the use of oral histories and archival records. Con-
            clusions suggest that the experience in Carneta, unlike that
            of Italian Americans studied in urban environments, was
            one which allowed the Carnetans to "unify their individual,
            family, communal, and ethnic images as they went about
            becoming American." Originally, Ph.D. dissertation, Uni-
            versity of Pennsylvania, 1968.

924.   Vanderbilt, Gertrude L[efferts]. The Social History of Flat-
        bush and Manners and Customs of the Dutch Settlers in Kings
        County. 2nd ed. Brooklyn: Frederick Loeser, 1909.
            Deals with the developments and changes in traditions,
            customs, and manners of the Dutch in the town of Flatbush,
            New York. Covers the time from the original settlement
            in the 1600's up to 1880. Addressed to the descendants of
            the early settlers, the work was written because the author
            felt that Flatbush was rapidly losing all traces of its in-
            dividuality as a Dutch settlement. Each chapter is devoted
            to a different topic, such as dress, weddings, furniture,
            cooking, gardens, churches, societies.

925.   Van Rensselaer, [Mrs.] John King. The Goede Vrouw of
        Mana-ha-ta at Home and in Society, 1609-1760. New York:
        Charles Scribner's Sons, 1898. Reprint. New York: Arno
        Press, 1972.
            Presents a description of the history of New Netherland
            and colonial New York through a discussion of the lives
            of the women of this time and place. The emphasis is on
            social history, household affairs, customs, manners, life-
            style, and so forth. The author writes "between the lines
            of contemporaneous history," placing the women in the
            foreground. Records and correspondence concerning the
            women of this setting are scarce. The description neces-
            sarily revolves around the women of the most prominent
            Dutch families of the time. Along with family papers, also
            uses records and published histories of the area.

926. Venturelli, Peter J. "Tuscan-American Families." In Richard N. Juliani, ed., The Family and Community Life of Italian Americans (Staten Island, N.Y.: The Italian American Historical Association, 1983), pp. 69-80.
Conclusions: "The North Italian District on Chicago's Lower West Side is home for 1,200 Italians originally from the Tuscan province in central Italy. Using a case study of this ethnic community, a study which included participant observation and extensive interviews, this paper describes and analyzes how ethnicity and territory affect the Tuscan family across generations; how the Tuscan American family and its members adjust to suburban living; how ethnic identity changes form as a result of migration from the local Tuscan district; how and to what extent Tuscan-American families assimilate into mass society; and how, in this particular community, the ethnic family and its surroundings share a symbiotic relationship" (p. 69).

927. Wade, Joseph S. "The Teaching of English to Foreigners in the First Two Years of Elementary School." School Work, 2 (November 1903): 285-292.

928. Walter, I. "One Year Arrival. The Adjustment of Indochinese Women in the United States: 1979-1980." International Migration, 19 (1981): 129-152.

929. Webster, Hanson H. Americanization and Citizenship. Boston: Houghton Mifflin, 1919.

930. Webster, Janice Reiff. "Domestication and Americanization: Scandinavian Women in Seattle, 1888 to 1900." Journal of Urban History, 4 (1978): 275-309.
Maintains that the dynamics of the city and the cultural patterns of Scandinavian immigrants in Seattle caused these immigrant women to discard their traditional roles and responsibilities.

931. Weet, Herbert S. "Citizenship and the Evening Use of School Buildings." The Common Good, 4 (1911): 7-9.

932. Wheaton, H. H. "Education of Immigrants." In Annual Report, U.S. Commissioner of Education, 1916 (Washington: Government Printing Office, 1917), Vol. I, pp. 339-351.

933. Wheaton, H. H. "Recent Progress in the Education of Immigrants." In Annual Report, U.S. Commissioner of Education, 1914. (Washington: Government Printing Office, 1915), Vol. I, pp. 425-54.

934. Wheaton, H. H. "Survey of Adult Immigrant Education." Immigrants in America Review, I (June 1915): 42-71.

935. Wheaton, H. H. "United States Bureau of Education and the

Immigrant." Annals of the American Academy of Political
and Social Science, 67 (September 1916): 273-283.

936.   Williams, Phyllis H.   South Italian Folkways in Europe and
America: A Handbook for Social Workers, Visiting Nurses,
School Teachers and Physicians.   New Haven, Conn.:   Yale
University Press, 1938.   Reprint.   With Introductory Note by
Francesco Cordasco.   New York: Russell & Russell, 1970.
This "is a pragmatically structured handbook of comparative
social anthropology which presents a detailed overview of
south Italian cultural attributes in capsuled areas of social
behavior and interaction (Employment, Housing, Marriage
and the Family, Education, etc.), and then relates these
to the American society to which they had been transplanted."

937.   Winsey, Valentine Rossilli.   "The Southern Italian Immigrant
Family in the United States."   In Humbert Nelli, ed., The
United States and Italy: The First Two Hundred Years.   (New
York: The American Italian Historical Association, 1977),
pp. 200-205.

938.   Woodward, Elizabeth A.   Report on Elementary Education of
Non-English-Speaking Adults: Survey and Tendencies of Work,
1919-1921.   Washington: National Education Association.   Commission of Revision of Elementary Education, 1920.

939.   Wortman, Marlene Stein.   "Domesticating the Nineteenth-
Century American City."   Prospects, 3 (1977):   531-72.
Maintains that historians have neglected the feminine characteristics of urban progressivism and that much of the re-
formist impulse flowed from a preoccupation with making
the city, as a physical and social environment, conform to
the demands of the ideal home environment.

940.   Yans-McLaughlin, Virginia.   Family and Community: Italian
Immigrants in Buffalo, 1880-1930.   Ithaca: Cornell University
Press, 1977.
Focuses on the family experience of working-class Italians
in Buffalo, stressing the factors that promoted family cohesion.   Sees the family as a flexible adaptive institution
which, nonetheless, can retain traditional patterns.   Emphasizes the danger of employing ideal types to specific
conditions among particular immigrant groups, as Handlin
does in The Uprooted.   The extended family household, for
example, rarely existed in southern Italy.   Therefore, the
prevalence of the nuclear form among immigrants in the
United States cannot be viewed as proof of disruption or
instability.   Other significant indexes of family disorganization and change, including percentages of matriarchal or
female-dominated households, desertion by male family
heads, illegitimacy rates, intergeneration conflict, and
exogamous marriages remained relatively low.   See review,
J. W. Briggs, International Migration Review, 12 (1978):
579-580.

941. Yans-McLaughlin, Virginia. "A Flexible Tradition: South
      Italian Immigrants Confront a New Work Experience." Journal
      of Social History, 7 (1974): 429-45.
      Argues that the factory system in New York canneries and
      other businesses had a much less devastating effect upon
      southern Italian culture, and especially family relationships,
      than is usually alleged. Asserts that canneries permitted
      families to work together and that homework also permitted
      continuance of that tradition.

942. Yans-McLaughlin, Virginia. "Patterns of Work and Family
      Organization: Buffalo's Italians." Journal of Inter-Disciplinary
      History, 5 (1971): 299-314.
      An investigation of female occupational patterns and family
      organization among Buffalo's Italian Americans between
      1900 and 1930, from which the author concludes that work-
      ing wives did not alter family power arrangements or dis-
      rupt the traditional family. Concludes that generalization
      of the impact of female labor upon family arrangements
      must be qualified by class, ethnic and religious background,
      region, and city.

943. Young, Pauline V. "Social Problems in the Education of the
      Immigrant Child." American Sociological Review, I (June
      1936): 419-29.
      The assimilation of the immigrant child and youth living
      with their foreign-born parents is in the last analysis only
      surface deep. They may appear assimilated in public, but
      in their private life they remain hyphenated in attitudes
      with the inevitable duality of personality. The school must
      have adequate knowledge of the life of the immigrant com-
      munity before efforts to Americanize the child can be suc-
      cessful.

944. Ziegler, Suzanne. "The Family Unit and International Migra-
      tion: The Perceptions of Italian Immigrant Children." Inter-
      national Migration Review, 11 (Fall 1977): 326-333.
      Examines the centrality of the family, both nuclear and
      extended, in the Italian postwar migratory process to Canada
      and in their post-migratory adjustment. In a series of
      interviews with first generation immigrant children, two
      themes emerged: The necessity of keeping the nuclear
      family together and the importance of intergenerational
      ties and commitments. The respondents tended to view
      their parents' decision to migrate as one primarily motivated
      by familial considerations. That is, it was seen as a
      decision based on their future as a family, whether for re-
      unification, or for greater opportunities for the children.
      For these respondents, family ties have not only survived
      migration but have been fortified by it.

945. Zinn, Maxine Baca. "Employment and Education of Mexican-
      American Women: The Interplay of Modernity and Ethnicity in

Eight Families." Harvard Education Review, 50 (February 1980): 47-62.

946.   Addams, Jane.   A New Conscience and an Ancient Evil.   New
       York: Macmillan, 1912.
           This work, describing dangers facing young immigrant fac-
           tory women at the turn of the century, helped incite a
           crusade against prostitution.

947.   Aiken, John R.   "New Netherlands Arbitration in the 17th
       Century."   The Arbitration Journal, 29 (September 1974):
       145-60.
           It has been assumed that the earliest mercantile arbitration
           on the American continent was derived from the English
           common law used in the British colonies.   This article
           has found evidences of arbitration in the Dutch colony of
           New Netherland.   The author has found the earliest example
           (1662) of a woman serving as an arbitrator.   Contends that
           arbitration in New Netherland was relatively swift and
           simple compared to that in the British colonies, and that
           the codified provisions for arbitration established by the
           English in New York (after 1664) were influenced by the
           Dutch arbitration practices.

948.   Aleandri, Emelise.   "Women in the Italian-American Theatre
       of the Nineteenth Century."   In Betty Boyd Caroli, Robert F.
       Harney, and Lydio F. Tomasi, eds. The Italian Immigrant
       Woman in North America (Toronto: Multicultural History So-
       ciety of Ontario, 1978), pp. 358-368.
           Conclusions: The history of the Italian-American theatre
           in New York City remains consistent with the history of all
           theatre in that it reflects the society and time which pro-
           duced it.   The special characteristics of this particular
           ethnic theatre and the women who participated in it depended
           ultimately on the sociological patterns and make-up of the
           Italian immigrant society in America, specifically in New
           York City.

949.   Alnaes, Barbara Ann.   Borghild Dahl.   Second-Generation
       Norwegian-American Author.   Master's thesis, University of
       Oslo, 1970.
           Looks at Borghild Dahl's views on the Norwegian-American
           immigrant family as compared with Norwegian-American
           history and with other fiction on this subject.   Borghild
           Dahl wrote numerous novels for young people in which she
           hoped to describe the way their parents and grandparents
           lived in the Midwest in previous years.   Her books cover

the period between 1870 and 1940 and emphasize the immigrant woman. Borghild Dahl's parents came to Minneapolis in 1882 where her father became a successful surveyor and engineer, and did much of the planning of Minneapolis and other parts of the state. Borghild Dahl became a popular teacher on the high school and college levels in spite of her near blindness. In 1978, she was still leading an active life at 88 in New York City.

950.   Ames, Azel. Sex in Industry: A Plea for the Working Girl. Boston: J. R. Osgood, 1875.

951.   Anderson, Eric. "Prostitution and Social Justice: Chicago, 1910-1915." Social Service Review, 48 (1974): 203-28. Examines the report of the Chicago Vice Commission and the eventual closing of the city's red-light district, and concludes that the antiprostitution crusade drew its support from a coalition of business leaders and professional altruists. Sees vice reform as a combination of municipal and social justice reform elements.

952.   Aquino, Belinda. "Filipino Women in Hawaii: An Overview." (Paper presented at the 6th Annual Conference on Ethnic and Minority Studies, University of Wisconsin, La Crosse, April 19-22, 1978, Educational Resources Information Center [ERIC] document ED 160 493).

953.   Arizpe, L. "Mujeres Migrantes y Economía Campesina: Análisis de una Cohorte Migratoria a la Ciudad de México, 1940-1970." America Indígena, 38 (April-June 1978): 303-326.

954.   Arnopoulos, S. Problems of Immigrant Women in the Canadian Labour Force. Ottawa: Conseil Consultatif Canadien de la Situation de la Femme, 1979.

955.   Atkinson, Mary M. "Women in Farm Life and Rural Economy." Annals of the American Academy of Political and Social Sciences, 143 (May 1929): 188-94.

956.   Avery, Evelyn G. "Tradition and Independence in Jewish Feminist Novels." Melus, 7 (1980): 49-55. Conclusions: More than fifty years ago, Anzia Yezierska, a struggling immigrant writer, depicted the anguish of poor Jewish women, burdened by heritage, gender, and class. In her novel Bread Givers (1925), Yezierska passionately portrays the trials of Sara Smolinsky, who battles an environment more impoverished, sexist, and tyrannical than most contemporary heroines confront. Determined to survive with dignity, Sara acquires an education, career, and husband, and finally achieves partial reconciliation with her authoritarian father. Such resolutions, however, have been rare in Jewish-American novels. In fact, before the

seventies, Jewish women writing fiction generally neglected Yezierska's concerns. Memorable stories such as Tillie Olsen's "Tell Me a Riddle" and Grace Paley's "Faith," reveal feminine predicaments, but they were not representative of the literature.

957. Barron, Milton L., ed. The Blending American: Patterns of Intermarriage. Chicago: Quadrangle Books, 1972.

958. Bebel, August. Woman Under Socialism. New York: Schocken Books, 1971. Published originally in Germany in 1883.
Focuses on women's situation in contemporary nineteenth-century society, especially in the labor force. Bebel did not seek to restore women to the home, but instead encouraged their broader participation in economic and political life. He appealed to woman "not to remain behind in this struggle in which her redemption and emancipation are at stake," but to join the working class in its struggle for a better future.

959. Bell, Ernest A. Fighting the Traffic in Young Girls, or War on the White Slave Trade. New York: Nichols, 1910.

960. Bernardy, Amy. "Sulle Condizioni delle Donne e dei Fanciulli Italiani negli Stati Uniti del Centro e dell'ovest della Confederazione del Nord America." Bollettino dell'Emigrazione, 1 (1911), pp. 3-170.

961. Bernardy, Amy. "La Tutela delle Donne e dei Fanciulli Italiani negli Stati Uniti d'America." In Atti del II Congresso degli Italiani all'Estero, pp. 46-73. Roma: Tipografia Editrice Nazionale, 1911.
Perceptive commentary by Italian journalist on the social needs of Italian immigrant women and children in the United States.

962. Bieler-Bretell, C. Portuguese Emigration and "Local Group." Variations on a Theme. Lisbon: Universidade Nova, 1975.
A study of the family in the context of the migration experience, with particular reference to Portuguese women.

963. Birnbaum, Lucia Chiavola. "Education for Conformity: The Case of Sicilian American Women Professionals." In Remigio U. Pane, ed., Italian Americans in the Professions (New York: American Italian Historical Association, 1983), pp. 243-252.

964. Blau, Zena Smith. "In Defense of the Jewish Mother." Midstream, 18 (February 1967): 42-49.

965. Blicksilver, Edith. "The Japanese-American Woman, the Second World War and the Relocation Camp Experience." Women's Studies International Forum, 5 (1982): 351-353.

966.   Bodnar, John E. "The Formation of Ethnic Consciousness:
        Slavic Immigrants in Steelton." In John E. Bodnar, ed.,
        The Ethnic Experience in Pennsylvania (Lewisburg, Pa.:
        Bucknell University Press, 1973), pp. 309-311.
            Includes notices of Croats, Serbs, Slovenes, Bulgarians,
            and the patterns of family adjustment.

967.   Bogen, Boris D. Jewish Philanthropy: Methods of Jewish
        Social Service in the United States. New York: Macmillan,
        1907.

968.   Boody, Bertha. A Psychological Study of Immigrant Children
        at Ellis Island. Baltimore: Williams & Wilkins, 1926. Re-
        print. New York: Arno Press, 1970.
            An examination of immigrant children in 1922 (August and
            September) and 1923 (July and August) with review of pro-
            cedures at Ellis Island, literature on immigrant testing,
            and application of conclusions to Immigration Law of 1924.
            Conclusion: "The smaller number of immigrants arriving,
            the more careful selection at the source, the lower quotas
            for races which have come to this country in the last few
            years, in numbers impossible of assimilation, the oppor-
            tunity for more intensive physical and mental examination
            on arrival, and for greater leisure in getting the facts
            necessary to determine the fitness of the individual, all
            give promise of the establishment of improved conditions
            throughout the country." Originally, Ph.D. dissertation,
            Johns Hopkins University, 1924.

969.   Boswell, Thomas D., and James R. Curtis. The Cuban-
        American Experience: Culture, Images and Perspectives.
        Totowa, N.J.: Rowman & Allanheld, 1984.

970.   Boyd, Monica. "The Status of Immigrant Women in Canada."
        The Canadian Review of Sociology and Anthropology, 12 (No-
        vember 1975): 406-416.

971.   Boyd, Monica. "Occupations of Female Immigrants and North
        American Statistics." International Migration Review, 10
        (1976): 73-79.
            Findings: The exclusion of most married women from oc-
            cupational tabulations compounds the problems associated
            with the use of summary occupational data appearing in the
            Canadian Immigration Statistics and the United States Immi-
            gration and Naturalization Service (Annual Report[s]). Fu-
            ture publications of these data sources should present sex-
            specific occupational tabulations. Not only would such tab-
            ulations facilitate investigations on the status of immigrant
            women, but they also would permit adjustments for the
            changing sex-composition of immigrant workers. If the
            underrepresentation of married women in occupational tab-
            ulations persists, the researcher would have the choice of
            using either the summary occupational data or the occupational

data for male immigrants. The result would be an improved, if not more accurate, analysis of the economic skills of immigrants to North America.

972. Bristow, Edward J. Prostitution and Prejudice: The Jewish Fight Against White Slavery, 1870-1939. New York: Schocken Books, 1983.
Represents a new genre of ethnic and social history, a study of the underside of Jewish life at a crucial stage in history. Set against the backdrop of rising economic dislocation and anti-Semitism, the breakdown of family ties and religious observances along with extensive migrations from Europe, the work examines widespread Jewish participation both in prostitution and the struggle against "white slavery." Relates the world of Jewish procurers and brothel-keepers to the international networks that supplied women in Europe, the Near East, Africa, and North and South America.

973. Brungot, Hilde Petra. Dorothea Dahl: Norwegian-American Author of Everyday Experience. A thesis presented to the English Department of the University of Oslo, 1977.
Presents an "account of the life and work of Dorothea Dahl." Dorothea Dahl in her numerous short stories and novel describes the second phase of Norwegian migration to America, from the Midwest to the Northwest. She was the best of the women writers describing this period and is often considered second only to Ole Rölvaag in the quality of her writing as a Norwegian-American. Much of her writing appeared in newspapers both in Norwegian and English.

974. Buchanan, S. H. "Haitian Women in New York City." Migration Today, 7 (September 1979): 19-25.

975. Buckley, Joan. "Martha Ostenso: A Critical Study of Her Novels." Unpublished Ph.D. dissertation, University of Iowa, 1976.
Offers an overview of the events of Ostenso's life; an analysis of her novel Wild Geese; studies of the fourteen other novels written by Ostenso; and an evaluation of Ostenso's accomplishments and limitations as a writer. Two appendixes provide a detailed bibliography of writings by and about Martha Ostenso.

976. Buckley, Joan N. "Martha Ostenso: Norwegian-American Immigrant Novelist." Norwegian-American Studies, 28 (1979): 69-81.
Examines the reasons why Martha Ostenso, "the first Norwegian-American woman to support herself and family by her writing," should be considered an immigrant writer.

977. Burchell, R. A. The San Francisco Irish, 1848-1880. Berkeley: University of California Press, 1980.

Depicts the Irish family during the thirty years following
the Gold Rush, and finds that by and large San Francisco
was much more hospitable to it than other major U. S.
cities. Based entirely on primary sources, this monograph
illuminates the experience of one of the major groups who
made San Francisco into a major modern metropolis.

978.   Carreiro, M. C. "The Participation of the Portuguese Immigrant Female in Higher Education." Unpublished report.
Boston College, 1968.

979.   Caswell, L. E. "The Portuguese in Boston." North End
Mission Magazine, 2 (1873): 57-72.

980.   [Center on Pre-Retirement and Aging of Catholic University
of America and the National Center for Urban Ethnic Affairs].
Symposium on Older Americans of Euro-Ethnic Origin. Washington, D. C., 1979.

981.   Chaney, E. M. "Women Who Go and the Women Who Stay
Behind." Migration Today, 10 (1982): 6-13.

982.   Cheng, Lucie, and Edna Bonacich, eds. Labor Immigration
Under Capitalism. Asian Workers in the United States Before World War II. Berkeley: University of California Press,
1984.
The plight of the Asian immigrant worker (considerable attention to women) in the United States prior to World War
II is well-documented in this monograph. This immigration is well placed in the larger political and economic context
in which it arose--namely, the development of capitalism
in the United States and the emergence of imperialism,
especially in relation to Asia.

983.   Chiaravillo, Edvige. La Protezione della Donna Italiana all'
Estero. Turin: Tipographia Barvalle, 1911.
On various efforts to provide guidance and care by Italian
government agencies and private philanthropies to Italian
immigrant women.

984.   Child, Irwin L. Italian or American? The Second Generation
in Conflict. New Haven, Conn.: Yale University Press,
1943. Reprint. With an Introduction by F. Cordasco. New
York: Russell & Russell, 1970.
Study of second-generation Italians in New Haven. Socio-
psychological approach to immigrant groups and the family
and their acculturation.

985.   Chotzinoff, Samuel. A Lost Paradise. New York: Alfred
A. Knopf, 1955.
Immigrant life in the Lower East Side (New York City)
Jewish community. Extraordinarily rich in the details of
everyday life, and one of the most important immigrant
memoirs.

986.   Christianson, J. R.   "Literary Traditions of Norwegian-
       American Women." In Odd S. Lovoll, ed., Makers of an
       American Immigrant Legacy: Essays in Honor of Kenneth O.
       Bjork (Northfield, Minn.:   The Norwegian-American Historical
       Association, 1980), pp. 92-110.
          The "sources and setting of immigrant culture" are set
       out and defined.   Aims to illustrate the thesis that Ameri-
       can culture must constantly renew its ties to the "lands,
       languages, and cultures of its roots" by "describing the
       literary traditions of Norwegian-American women writers
       from the years between 1850 and 1950 and by relating them
       to the literary traditions of Scandinavian women throughout
       the world."

987.   Claghorn, Kate H.   "Methods of Evaluating Our Immigrant
       Peoples." Mental Hygiene, 7 (January 1923):   20-31.
          Generally critical of intelligence tests and their widespread
       use in evaluating immigrants: "Those who are actively
       engaged in dealing with social problems are skeptical as to
       the generalizations based on intelligence tests, for instance,
       those that show a high percentage of mental defect among
       special classes."   Claghorn was a faculty member of the
       New York School of Social Work.

988.   Cohen, Lucy M.   "The Female Factor in Resettlement." So-
       ciety, 14 (September/October 1977):   27-30.

989.   Cole, Donald B.   Immigrant City: Lawrence, Massachusetts,
       1845-1921.   Chapel Hill: University of North Carolina Press,
       1963.
          Important study on immigrant's search for security in
       America;   immigrant acculturation; and life in the urban
       immigrant community.   Focus is on the I. W. W. textile
       strike in Lawrence in 1912 (in which immigrant women
       played a critical role) and the role of the immigrant com-
       munities.   Originally, Ph.D. dissertation, Harvard Uni-
       versity, 1957.

990.   Connelly, Mark T.   "Fear, Anxiety, and Hope: The Response
       to Prostitution in the United States, 1900-1920." Unpublished
       Ph.D. dissertation, Rutgers University, 1977.
          Views prostitution as a symbol for a variety of social fears
       and anxieties caused by immigration, rural decay, urban
       graft and corruption, industrial squalor, venereal disease,
       and changing sexual mores.   Examines the differing re-
       sponses of reformers at all governmental levels to prosti-
       tution.

991.   Cook, Alice H.   "Women and Work in Industrial Societies."
       In Noel Iverson, ed., Urbanism and Urbanization: Views,
       Aspects, and Dimensions (Leiden: E. J. Brill, 1984), pp.
       209-234.

992.   Corcos, L. "Una Inchiesta Sui Matrimoni fra Immigranti e
        Nazionali." Italiani nel Mondo, 23 (January 1967): 6-10.

993.   Cordasco, Francesco, and Rocco Galattioto. "Ethnic Dis-
        placement in the Interstitial Community: The East Harlem
        (New York City) Experience." Phylon: The Atlanta Uni-
        versity Review of Race & Culture, 31 (Fall 1970): 302-312.
        The Jewish, Italian, and Puerto Rican communities, inter-
        ethnic relations, and the patterns of evolving change.

994.   Cordasco, Francesco, and Thomas M. Pitkin. The White
        Slave Trade and The Immigrants. Detroit: Blaine Ethridge,
        1981.
        Delineates the historical contents (largely from contempo-
        rary sources) in which the white slave trade existed in the
        period of the great migrations to the United States. The
        account begins in 1902 and includes a source document,
        "Importation and Harboring of Women for Immoral Pur-
        poses." A select bibliography and note on immigration
        literature are included.

995.   Costin, Lela B. Two Sisters for Social Justice: A Biogra-
        phy of Grace and Edith Abbott. Urbana: University of Illi-
        nois Press, 1983.
        Edith and Grace Abbott were born in Nebraska in the late
        1870's. They were lifelong leaders in movements for so-
        cial justice from the Progressive period through the New
        Deal. In their lives, the Abbott sisters were involved with
        issues concerning immigrants, mothers and infants, child
        labor, women's suffrage, and world peace. Grace is per-
        haps best known as the successor to Julia Lathrop in head-
        ing the U. S. Children's Bureau; Edith for her pioneering
        study Women in Industry (1909), and for her role in the
        development of the University of Chicago's School of Social
        Service and Administration. The Abbotts were also among
        that group of women who centered around Jane Addams and
        Hull House--a group that included Addams herself, Florence
        Kelley, and Sophonisba P. Breckinridge.

996.   Crocker, Bertram. "A Study of the Cultural Integration of
        a Welsh Community With Its American Environment." Un-
        published Ph. D. dissertation, Columbia University, 1952.

997.   Cropsey, Edward. The Nether Side of New York, or, The
        Vice, Crime and Poverty of the Great Metropolis. New York:
        Sheldon, 1872.

998.   Cummings, Judith. "Indochinese Women Find Life in Ameri-
        ca Fraught with Barriers." The New York Times, 84 (No-
        vember 1, 1984): C1, C12.
        An overview of the difficulties faced by women from South-
        east Asia "struggling with special barriers to a smooth re-
        settlement in the United States." Notices of Vietnamese,
        Cambodian, and Laotian women.

999.   Davison, L. "Women Refugees: Special Needs and Pro-
        grams." Journal of Refugee Resettlement, 3 (May 1981):
        16-26.
            Summarizes the main findings of a study, undertaken by
            the Equity Policy Center with support from the Asia
            Foundation, which identifies the major problems facing
            Indochinese refugee women being resettled in the U.S.,
            reviews programs available to them, and suggests changes
            in current programs.

1000.   Denis, A. B. "Femmes: Ethnie et Occupation au Quebec
        et en Ontario, 1931-1971." Canadian Ethnic Studies, 13
        (1981): 75-90.

1001.   Dick, Everett. "The Frontier Women." In his The Dixie
        Frontier: A History of the Southern Frontier from the First
        Transmontane Beginnings to the Civil War, Chap. 26. New
        York: Alfred A. Knopf, 1948. Reprint. New York: G. P.
        Putnam's Sons, 1964.

1002.   Di Leonardo, Marcaela. The Varieties of Ethnic Experience:
        Kinship, Class and Gender Among California Italian-Ameri-
        cans. Ithaca, N.Y.: Cornell University Press, 1984.
            Sees the ethnics and their families as people shaped by
            the "overarching effects of the global economy . . . the
            variety and malleability of kin forms, the linked contin-
            uities of class division and male dominance and the crea-
            tivity and adaptability of the human construction and re-
            construction of social reality." Strongly feminist view
            articulated in a neo-marxian perspective.

1003.   Dobbert, Guido Andre. The Disintegration of an Immigrant
        Community: The Cincinnati Germans, 1870-1920. New York:
        Arno Press, 1980.
            Cincinnati's German community was moribund before
            World War I had begun in Europe. If it died during the
            war, its death was of its own making. The war served
            only to heighten its agony. Nativism, upon reaching its
            full strength at war's end, had found only a dead or dying
            community. In the case of Cincinnati, decay was mani-
            fested primarily by two major symptoms: one physical,
            the other sociopsychological, with considerable interaction.
            The community's physical disintegration showed itself not
            only biologically in the decrease of new blood coming from
            Germany, but also geographically in its members being
            spread increasingly thin over an ever expanding metro-
            politan area. This led to a physical separation of the
            community's elite from its rank and file. The elite, by
            living now in one of the more exclusive residential sec-
            tions of the city, had simply exchanged one ghetto for
            another. An enormous gap grew between the German im-
            migrant who had done well and the immigrant who had
            not done so well. It was manifested immediately in the

community's lack of competent leadership the moment
Cincinnati began to become a metropolis. Originally,
Ph. D. dissertation, University of Chicago, 1965.

1004.   Donelin, Mary C. "American Irish Women Firsts." Journal
of the American Historical Society, 24 (1925): 215-21.

1005.   Douglass, William A., ed. Anglo-American Contributions
to Basque Studies. Essays on Basque Immigrant Culture,
and on the Basque Homeland. Reno, Nev.: Social Sciences
Center, 1978.

1006.   Draper, J. "La Migration Est Aussi Une Question qui Af-
fecte Les Femmes." Migrations, 29 (1982): 12-17.

1007.   Dublin, Thomas, ed. Farm to Factory: Women's Letters,
1830-1860. New York: Columbia University Press, 1979.
Dublin's introduction, notes, and afterword shed new light
on women's economic interests and their other plans and
aspirations in the pre-Civil War generation.

1008.   Duncan, Hannibal C. Immigration and Assimilation. Boston:
D. C. Heath, 1933.
Book I deals with conditions in other countries which bear
on immigration to the United States. Book II is a collection of life histories of immigrants, the children and
grandchildren of immigrants.

1009.   Edger, Henry. Prostitution and the International Women's
League. New Bedford, Mass.: Benj. R. Tucker, 1878.

1010.   Ellett, Elizabeth F. The Pioneer Women of the West.
Philadelphia: Porter & Coates, 1852. Reprint. Freeport,
N. Y.: Books for Libraries, 1973.

1011.   Ellington, George. The Women of New York: Or the Under-
World of the Great City. Illustrating the Life of Women of
Fashion, Women of Pleasure, Actresses and Ballet Girls,
Saloon Girls, Pickpockets and Shoplifters, Artists' Female
Models, Women-of-the-Town, etc., etc., etc., with Numerous Engravings. [1869]. New York: Arno Press, 1976.
An example of the male-made popular literature of the
day that "rips the veil from shame and explores the evils
that drag innocent women into sin and honorable men into
disease and moral destruction." Attempts a measured
report of the transformation of virtue into vice that hits
rich and poor alike. It anticipates the populist idea of
the curse of the big cities of the East. A tour of the
nether world of crime in palace and slum, into the gam-
bling dens, the dames and demi-mondes, the mansions
and houses of ill repute.

1012.   Erickson, Charlotte. "English Women Immigrants in America

in the Nineteenth Century: Expectations and Reality." Faw-
cett Library Papers, No. 7. [LLRS Publications, 1983].

1013.   Falk, Candace. Love, Anarchy, and Emma Goldman. New
York: Holt, Rinehart & Winston, 1984.
Falk (editor of the Emma Goldman Papers Project, National Archives) deals primarily with Goldman's private
life.

1014.   Fanning, Charles. "Elizabeth Cullinan's House of Gold:
Culmination of an Irish-American Dream." Melus, 7 (1980):
31-48.
Findings. Fiction about the Irish experience in America
contains a recurrent conjunction of characterization and
symbolism: the dominant mother who controls a house
that also functions as a central organizing symbol. The
persistence of this literary theme suggests that it reflects
observable truths of Irish-American life. The reasons
behind the development of such a figure and her establishment in the house-as-fortress most probably lie in con-
sideration of the salient defining elements of the experience
of the Irish ethnic group--Ireland, Catholicism, and immigration. In the first place, conditions in Ireland were
detrimental to the male self-image of the Catholic peasantry who made up the bulk of the nineteenth-century immigration. As unwilling colonial dependents under British
imperial rule, the Irish were oppressed politically, culturally, and economically. Of course, the women suffered
along with the men.

1015.   Feingold, Gustave. "Intelligence of the First Generation of
Immigrant Groups." Journal of Educational Psychology, 15
(February 1924): 65-82.
Study of nationality and IQ in secondary school students.
IQ's ranged from 105 (Scotch and English) to 97 (Polish
and Italian).

1016.   Fine, David. "Abraham Cahan, Stephen Crane and the R
mantic Tenement Tale of the Nineties." American Studie
14 (Spring 1973): 95-108.

1017.   Fine, David. "Attitudes Toward Acculturation in the En
Fiction of the Jewish Immigrant, 1900-1917." America
Jewish Historical Quarterly, 63 (September 1973): 45-5

1018.   Fine, David. "Immigrant Ghetto Fiction, 1885-1918:
Annotated Bibliography." American Literary Realism
1910, 6 (Summer 1973): 169-196.

1019.   Fine, David M. The City, the Immigrant and Ameri
Fiction, 1880-1920. Metuchen, N.J.: Scarecrow Pr
1977.
Examines novels and stories written by both imm

and native-born authors during the peak ghetto years,
1880-1920, the period bounded by the beginning of the
massive influx of southeastern European immigrants into
America's large cities and the beginning of the decline of
immigrant ghetto communities with the post-World War I
restriction laws.   Reflects the attempt throughout to emphasize both the literary and historical contexts of the
fiction.   Ghetto fiction was a response to an unsettling
contemporary reality, but the conventions it drew on were
part of a long history of slum portraiture in literature.
Major concern of the study is to trace the literary antecedents of immigrant ghetto fiction in eighteenth- and
nineteenth-century novels.   At the same time concerned
with the contemporary social issues and historical factors
which conditioned the fiction.   Individual chapters are devoted to the literature of nativism and xenophobia, urban
reform and the cosmopolitan ideal, the "tenement tale"
tradition, the literary discovery of the ghetto, the immigrant labor novel, the immigrant as author, and the works
of Abraham Cahan, the most important of the first-
generation immigrant authors of the period.

1020.   Flower, B. O.   Civilization's Inferno: Or, Studies in the
        Social Cellar.   Boston: Arena Publishing, 1893.

1021.   Frittelli, A. T.   "Report on Migrant Women in Their Coun-
        try of Origin."   International Migration, 19 (1981):   114-128.

1022.   Frumkin, Boris, and Shimon Ginzburg.   On Jews, America,
        and Immigration: A Socialist Perspective.   Translated and
        edited by Uri D. Herscher and Stanley F. Chyet.   New York:
        Ktav Publishing House, 1980.
            Originally a report to the International Socialist Congress
        written in 1907 concerning the recent immigrant Jewish
        workers in the United States.   The authors were Marxist
        socialists active in the Jewish Bund.   They believed that
        the Jews had traded the tyranny of the czar for abuse by
        the great industrialists who ran the factories and sweat-
        shops with more concern for their machines than their
        employees.   Frumkin and Ginzburg could not understand
        why the American labor movement was not attracted to
        Socialism to end its exploitation.   The forces at work
        during this formative period of the Jewish community and
        its labor unions, including the restrictionist policy of im-
        migration by the U. S. government, are illuminated in this
        historical document through the issue of emigration and
        immigration from the Socialist point of view.

1023.   Gabaccia, Donna R.   From Sicily to Elizabeth Street: Hous-
        ing and Social Change Among Italian Immigrants, 1880-1930.
        Albany: State University of New York Press, 1984.
            Analyzes the relationship of environment to social behavior.
        It revises our understanding of the Italian-American family

and challenges existing notions of the Italian immigrant
experience by comparing everyday family and social life
in the agrotowns of Sicily to life in a tenement neighborhood in New York's Lower East Side at the turn of the
century. Change in immigrant family and community life
resulted when former Sicilian peasants painlessly abandoned familiar social practices in order to realize some
Old World social ideals. Within this general pattern there
was, of course, considerable variation. One important
group of immigrants--artisans--experienced relatively
little change during migration. And women immigrants
sometimes ignored Sicilian social ideals, while overcoming
considerable new environmental restraints, to continue to
form familiar social ties with their neighbors in the
tenements.

1024.   Gartner, Carol B. "A New Mirror for America: The Fic-
        tion of the Immigrant of the Ghetto, 1890-1930." Unpublished
        Ph.D. dissertation, New York University, 1970.

1025.   Gartner, Lloyd. "The Jews of New York's East Side, 1890-
        1893." American Jewish Historical Quarterly, (March 1964):
        264-275.

1026.   Geyer, Carolyn. "Beret in the Prairie Trilogy of Ole E.
        Rölvaag: A Study of Character-Symbol Relationships." Un-
        published Master's Thesis. Auburn University, 1965.
        An intelligent and sensitive interpretation of Beret, the
        main female character in Rölvaag's classic novel about
        Norwegian immigrants.

1027.   Glanz, Rudolf. Studies in Judaica Americana. New York:
        Ktav Publishing House, 1970.
        Fifteen scholarly essays on the history of the immigration,
        adjustment, and socioeconomic-cultural activities of Ger-
        man Jews in America during the nineteenth and early
        twentieth centuries. The first chapter, reprinted from
        the Yivo Annual of Jewish Social Science (vol. 6, 1951),
        contains 150 documents on the history of German Jewish
        immigration to the United States, 1800-1880.

1028.   Goddard, Henry H. "Mental Tests and the Immigrant."
        Journal of Delinquency, 2 (1917): 253-277.
        See also the author's Feeble-Mindedness and Immigration
        (Training School Bulletin, vol. 9, no. 6, 1912): and
        Human Efficiency and Levels of Intelligence (Princeton
        University Press, 1920). Goddard served as director of
        studies of hereditary feeblemindedness at the Training
        School at Vineland, N.J. See also Goddard's The Kallikak
        Family: A Study in the Heredity of Feeblemindedness
        (1912); and his School Training of Defective Children
        (1914). In a study for the U.S. Public Health Service at
        Ellis Island in 1912, Goddard reported that, based upon

his examination of the "great mass of average immigrants, 83 percent of Jews, 80 percent of Hungarians, 79 percent of Italians, and 87 percent of Russians were feebleminded." ["The Binet Tests in Relation to Immigration," Journal of Psychoasthenics, 18 (1913): 105-117].

1029.   Goldscheider, Calvin, and Alan S. Zuckerman. The Transformation of the Jews. Chicago: University of Chicago Press, 1984.
A comparative and historical study tracing the effects of industrialization, urbanization, and modernization on Jews as an ethnic group as they moved from the poor and isolated shtetls of nineteenth-century Europe to the affluence of twentieth-America and Israel.

1030.   Gordon, Nicholas. "Jewish and American: A Critical Study of the Fiction of Abraham Cahan, Anzia Yezierska, Waldo Frank, and Ludwig Lewisohn." Unpublished Ph.D. dissertation, Stanford University, 1967.

1031.   Goren, Arthur S. New York Jews and the Quest for Community: The Kehillah Experiment, 1908-1922. New York: Columbia University Press, 1970.
East European Jews and an experiment in disciplined community structure, i.e., the Kehillah, an organ of Jewish communal control whose history goes back to the Middle Ages.

1032.   Green, Rose Basile. The Italian American Novel: A Document of the Interaction of Two Cultures. Cranbury, N.J.: Fairleigh Dickinson University, 1974.
A descriptive register of Italian American novels (with invaluable summaries), and a significant milestone in American literary history which makes available to the social historian a little known and at times ephemeral literature out of which a neglected dimension of American ethnic experience can be assessed. See review F. Cordasco, Journal of Ethnic Studies, 2 (February 1975): 104-112.

1033.   Green, Rose Basile. The Italian Woman, Toga Wearer of a New World: Response to Presentation of the Woman of the Year Award. Pittsburgh: Grand Lodge of Pennsylvania, Order Sons of Italy in America, 1975.

1034.   Green, Rose Basile. "The Italian Immigrant Woman in American Literature." In Betty Boyd Caroli, Robert F. Harney, and Lydio F. Tomasi, eds., The Italian Immigrant Woman in North America (Toronto: Multicultural History Society of Ontario, 1978), pp. 341-349.
Conclusions: The Italian-American woman in American literature has been discussed previously in terms narrowed down by comparison and selection. For our purpose there

is an added illuminating value in analyzing in depth the
Italian woman who came to this country with the hope of
becoming an American. However, the difficulty in making
this analysis lies in the fact that Italian-American writers
have depicted the immigrant Italian woman effectively,
while non-Italian-American writers in American literature
have noticed her almost not at all.

1035.   Gulbenkian, Vahe. "The Slum Movement in English and
American Fiction, 1880-1920: A Chapter in the History of
the American Novel." Unpublished Ph. D. dissertation, Case
Western Reserve University, 1951.

1036.   Gurak, D. T. "Dominican and Colombian Women in New
York City." Migration Today, 10 (1982): 14-21.

1037.   Guttman, Allen. The Jewish Writer in America: Assimilation and the Crisis of Identity. New York: Oxford University
Press, 1971.

1038.   Hammerton, A. James. "Feminism and Female Emigration,
1861-1886," in Martha Vicinus, ed., A Widening Sphere:
Changing Roles of Victorian Women (Bloomington: Indiana
University Press, 1977), pp. 181-196.

1039.   Hansen, Marcus L. The Problem of the Third Generation
Immigrant. Rock Island, Ill.: Augustana Historical Society,
1938.
            A historical interpretation of migration with special refer-
ence to the problems confronting the historian in his study
of the third-generation immigrant. With the third generation there develops a spontaneous and almost irresistible
impulse to interest themselves in their common heritage.
Hansen was concerned with how to direct this impulse
toward a dignified contribution to the development of the
receiving country.

1040.   Hapgood, Hutchins. The Spirit of the Ghetto: Studies of
the Jewish Quarter in New York. Edited by Moses Rischin.
Cambridge, Mass.: Harvard University Press, 1967.
            Originally published in 1902. Vignettes of immigrant life
by a reformer-journalist. See also Hapgood's Types from
City Streets (1910); and his autobiography, A Victorian in
the Modern World (1939).

1041.   Harmon, Sandra D. "Florence Kelley in Illinois." Journal
of the Illinois State Historical Society, 74 (Autumn 1981):
163-78.
            Records Kelley's work as chief factory inspector for the
state of Illinois, 1893-1897. As chief factory inspector,
Kelley acted forcefully to improve the working conditions
of women and children, a campaign she later developed
under the auspices of the National Consumers' League.

1042. Harris, O., ed. <u>Latin American Women.</u> New York: Mi-
       nority Rights Group, 1983.

1043. Haugen, Einar. <u>Ole Edvart Rölvaag.</u> Boston: G. K. Hall,
       1983.
       Points out that the author of <u>Giants in the Earth</u> is an
       "anomaly" who spent the first 20 years of his life in
       Norway and wrote all of his stories and novels in Nor-
       wegian. To label him an American writer forces us to
       consider the implications of the designation "American."
       Rölvaag's work exemplifies the divided identity that af-
       fects all ethnic groups seeking access to American life.
       Traces Rölvaag's life from his youth as a fisherman in
       Norway to his worldwide fame as a writer, but gives us
       less than a full-scale biography because it places most
       of its emphasis on Rölvaag's self-chosen role as mediator
       between Norway and America and on his crusade to keep
       immigrant Norwegian identity from being swallowed by
       American materialism. This emphasis extends the rele-
       vance of the study beyond the boundaries of the Norwegian-
       American community to include the dilemma of assimila-
       tion faced by all ethnic groups.

1044. Hercher, U. D., ed. <u>The East European Jewish Experience
       in America: A Century of Memories, 1882-1982.</u> New York:
       Ktav Publishing House, 1983.

1045. Hill, Robert Fred. <u>Exploring the Dimensions of Ethnicity:
       A Study of Status, Culture and Identity Among Polish-Ameri-
       cans.</u> New York: Arno Press, 1980.
       Through participant observation, focused interviews, li-
       brary research, survey questionnaire, and an analysis of
       historical documents, explores the dimensions of status,
       culture, and identity among Polish Americans in Pitts-
       burgh. Focusing on these three dimensions and the dy-
       namic interrelation between them at different units of
       analysis--the group, the community, the school, and the
       individual--it is concluded that observed intraethnic varia-
       tion can be explained by three adaptive strategies: en-
       clave security, passing, and militancy. Approaches which
       assume a homogeneity of human response to ethnicity,
       whether pluralist or assimilationist, are seen as more
       ideological than factual. The study includes ethnohistori-
       cal profiles of the Polish American group in time and
       space, a working class Polish-American community, a
       Roman Catholic high school where the students are of
       predominant Polish-American background, and the life
       histories of two Polish-American individuals. Originally,
       Ph. D. dissertation, University of Pittsburgh, 1975.

1046. Hoffman, George J. "Catholic Immigrant Aid Societies in
       New York City from 1880 to 1920." Unpublished Ph. D. dis-
       sertation, St. John's University, 1947.

1047.   Hoffman, Klaus D. "Sewing Is for Women, Horses Are for
        Men: The Role of German Russian Women." In Sidney
        Heitman, ed., Germans from Russia in Colorado (Ann Arbor,
        Mich.: Western Social Science Association, 1978), pp. 131-
        144.

1048.   Holli, Melvin G., and Peter d'A. Jones. The Ethnic Fron-
        tier: Essays in the History of Group Survival in Chicago
        and the Midwest. Grand Rapids, Mich.: William B. Eerd-
        mans Publishing, 1977.
              A series of essays on the population elements of Chicago
        from French times to the present, especially on Jews,
        Swedes, Poles, Italians, Blacks, and Mexicans.

1049.   Horna, J. "The Entrance Status of Czech and Slovak Immi-
        grant Women." In Jean Elliot ed., Two Nations, Many
        Cultures (Toronto: Prentice-Hall, 1979), pp. 270-279.

1050.   Howe, Irving. "The Lower East Side: Symbol and Fact."
        In Allon Schoener, ed., The Lower East Side: Portal to
        American Life, 1870-1924 (New York: The Jewish Museum,
        1966), pp. 11-14.

1051.   [Hunter College. Women's Studies Collective]. Women's
        Realities, Women's Choices. New York: Oxford University
        Press, 1983.
              A valuable text intended for introductory women's studies
        courses, with materials that illuminate the social contexts
        which immigrant women encountered. See particularly,
        (II) The Family Circle; and (III) Women in Society.

1052.   Ifkovic, Edward, ed. American Letters: Immigrant and
        Ethnic Writing. Englewood Cliffs, N.J.: Prentice-Hall,
        1975.
              A basic collection of ethnic literature drawn from most
        American immigrant (including Afro-American) groups.

1053.   "Illegitimate Births Among Immigrant Mothers." [Massa-
        chusetts, House]. Report of the Commissioners of Alien
        Passengers and Foreign Paupers, 1853. Doc. 18, Docu-
        ments, 1853 (Boston 1853): 14-19.

1054.   Indra, D. "The Invisible Mosaic: Women, Ethnicity and
        the Vancouver Press, 1908-1976." Canadian Ethnic Studies,
        13 (1981): 63-74.

1055.   James, Edmund J., ed. The Immigrant Jew in America.
        New York: Buck, 1907.
              Essays by non-Jewish and Jewish scholars on the adjust-
        ment of Russian Jewish immigrants in America, and on
        Jewish activities in philanthropy, religion, education,
        politics, and other aspects of life in the United States.
        In a preface, it is emphasized that the Russian Jewish

immigrants "struggle along patiently and honestly, making gradually a more and more decent home and livelihood for themselves, and sparing no privation to secure the education and advance of their children."

1056.   Jastrow, Marie.   A Time to Remember: Growing Up in New York Before the Great War. New York: W. W. Norton, 1979.
Jastrow's father, an Austrian Jew, came to America in the immigration wave of the 1900's, penniless and in search of the legendary gold that was to provide for his wife and child.   Jastrow's book is a memoir of these early years in New York, of the ordeals of the immigrants, and of the close-knit neighborhood of Jews and Germans in Yorkville where the family later settled.

1057.   Jerabek, Esther.   Czechs and Slovaks in North America. A Bibliography.   New York: Czechoslovakian Society of Arts and Sciences in America, 1976.

1058.   Joseph, Samuel.   History of the Baron De Hirsch Fund: The Americanization of the Jewish Immigrant.   New York: Baron De Hirsch Fund, 1935.   Reprint.   With a new Introduction by Philip S. Cohen and Francesco Cordasco.   Fairfield, N. J.:   Augustus M. Kelley, 1976.
A documented account of a half-century of a philanthropic program aimed at "the adjustment and assimilation of the immigrant Jewish population . . . [through] relief, temporary aid, promotion of suburban industrial enterprises, removal from urban centers, land settlement, agricultural training, trade and general education."   Illustrations and texts of documents.

1059.   Joseph, Samuel.   Jewish Immigration to the United States from 1881 to 1910.   New York: [The Author], 1914.
A Ph.D. dissertation at Columbia University analyzing the socioeconomic-political context of Jewish life in Eastern Europe, the immigration, and the socioeconomic-educational characteristics of the immigrants.   Appended statistics and a short bibliography in English, French, and German.

1060.   Juteau-Lee, D.   "Ethnicity and Femininity: D'apres Nos Expériences."   Canadian Ethnic Studies, 13 (1981): 1-23.

1061.   Kats, Rachel.   "The Immigrant Woman: Double Cost or Relative Improvement."   International Migration Review, 16 (Fall 1982): 661-677.
Findings: Women and immigrants in the labor market are viewed to be in a disadvantaged position because of ascribed rather than achieved characteristics.   In the case of the women, this is her sex, universal and rather fixed; for the immigrant, it is ethnicity and distance from

the dominant majority in the country of arrival. His position varies with the immigrant group to which he belongs
and the countries from which and/or to which the move
is made. Although the major channel for career mobility
for both groups is education and occupational training, the
assumed characteristics which attract or push workers
into the secondary labor market also form barriers to
promotion.

1062.   Kauffman, Reginald W. The House of Bondage. New York:
        Grosset & Dunlap, 1910.
        A semi-fictional account of prostitution and reform efforts.

1063.   Kaufman, Polly Wells. Women Teachers on the Frontier.
        New Haven, Conn.: Yale University Press, 1984.
        Described are the young, single women sent West in the
        decade after 1846 by the National Board of Popular Edu-
        cation. The women, nearly 600, were from New England
        and upper New York State. The frontier where they
        taught was Indiana, Wisconsin, Illinois, Iowa, and Oregon.
        A diary, a reminiscence, and letters make up most of
        the book. In an introduction, Kaufman finds common
        characteristics of these teachers: they came from modest
        farm homes; they were daughters of first-generation liter-
        ate women; they were inspired to go West by the motives
        of economic betterment and Protestant evangelical religion.

1064.   Kellor, Frances A. "The Immigrant Woman." Atlantic,
        100, 3 (1907): 401-7.

1065.   Kelly, Gail Paradise. From Vietnam to America: A Chron-
        icle of the Vietnamese Immigration to the United States.
        Boulder, Colo.: Westview Press, 1978.
        The first study of the exodus and of the transformation
        from refugees to immigrants, first in the camps to which
        they were sent, and subsequently in the communities which
        accepted them. The author spent 18 months with the
        refugees in the Fort Indian Town Gap, Pennsylvania camp.

1066.   Kelly, Myra. Little Citizens: The Humours of School Life
        Illustrated by W. D. Stevens. [1914]. New York: Arno
        Press, 1975.
        These narratives of America's newly arrived minority
        children include The Christmas Present for a Lady, When
        a Man's Widowed, and A Passport to Paradise.

1067.   Kelly, Myra. Little Aliens. [1910]. New York: Arno
        Press, 1975.
        Author of Little Citizens and Wards of Liberty, Myra
        Kelly in this companion volume, weaves together more
        schoolday episodes from the lives of "fifty-eight little
        children of Israel," sons and daughters of the turn-of-the-
        century East European immigration to New York's Lower

East Side. The central figure in these tenement sketches
is Miss Constance Bailey, the normal school teacher in
Gibson shirtwaist, who believes that the teacher must be
"wise as Solomon, as impartial as the telephone directory,
as untiring as a steam-engine, and as tender as a sore
throat."

1068.   Kessler-Harris, Alice, ed. An Anzia Yezierska Collection.
New York: Persea Books, 1979.

1069.   Kessler-Harris, Alice. Out to Work: A History of Wage-
Earning Women in the United States. New York: Oxford
University Press, 1983.
Traces the transformation of "women's work" into wage
labor in the United States from Colonial period to the
present, and identifies the social, economic and ideological
forces that have shaped expectations of what women do.
Examines the effects of class, ethnic, and racial patterns,
changing perceptions of wage-work for women and the
relationship between wage earning and family roles.

1070.   Kim, Elaine H. Asian American Literature: An Introduction
to the Writings and Their Social Context. Philadelphia:
Temple University Press, 1984.
A socio-literary examination of literature written in
English by Chinese, Japanese, Philippine and Korean
authors about the American experience. The genre begins in 1840 with the arrival of Chinese immigrants to
the United States. Examines major themes, analyzes
stereotypes, and discusses the search for social identity,
women's roles, and responses to America's discriminatory
rejection.

1071.   Kneeland, George J., with Katharine B. Davis. Commer-
cialized Prostitution in New York City. Publications of the
Bureau of Social Hygiene. New York: Century, 1913.

1071a. LaGuerre, Michel S. American Odyssey: Haitians in New
York City. Ithaca, N.Y.: Cornell University Press, 1984.
Assesses the development and adaptation of the Haitian
immigrant community in three boroughs of New York City.
Special attention is given to the Haitian female immigrant
worker.

1072.   Laska, Vera. The Czechs in America, 1633-1977. A
Chronology and Fact Book. Dobbs Ferry, N.Y.: Oceana
Publications, 1978.

1073.   Lehr, J. C. "The Government and the Immigrant: Per-
spectives on Ukrainian Block Settlement in the Canadian
West." Canadian Ethnic Studies, 9 (1977): 42-52.
Examines two powerful and opposed forces in the Ukrainian
Settlement: the immigrants' desire to settle near other

Ukrainians and the Canadian government's policy to dis-
perse them throughout the West to speed assimilation.
Shows the interaction of these two forces in shaping the
geography of this Ukrainian Settlement in the Canadian
West. Includes notices of Ukrainian women and family
life.

1074.   Levi, F. "L'Evolution de la Femme Portugaise Immigrée."
         Migration dans le Monde, 2 (1977): 1-9.

1075.   Logan, [Mrs.] John A. [Mary S.]. The Part Taken by Wom-
         en in American History. [1912]. New York: Arno Press,
         1976.
         An encyclopedic compendium by the wife of a prominent
         post-Civil War politician, herself active in public life
         and in Washington society. Hundreds of entries of the
         famous and not-so-famous, personal histories, professions,
         causes and careers of women, done with color and human
         interest. Especially valuable sections on outstanding
         Catholic and Jewish women.

1076.   Loomis, A. W. "Chinese Women in California." Overland
         Monthly, 10 (April 1969): 343-351.

1077.   Luchetti, Cathy, and Carol Olwell. Women of the West.
         St. George, Utah: Antelope Island Press, 1984.
         Narratives of eleven women who moved to or lived in the
         American West in the nineteenth century. The hardships
         and triumphs of Indian, Black, Jewish and Oriental women
         are discussed with specific reference to journal entries,
         newspaper items, and family letters.

1078.   Lussler, V. L., ed. Women's Lives: Perspectives on
         Progress . . . . Newark: University of Delaware Press,
         1977.

1079.   MacAodha, Brendan. "Letters from America." Ulster Folk-
         life, 3 (1957): 64-69.

1080.   McLeod, Arnopoulos, S. "Quel Est le Point? Les Problèmes
         des Femmes Immigrées sur le Marché du Travail Canadien."
         Migrations, 24 (1979): 25-26.
         An examination of seven ethnic groups, employment ex-
         periences with special attention to cultural variables and
         the contrasting experiences of men and women.

1081.   McMullen, L. "Ethnicity and Feminity: Double Jeopardy."
         Canadian Ethnic Studies, 13 (1981): 52-62.

1082.   Magganara, J. The Position of Women in Greek Migration
         and Study of Returnees to Rural Areas in Greece. Geneva:
         Alliance Mondiale, 1973.

1083.   Malone, Anne Patton. Women on the Texas Frontier. El
        Paso: Texas Western Press, The University of Texas at
        El Paso, 1983.

1084.   Mangano, Antonio. Sons of Italy: A Social and Religious
        Study of the Italians in America. New York: Missionary
        Education Movement of the United States and Canada, 1917.
        Reprint. With a Foreword by F. Cordasco. New York:
        Russell & Russell, 1972.
            An important social history by an Italian-American Baptist
            minister who was a vigorous force in the Italian com-
            munity. Special attention to the Italian immigrant family.

1085.   Marcus, Jacob R., and Abraham J. Peck, eds. Studies in
        the American Jewish Experience. New York: Ktav Publish-
        ing House, 1981.
            The six essays comprise the first volume of contributions
            of scholars participating in the fellowship programs of the
            American Jewish Archives. These programs are intended
            to aid in the development of theory and methods in Ameri-
            can Jewish studies. The essays in this volume are his-
            torical and, with one exception, biographical in nature.
            Norman Fain Pratt's "Immigrant Jewish Women in Los
            Angeles: Occupation, Family and Culture" describes the
            complexities involved in the transformation of identity of
            East European Jewish women during the first four decades
            of this century. Pratt notes that in addition to maintaining
            her traditional economic role in the family, the woman
            was also central in this group's acculturation. She con-
            tends that this group of women pioneered the inclusion
            of a public, extra-familial social component as a legiti-
            mate part of the identity of the Jewish woman.

1086.   Margolies, Maxine L. Mothers and Such: Views of Ameri-
        can Women and Why They Changed. Berkeley: University
        of California Press, 1984.
            Why was motherhood barely mentioned as a discrete role
            in eighteenth-century sermons? And why, beginning in
            the 1830's, did it become the focus of attention in do-
            mestic manuals and other forms of popular literature ad-
            dressed to women? Why, during the same decade, were
            women advised for the first time that housekeeping was
            a profession second to none? Why have beliefs about the
            compatibility of women's domestic roles and outside em-
            ployment changed over the course of American history?
            And why, until the last decade or so, did experts on child
            rearing insist that full-time mothering was essential to
            children's growth and development? Examines these and
            other questions about the changing roles of American wom-
            en. Conclusion, guided by the theoretical perspective of
            cultural materialism, is that "what we have come to think
            of as inevitable and biologically necessary is in great
            measure a consequence of our society's particular social

and economic system." Cites the influence of such variables as household versus industrial production, a manufacturing versus a service-oriented economy, the demand
or lack of demand for women's labor, the economy's need
for "high-quality" employees, and the changing costs and
benefits of rearing children who would become those employees. Argues that ideologies about the roles of middle-
class American women are deeply rooted in the changing
nature of the American economy. This analysis asserts
that there are well-defined material causes for contemporary attitudes toward women and work, for new ideas
about child-rearing, for the changing nature of housework,
and for the revival of feminism. Valuable for that background against which the acculturation of immigrant wom-
en evolved.

1087.   Matulich, Loretta Kay. A Cross-Disciplinary Study of the
European Immigrants of 1870 to 1925. New York: Arno
Press, 1980.
Two views of assimilation into American society are
presented in this study: Henry P. Fairchild's static definition of the goal of Americanization and Jane Addams'
dynamic definition of American cultural growth. Reject-
ing Fairchild's view that immigrants must lose all traces
of their foreign origin in order to become real Americans,
this study adopts Addams' belief that this majority of immigrants could only become Americans if one sees both
native- and foreign-born growing toward each other into
one culture. The portraits of the various ethnic groups
of immigrants as they appear in fiction, social science
writings, and autobiographies attempt to determine whether
the immigrants' personal and cultural characteristics,
motivations for immigration, and interactions with American communities are presented as similar in each genre.
Major areas of discussion are how immigrants have been
perceived, how they have viewed the American people and
institutions, and how they have adjusted to and have been
assimilated into American life, how Americans reacted
to the European immigrants, and how the immigrants have
contributed to American life. The viewpoint of the longer
established Americans is examined in terms of ethnic
stereotypes and predictions of American cultural change.
The immigrants' viewpoint concentrates on their hopes,
experiences, and achievements in their adopted country.
Originally, Ph.D. dissertation, University of New Mexico,
1971.

1088.   Melville, Marquarita B. "Mexican Women Adapt to Migration." International Migration Review, 12 (Summer 1978):
225-235.

1089.   Metzker, Isaac. A Bintel Brief: Sixty Years of Letters
from the Lower East Side to the Jewish Daily Forward. New
York: Doubleday, 1971.

Translations from the Yiddish of letters and editorial re-
plies on personal problems, as well as on political and
social issues. Interpretive foreword and notes by Harry
Golden. Many of the correspondents were Jewish immigrant women.

1090.   Meyer, Annie Nathan, ed. Women's Work in America. With
an Introduction by Julia Ward Howe. [1911]. New York:
Arno Press, 1976.
Eighteen articles by foremost authorities in their fields
describe the transition period when women were not abso-
lutely denied entry to job and profession, but were surely
not welcomed. Valuable factual surveys by Julia Ward
Howe, Mary Putnam Jacobi, Mary Livermore, Josephine
Shaw Lowell, Frances Willard, Clara Barton and others.
Focus is on the period when propriety, not capacity, had
become the issue, and kindly but patronizing resistance
rather than open objection had become the way of pre-
serving feminine dependence.

1091.   Miller, Beth, ed. Women in Hispanic Literature: Icons
and Fallen Idols. Berkeley: University of California Press,
1983.
While this collection shows ample evidence of the dual
archetype of woman as icon and woman as fallen idol,
the 18 essays reach beyond these stereotypes to more
complex sociological and theoretical concerns, with perceptive analyses of the American milieu and the Hispanic
woman.

1092.   Miller, Herbert A., and Robert E. Park. Old World Traits
Transplanted. New York: Harper & Brothers, 1921.
Primary author of this work was actually W. I. Thomas,
the Chicago sociologist. The book was a counterthrust to
the arguments favoring compulsory Americanization. Part
of the "Americanization Studies: The Acculturation of
Immigrant Groups into American Society" commissioned
by the Carnegie Corporation.

1093.   Mincer, Jacob. "Family Migration Decision." Journal of
Political Economy, 86 (October 1978): 749-773.

1094.   Mohl, Raymond A., and Neil Betten. "Paternalism and
Pluralism: Immigrants and Social Welfare in Gary, Indiana,
1906-1940." American Studies, 15 (Spring 1974): 5-30.

1095.   Montero, Darrel. "Vietnamese Refugees in America: Toward a Theory of Spontaneous International Migration." International Migration Review, 13 (1979): 624-648.

1096.   Morokvasic, Mirjana. "Why Do Women Migrate? Towards
an Understanding of the Sex-Selectivity in the Migratory Movements of Labour." Studi Emigrazione, 20 (June 1983): 132-
138.

Analyses of female migrants' conditions as presented in
some recent surveys. On the one hand the role of migrant women is tied up with general migratory problems,
e.g., women's sociocultural and psychological integration.
On the other hand it is connected with more specific situ-
ations of the female role. Maintains that the women's
presence in the labor market reflects the traditional and
hierarchical division of male and female labor.

1097. Mortimer, D. M., ed. Female Immigrants to the United
States: Caribbean, Latin American and African Experience.
Washington: Smithsonian Institution, 2, 1981.

1098. Nies, Judith. Seven Women: Portraits from the American
Radical Tradition. New York: Penguin Books, 1977.
Portraits are of Sarah Moore Grimké (1792-1873), Harriet
Tubman (1820-1913), Elizabeth Cady Stanton (1815-1902),
Mother Jones (1830-1930), Charlotte Perkins Gilman
(1860-1935), Anna Louis Strong (1885-1970), and Dorothy
Day (1897-1980). Epilogue: The Legacy of the Radical
Tradition.

1099. O'Farrell, M. Brigid, and Lydia Kleiner. "Anna Sullivan:
Trade Union Organizer." Frontiers, 2 (Summer 1977): 29-
36.
Description of the collaborative model of the oral history
project, "The Twentieth Century Trade Union Woman:
Vehicle for Social Change," with excerpts from an interview with Anna Sullivan, born in 1904, a union organizer.

1100. Panayotakopoulou, E. "Specific Problems of Migrant Women
Returning to the Country of Origin, Particularly as Regard
Employment and Social Services." International Migration,
19 (1981): 219-224.

1101. Passi, Michael M. "Immigrants and the City: Problems
of Interpretation and Synthesis in Recent White Ethnic History." Journal of Ethnic Studies, 4 (1976): 61-72.
Reviews three books: Immigrants and the City: Ethnicity
and Mobility in a Nineteenth Century Midwestern Community by Dean R. Esslinger (1975); Polish American
Politics in Chicago, 1880-1940 by Edward R. Kantowicz
(1975); and Peasants and Strangers: Italians, Rumanians
and Slovaks in an American City by Josef Barton (1975),
whose central theme is "the confrontation of immigrant
cultures with American urban-industrial society, recon-
sidered in light of the new sensitivity to the history of
non-elite groups, the new quantitative methods, and the
revised theoretical assumptions about the nature of assimilation."

1102. Peragallo, Olga. Italian American Authors and Their Contribution to American Literature. New York: S. F. Vanni,
1949.

1103.   Peterson, Susan. "From Paradise to Prairie: The Presen-
         tation Sisters in Dakota, 1880-1896." South Dakota History,
         10 (Summer 1980): 210-222.
             The Sisters arrived in Dakota Territory in 1880 from
         Ireland. Their story provides insights into the similari-
         ties and differences between the adjustments made by these
         women and typical pioneer women. They too were affected
         by the 1880-81 blizzards and the spring floods that fol-
         lowed. Their work required that they move frequently
         during their first years until in 1886 they settled in Aber-
         deen and opened a school. In the early 1890's they were
         plagued by drought and depression, but by 1896 they were
         firmly established and thriving.

1104.   Pivar, David J. Purity Crusade: Sexual Morality and So-
         cial Control, 1868-1900. Westport, Conn.: Greenwood
         Press, 1973.

1105.   Platt, Anthony M. The Child Savers: The Invention of
         Delinquency. Chicago: University of Chicago Press, 1969.
             Important for understanding the world of the immigrant
         child and family. "Contemporary programs of delinquency
         control can be traced to enterprising reforms of the child
         savers who, at the end of the nineteenth century, helped
         to create special judicial and correctional institutions for
         the labeling, processing, and management of 'troublesome'
         youth." See Enoch C. Wines, The State of Prisons and
         Child-Saving Institutions in the Civilized World (1880),
         which was widely used as a comprehensive treatise until
         the early 1900's.

1106.   Portes, Alejandro, and Robert L. Bach. Latin Journey:
         Cuban and Mexican Immigrants in the United States. Berk-
         eley: University of California Press, 1984.
             The authors maintain that U.S. immigration policy is
         guided primarily by classic assimilationist theories based
         on the experiences of turn-of-the-century European immi-
         grants, and ask do these theories match the reality faced
         by modern immigrants? Details a unique eight-year sur-
         vey of Mexican and Cuban immigrants--the first and third
         largest contingents coming to the U.S. in the 1970's (with
         special attention to women and the family). Describe
         patterns of occupational and economic development, cul-
         tural adaptation, and social relationships both within the
         ethnic circle and in the larger community.

1107.   Pozzetta, George E. "Immigrant Women in Tampa: The
         Italian Experience." Florida Historical Quarterly, 61 (Janu-
         ary 1983): 296-312.

1108.   Prisland, Marie, and Albina Novak. Women's Glory. Chi-
         cago: Slovenian Women's Union of America, 1963.

1109. Prisland, Marie. From Slovenia--to America. Chicago:
       Slovenian Women's Union of America, 1968.
       A historical and cultural analysis with particular attention
       to Slovenian women.

1110. Prpic, George J. The South Slavic Immigration in America.
       Boston: Twayne Publishers, 1978.

1111. Ralph, Julian. People We Pass. Stories of Life Among the
       Masses of New York City. New York: Harper & Brothers,
       1896.

1112. Rasmussen, Janet E. "Sisters Across the Sea: Early Nor-
       wegian Feminists and Their American Connections." Wom-
       en's Studies International, 5 (1982): 647-654.

1113. Reishus, Martha. The Rag Rug. Vantage: New York,
       1955.
       Fictional account of the author's grandmother and her
       family who settled in Minnesota after emigration from
       Telemark, Norway.

1114. Ribes Tovar, Frederico. The Puerto Rican Woman: Her
       Life and Evolution Throughout History. Trans. from the
       Spanish by Anthony Rawlings. [New York]: Plus Ultra Edu-
       cational Pub., 1972.

1115. Riegel, Robert. "Changing American Attitudes Toward Pros-
       titution 1800-1920." Journal of the History of Ideas, 29
       (1968): 437-452.

1116. Rischin, Moses. "Abraham Cahan and the New York Com-
       mercial Advertiser, 1897-1900: A Study in Acculturation."
       American Jewish Historical Quarterly, 43 (Sept. 1953): 10-
       36.

1117. Roniger, M. Stella Maris. "Contributions of the Missionary
       Sisters of the Sacred Heart to Education in Italy and the
       United States." Unpublished M. A. thesis, Fordham Univer-
       sity, 1938.
       The origin, growth, and educational activities of the Mis-
       sionary Sisters of the Sacred Heart, in an evaluation of
       the contributions of their community to the field of Chris-
       tian education in Italy and the United States. Centered
       on the biography of the foundress of the Order, St. Frances
       Xavier Cabrini.

1118. Rose, Arnold M. "A Research Note on the Impact of Immi-
       gration on the Birth Rate." American Journal of Sociology,
       47 (Jan. 1942): 614-621.
       A study of 1,348 Italian-born women in Chicago showing
       that birth rates were higher after immigration than in the
       homeland.

1119.   Rothman, David J., ed. The Almshouse Experience: Collected Reports. New York: Arno Press, 1971.
         Includes: Philadelphia Board of Guardians, Report of the Committee Appointed by the Board of Guardians of the Poor of the City and Districts of Philadelphia, to Visit the Cities of Baltimore, New York, Providence, Boston, and Salem (1827); [Massachusetts General Court] (Josiah Quincy), Report of the Committee on the Pauper Laws of this Commonwealth (1821); John Yates, Report of the Secretary of State in 1824 on the Relief and Settlement of the Poor (1824). These three most famous and influential reports in the Jacksonian period sparked the rise and spread of almshouses throughout America. The results of extensive investigations, the reports not only offer an unusually complete picture of the treatment of the poor, but announce the goals of reformers for the next fifty years.

1120.   Rothman, David J., ed. The Jacksonians on the Poor: Collected Pamphlets. New York: Arno Press, 1971.
         Includes: Charles Burroughs, A Discourse Delivered in the Chapel of the New Alms-house, in Portsmouth, New Hampshire, December 15, 1834 on the Occasion of Its First Being Opened for Religious Services (1835); Mathew Carey, Essays on the Public Charities of Philadelphia, intended to vindicate the Benevolent Societies of this City from the Charge of encouraging Idleness, and to place in strong Relief, before an enlightened Public, the Sufferings and Oppression under which the greater part of the Females labour, who depend on their industry for a support for themselves and Children (1828); Mathew Carey, A Plea for the Poor, Particularly Females. An Inquiry How Far the Charges Alleged Against them of Improvidence, Idleness, and Dissipation, are Founded in Truth (1837); Walter Channing, An Address on the Prevention of Pauperism (1843); Josiah Quincy, Remarks on Some of the Provisions of the Laws of Massachusetts, Affecting Poverty, Vice, and Crime; Being the General Topics of a Charge to the Grand Jury of the County of Suffolk, in March Term, 1822 (1822); R. C. Waterston, An Address on Pauperism, Its Extent, Causes, and the Best Means of Prevention; Delivered at the Church in Bowdoin Square, February 4, 1844 (1844). Brought together expressly for this series, these important pamphlets on poverty in the Jacksonian period reflect the major trends in contemporary thinking on the subject. Included in the collection is Mathew Carey's careful analysis and critique of these developments.

1121.   Ruud, Curtis D. "Beret and the Prairie in Giants in the Earth." Norwegian-American Studies, 28 (1979): 217-244.
         An analysis of the prairie theme in Rölvaag's work about Norwegian immigrants, particularly in relation to Beret, the main female character.

1122.   Ruud, Helga M.   A History of the Norwegian Woman's Club
        of Chicago.   n. p. ,   1942.
        Founded to achieve "intellectual culture and true fellow-
        ship, " this club is an example of organizations created
        by Norwegian immigrant women.   The history is written
        in report form.

1123.   Sabaugh, George, and Dorothy Thomas.   "Changing Patterns
        of Fertility and Survival among the Japanese on the Pacific
        Coast. "   American Sociological Review, 10 (October 1945):
        651-658.

1124.   Sachs, Carolyn E.   The Invisible Farmers.   Women in
        Agricultural Production.   Totowa, N. J. :   Rowman & Allan-
        held, 1983.
        U. S. agricultural policy has always emphasized the im-
        portance of the "family farm, " but research has focused
        on the male of that family, relegating the female to only
        minor roles--invisible, as the title suggests.   Sachs's
        study fills this gap.   It documents the extensive participa-
        tion of rural women (including immigrant) in U. S. agri-
        culture as owners, workers, and household producers,
        paid and unpaid, farm and off-farm.

1125.   Sager, Gertrude A.   "Immigration: Based upon a Study of
        the Italian Women and Girls of Chicago. "   Unpublished Ph. D.
        dissertation, University of Chicago, 1914.

1126.   Salmon, Lucy Maynard.   Domestic Service.   [1897].   New
        York: Arno Press, 1976.
        A legion of ladies spent their lives earning bread and
        board by serving in strange homes.   Lucy Salmon, a
        person of strong democratic beliefs, an aspiring teacher
        at Vassar and pioneer social historian, first woman to
        serve on the executive council of the American Historical
        Association, presents a devastating, meticulously re-
        searched analysis of the life of anonymous thousands
        trapped in endless days of subservience to master and
        mistress.

1127.   Sandell, Steven H.   "Women and the Economics of Family
        Migration. "   Review of Economics Statistics, 59 (November
        1977):   406-414.

1128.   Sanders, Ronald.   The Downtown Jews: Portrait of an Im-
        migrant Generation.   New York: Harper & Row, 1969.
        An account of Jewish life, labor, and culture on the
        Lower East Side of New York City in the early twentieth
        century against the background of the Russian situation
        which led to the immigration to America.   The focus is
        on the life of Abraham Cahan, Yiddish journalist and edi-
        tor of the Jewish Daily Forward (Forverts).   Photographs,
        glossary of Yiddish, Hebrew, and Russian terms, and
        brief bibliography.

1129.   Sanger, William W. The History of Prostitution: Its Extent,
         Causes, and Effects Throughout the World, Being an Official
         Report to the Board of Alms-House Governors of the City
         of New York. New York: Harper & Brothers, 1859. Re-
         print. Arno Press, 1976.
             The official report of the Board of Alms-House Governors
             of the City of New York, compiled under the direction of
             the resident physician at Blackwell's Island. A massive
             survey, one-third devoted to New York City and based on
             interviews with 2,000 women replying to the question,
             "What was the cause of your becoming a prostitute?"
             Concern is with community safety, disease, female honor,
             crime and the callousness of wealth, the futility of punish-
             ment, the experience of regulation, and the hypocrisy of
             whispering.

1130.   Sartorio, Enrico C. Social and Religious Life of Italians
         in America. Boston: Christopher Publishing House, 1918.
         Reprint. With a Foreword by F. Cordasco. Clifton, N.J.:
         Augustus M. Kelley, 1974.
             One of a handful of volumes written by Italians in English
             on the life of Italians during the period of the great mi-
             grations. Sartorio deals with the "round-of-life" in the
             Italian community; the twin dynamics of conflict and ac-
             culturation in a discussion of "Americanization"; and the
             role of churches from the viewpoint of the Protestant
             minister.

1131.   Scarpaci, Jean. "La Contadina: The Plaything of the Middle
         Class Woman Historian." Journal of Ethnic Studies, 9 (Sum-
         mer 1981): 21-38.

1132.   Scourby, Alice. The Greek Americans. Boston: G. K.
         Hall, 1984.
             A sociological survey articulating a framework of Greek
             American cultural and social values. Special attention
             is given to Greek immigrant women. Five community
             studies are summarized to show the "elusive chameleon"
             quality of Greek American life.

1133.   Sealy, N. "Acadian Women. Economic Development, Eth-
         nicity, and the Status of Women." In Jean Elliot, ed., Two
         Nations, Many Cultures (Toronto: Prentice-Hall, 1979), pp.
         270-279.

1134.   Seltzer, Mildred. "Jewish-American Grandmothers." In
         Lillian E. Troll, Joan Israel and Kenneth Israel, eds., A
         Woman's Guide to the Problems and Joys of Growing Older
         (Englewood Cliffs, N.J.: Prentice Hall, 1977), pp. 157-161.
             Social and personality characteristics of Jewish-American
             grandmothers. Contends that old women of all ethnic
             groups may have more in common with one another than
             with younger families, and that the strength that enabled

them to survive until old age in a hostile environment
may be the very characteristic upon which negative stereotypes are based.

1135. Semmingsen, Ingrid. Norway to America: A History of the
Migration. Translated by Einar Haugen. Minneapolis: University of Minnesota Press, 1978.
A revision and condensation of her two-volume work in
the Norwegian language. A well-written, scholarly, interpretive survey.

1136. Seskin, Jane. More Than Mere Survival: Conversations
with Women Over 65. New York: Newsweek Books, 1980.
Transcripts of interviews with 22 women over the age of
65 and of varying ethnic and religious backgrounds and
life-styles.

1137. Shaheen, G. "Clothing Practices of Pakistani Women Re-
siding in Canada." Canadian Ethnic Studies, 13 (1981):
120-126.

1138. Shaler, Nathaniel S. "European Peasants as Immigrants."
Atlantic Monthly, 71 (May 1893).
A supra-organic evolutionist, and immigration restriction-
ist. See Walter L. Berg, "Nathaniel S. Shaler: A
Critical Study of an Earth Scientist," unpublished Ph.D.
dissertation, University of Washington, 1957.

1139. Sheehan, Susan. Kate Quinton's Days. Boston: Houghton
Mifflin, 1984.
A factual chronicle of the pseudonymous Kate O'Donoghue
Quinton, a widowed Scottish immigrant, who has lived
most of her 80 years in a working-class section of
Brooklyn (N.Y.), and her unmarried daughter who takes
care of her elderly parent. Includes retrospective vignettes of Kate Quinton's early years in Scotland, her
work as a maid after immigrating to America, and her
years as wife and mother.

1140. Shepard, [Mrs.] Frederick J. "The Women's Educational
and Industrial Union in Buffalo." Buffalo Historical Society
Publications, 22 (1918): 147-200.

1141. Sicherman, Barbara. Alice Hamilton: A Life in Letters.
Cambridge, Mass.: Harvard University Press, 1984.
Founder of industrial toxicology, co-worker of Jane Addams,
and first woman professor at Harvard, Alice Hamilton's
life spanned the Victorian and Vietnam War eras. Sicherman's book integrates letters and biography to illuminate
the life of this pioneer in medicine and social reform,
and to show the ways in which Hamilton's nineteenth-
century ideals conflicted with the twentieth-century reality
she helped to create.

1142.   Silverman, Eliane. "In Their Own Words: Mothers and
         Daughters on the Alberta Frontier, 1890-1929." Frontiers,
         2 (Summer 1977): 37-44.
             A discussion, with excerpts from interviews with women
         who arrived in Alberta (where the last land rush in North
         America took place) before 1929, on the theme of daugh-
         ters' perceptions of their mothers. The frontier women
         came from a variety of social classes and of ethnic, re-
         ligious and regional backgrounds. In some cases, the
         strong bond between mothers and daughters documented
         in their narratives formed the basis of their strength and
         courage.

1143.   Smith, M. Estellie. "The Portuguese Female Immigrant:
         The 'Marginal Man.'" International Migration Review, 14
         (Spring 1980): 77-92.
             Presents an analysis of the role of Portuguese women in
         the migration decision of typical Portuguese "male-domi-
         nated" families; their continued importance in the actual
         departure and in the acculturative process upon arrival.
         Seeks to redress a previous imbalance in migration liter-
         ature neglecting the role of women in these processes.

1144.   Smith, Timothy L. "Immigrant Social Aspirations and
         American Education, 1880-1930." American Quarterly 21
         (Fall 1969): 523-43.
             Asserts that immigrants (i.e., Central European Slavs,
         Magyars, Romanians, Jews, Greeks, and Italians) had a
         "commitment" to personal advancement through schooling.

1145.   Sochen, June. Consecrate Every Day: The Public Lives
         of Jewish American Women, 1880-1890. Albany: State Uni-
         versity of New York Press, 1981.
             Documents the contributions of Jewish women to American
         life. A chapter on radical Jewish women activists fea-
         tures Emma Goldman.

1146.   Solomon, Barbara M. Pioneers in Service: A History of
         the Associated Jewish Philanthropies of Boston. Boston:
         Associated Jewish Philanthropies, 1956.

1147.   Stellos, Marie H. "The Greek Community in St. Louis
         (1900-1967): Its Agencies for Value Transmission." Un-
         published Ph.D. dissertation, St. Louis University, 1968.

1148.   Stensland, Doris. Haul the Water, Haul the Wood. Aber-
         deen, S.D.: North Plains Press, 1977.
             A fictional work based on historical fact. The author re-
         constructs the life and times of her great-grandmother,
         Johanna Overseth, and her husband, Ole. They were
         early immigrant pioneers to Lincoln County, South Dakota.

1149.   Stolarik, M. Mark. "From Field to Factory: The Historiography of Slovak Immigration to the United States." _Inter-national Migration Review_, 10 (Spring 1976): 81-102.

1150.   Sunoo, S. S. "Korean Women Pioneers of the Pacific North-west." _Oregon Historical Quarterly_, 79 (Spring 1978): 51-63.
>   Over 1,000 young Korean women emigrated between 1910 and 1924, most of whom were sent abroad on marriage contracts. Describes the experiences of six of these "picture brides" who went to the Pacific Northwest.

1151.   Taft, Donald R. _Two Portuguese Communities in New England._ New York: Longmans, Green, 1923.

1152.   Taft, R., and R. Johnson. "The Assimilation of Adolescent Polish Immigrants and Parent-Child Interaction." _Merrill Palmer Quarterly_, 13 (1967): 111-120.
>   Suggests that Polish girls are more likely than boys to conform to parental ethnic models, and describes role of Polish immigrant mother in acculturation.

1153.   "Tenement Life in New York." _Harper's Weekly_, 23 (1879): 246, 266-67.

1154.   Thernstrom, Stephan. "Immigrants and WASPs: Ethnic Differences in Occupational Mobility in Boston, 1890-1940." In Stephan Thernstrom and Richard Sennett, eds., _Nineteenth-Century Cities: Essays in the New Urban History_ (New Haven, Conn.: Yale University Press, 1969), pp. 125-64.
>   Includes (1) career mobility: natives vs. foreign-born; (2) career mobility for three ethnic generations; (3) the influence of class origins; (4) some hints of differences between specific ethnic groups.

1155.   Thorson, Gerald. "Tinsel and Dust: Disenchantment in Two Minneapolis Novels in the 1880's." _Minnesota History_, 45 (1977): 211-222.
>   Describes the woman Norwegian immigrant novelist Drude Janson and her husband, both of whom wrote novels about Minneapolis in the 1880's. Thorson describes Drude Janson as "a gifted and intelligent woman" and "an active participant in current affairs." She was involved in the women's rights movements in Norway and America. She left America in 1893.

1156.   Tobenkin, Elias. "The Immigrant Girl in Chicago." _Survey_, 23 (1909): 189-204.

1157.   Toll, William. "The Female Life Cycle and the Measure of Social Change: Portland, Oregon, 1880-1930." _American Jewish History_, 72 (March 1983): 309-333.

1158.   Tomasi, Silvano. _Piety and Power: The Role of Italian_

Parishes in the New York Metropolitan Area, 1880-1930.
New York: Center for Migration Studies, 1975.
Includes materials on Catholic parish schools and Italian
immigrant children. Immigrant women formed the larger
number of the Church's congregants.

1159.   Townsend, Edward W. A Daughter of the Tenements. New
York: Lovell, Coryell, 1895.

1160.   U. S. Immigration Commission. Report of the Immigration
Commission. "Fecundity of Immigrant Women." 61st Congress, 2nd Session, Document No. 282, pp. 731-826. Washington: Government Printing Office, 1911.
"In any comprehensive study of immigration the relative
fecundity of different foreign races in the United States
becomes an important subject of inquiry, especially in
comparison with the fertility of the native American stock
represented by the native white whose parents also were
native American. . . . Recognizing the great value of
information relative to the fecundity of foreign races in
the United States, the Immigration Commission obtained
permission to use the original data which the census had
collected. This action was taken not with any idea of
making a comprehensive tabulation covering the entire
United States, or doing the work which the census had
not found the opportunity to do, but with the intention
simply of selecting and studying certain limited but more
or less typical sections or areas. It was believed that
with comparatively small labor and expense results could
be obtained which would present statistically a very interesting and significant comparison as regards fecundity
between the immigrants, the native-born children of immigrants representing the second generation of foreign stock,
and the native Americans born of native American parents"
(p. 737).

1161.   U. S. Immigration Commission. Report of the Immigration
Commission. 61st Congress, 2nd & 3rd Sessions, 1911.
41 vols. "Importing Women for Immoral Purposes: A Partial Report of the Immigration Commission on the Importation
and Harboring of Women for Immoral Purposes," vol. 37,
pp. 57-101.
A harrowing document, presented to the Congress on
December 10, 1909, and following which "steps were immediately taken to amend the immigration law of 1907 to
more effectively prevent the importation of women and
girls for immoral purposes, and their control by import-
ers or others after admission to the United States." The
report was somber in its advisements: "The importation
and harboring of alien women and girls for immoral purposes and the practice of prostitution by them--the so-
called 'white slave traffic'--is the most pitiful and the
most revolting phase of the immigration question. It

is in violation of the immigration law and of the agreement of 1904 between the United States and other powers
for the repression of the trade in white women.   This
business had assumed such large proportions and was
exerting so evil an influence upon our country that the
Immigration Commission felt compelled to make it the
subject of a thorough investigation.   Since the subject is
especially liable to sensational exploitation, the Commission's report is primarily a statement of undeniable facts
calculated to form a basis of reasonable legislative and
administrative action to lessen its evils" (p. 57).

1162.   Ussach, Betty I.   The Portuguese in Rhode Island.   Unpublished Report.   Providence College, 1973.

1163.   Van Hoeven, James W., ed.   Piety and Patriotism: Bicentennial Studies of the Reformed Church in America, 1776-
1976.   Grand Rapids, Mich.:   Wm. B. Eerdmans Publishing,
1976.
The essays are intended as a history of the Reformed
Church in America from the Revolution to the present.
While stressing the church's history the writers have
attempted to show the interaction of the history of this
Dutch church with the history and culture of the United
States.   Includes "The Role of Women in the India Mission, 1819-1880" by Barbara Fassler.

1164.   Vecoli, Rudolph J.   "The Contadini in Chicago: A Critique
of The Uprooted."   Journal of American History, 51 (1964):
404-17.
Utilizes experience of Chicago's Sicilian Americans to
dispute notion that New Immigrants were decimated by
urban-industrial life.   Argues that the cultural heritage
of the rural southern Italian immigrants was successfully
resistant to pressures for assimilation in Chicago.

1165.   Vecoli, Rudolph J.   "European Americans: From Immigrants
to Ethnics."   International Migration Review, 6 (Winter 1972):
403-434.
An analysis of immigration historiography.   Also, with
some change, in William H. Cartwright and Richard L.
Watson, eds., The Reinterpretation of American History
and Culture (1973), pp. 81-112.   See also Moses Rischin,
ed., Immigration and the American Tradition (1976).

1166.   "The View of Migrant Women."   Language for Living, 7
(1977):   22-40.

1167.   Vorse, Mary Heaton.   "The Portuguese of Provincetown."
Outlook, 97 (January-April, 1911):   409-416.

1168.   Walden, Daniel, ed.   Jewish Women Writers and Women in
Jewish Literature.   Albany: State University of New York
Press, 1983.

Twenty essays by contemporary scholars, making up a
valuable contribution to the study of both women's literature and Jewish literature as well as to American literature. Eleven of the essays examine women characters
in fiction by women and nine essays discuss women in
fiction by male authors: Cahan, Lewisohn, Bellow,
Malamud, Roth, and Borges. The women writers, Yezierska, Ozick, Rosen, Paley, and Margolin, are signigicant
and interesting.

1169. Walkowitz, Judith R. Prostitution and Victorian Society:
       Women, Class and the State. Cambridge, Eng.: Cambridge
       University Press, 1980.

1170. Ward, David. Cities and Immigrants: A Geography of
       Change in Nineteenth Century America. New York: Oxford
       University Press, 1972.
       Urban change in the nineteenth century with immigration
       impact on cities, and valuable notices of immigrant family
       life in the cities.

1171. Ware, Caroline F. Greenwich Village, 1920-1930. A Com-
       ment on American Civilization in the Post-War Years. New
       York: Harper, 1935. Reissued with a New Preface, 1965.
       Includes "The Italian Community," pp. 152-202; and A. E.
       Bromsen, "The Public School's Contribution to the Mala-
       daptation of the Italian Boy," pp. 455-461.

1172. Ware, Helen. "Immigrant Fertility: Behavior and Attitudes."
       International Migration Review, 9 (August 1975): 361-378.

1173. Weed, Thurlow. "The Ruin of Female Honour," in John F.
       Maguire, The Irish in America (London: Longmans, Green,
       1868), p. 340.
       Thurlow Weed, member of the N.Y. Commissioners of
       Emigration, addressed the plight of immigrant girls in
       his speech at opening of the Emigrant Hospital on Ward's
       Island, 1864.

1174. Weiss, Milford. "Selective Acculturation of the Dating Pro-
       cess: The Patterning of Chinese Caucasian Interracial Dat-
       ing." Journal of Marriage and the Family, 32 (May 1970):
       273-278.
       Suggests that girls are more at ease in interracial dating
       than boys because they feel no obligation to carry on the
       family name and ethnic traditions.

1175. Welter, Barbara. Dimity Convictions: The American Wom-
       an in the Nineteenth Century. Athens: Ohio University
       Press, 1976.
       The conditioning of young women to the sexist social
       norms. Intellectual and social history.

1176. Wexler, Alice. Emma Goldman: An Intimate Life. New
York: Pantheon, 1984.
Deals with Goldman's early life in Eastern Europe and
immigrant America, her Jewish background, and family
influences against which she reacted. Concludes with
Goldman's deportation from the United States in 1919.

1177. Wexler, Alice. "Emma Goldman on Mary Wollstonecraft."
Feminist Studies, 7 (Spring 1981): 113-33.
Reprints in full the text of Goldman's lecture "Mary Woll-
stonecraft, the Pioneer of Modern Womanhood."

1178. Wheeler, Thomas C., ed. The Immigrant Experience: The
Anguish of Becoming an American. New York: Dial, 1971.
Immigrant narratives in conflict and acculturation, and
the maintenance of cultural identity.

1179. White, George C. "Immigration and Assimilation: A Survey
of Social Thought and Public Opinion, 1882-1914." Unpublished Ph.D. dissertation, University of Pennsylvania, 1952.

1180. Whiteford, Michael B. "Women, Migration and Social Change:
A Colombian Case Study." International Migration Review,
12 (1978): 236-246.

1181. Williams, Phyllis H. South Italian Folkways in Europe and
America: A Handbook for Social Workers, Visiting Nurses,
School Teachers, and Physicians. New Haven, Conn.: Yale
University Press, 1938. Reprint. With an Introductory note
by F. Cordasco. New York: Russell & Russell, 1969.
In a socio-anthropological context, examines Italian folk-
ways, mores, and institutions which have continuing rele-
vancy. Particularly, (IV.) Diet and Household Economy;
(VI.) Marriage and the Family; (X.) Health and Hospitals.

1182. Winick, Charles, and Paul M. Kinsie. The Lively Com-
merce: Prostitution in the United States. Chicago: Quadrangle Books, 1971.

1183. Winsey, Valentine R. "The Italian Immigrant Women Who
Arrived in the United States Before World War I." In
Francesco Cordasco, ed., Studies in Italian American So-
cial History: Essays in Honor of Leonard Covello (Totowa,
N.J.: Rowman & Littlefield, 1975), pp. 199-210.

1184. Woolston, Harriet B. Prostitution in the United States.
New York: Century, 1921. Reprint. Montclair, N.J.:
Patterson Smith, 1969.
Focuses on prostitution in the United States prior to World
War I and efforts at reform.

1185. [World Council of Churches]. Filipino Workers: A Case of
Exported Women Workers. Geneva: Migration Secretariat,
World Council of Churches, 1980.

1186.   Wunsch, James Lemuel. "Prostitution and Public Policy:
         From Regulation to Suppression, 1858-1920."   Unpublished
         Ph. D. dissertation, University of Chicago, 1976.
              Attributes the change from regulation to suppression to
              a constellation of motives ranging from medical discov-
              eries to the linkage of prostitution and low wages.   The
              closing of brothels by World War I caused prostitutes to
              adjust their methods of doing business.

1187.   Yezierska, Anzia. "Soap and Water and the Immigrant."
         The New Republic, 18 (February 22, 1919):   117-119.

1188.   Yoffeh, Zalman. "The Passing of the East Side."   Menorah
         Journal, 17 (December 1929):   265-275.

1189.   Yung, Judy.   " 'A Bowlful of Tears':   Chinese Women Immi-
         grants on Angel Island."   Frontiers, 2 (Summer 1977):   52-
         55.
              Visiting the Immigration Station in 1975, Yung was deeply
              touched by the poetry and other records scratched on the
              walls by the detainees.   The experiences related in this
              article are based upon oral history interviews with women
              detained there between 1910 and 1941.

1190.   Zangwill, Israel.   The Melting Pot: A Drama in Four Acts.
         New York: Macmillan, 1914.
              New and revised edition with important "Afterword" by
              Zangwill on his theories of Americanization and the immi-
              grant in America.

INDEX

Numbers refer to entries, not pages.